Meals Worth Stopping for in

Florida

Local Restaurants within 10 Miles of the Interstate

by the Gourmettes: Nancy Barber and Jane Bolding

gpp

travel

Guilford, Connecticut

The prices and rates in this guidebook were confirmed at press time. We recommend, however, that you call establishments before traveling to obtain current information.

To buy books in quantity for corporate use or incentives, call **(800) 962–0973** or e-mail **premiums@GlobePequot.com.**

Photo credits: All restaurant photos are by Nancy Barber unless otherwise specified.
Spot photography © Shutterstock, except p. 5 © iphoto.com; pp. 27, 73, 106 © photos.com.

Text design by Libby Kingsbury

Maps by Melissa Baker © Morris Book Publishing, LLC

Library of Congress Cataloging-in-Publication Data

Barber, Nancy.
    Meals worth stopping for in Florida : local restaurants within 10 miles of the interstate / by the gourmettes, Nancy Barber and Jane Bolding.
        p. cm.
    ISBN 978-0-7627-4528-9
  1. Restaurants—Florida—Guidebooks. I. Bolding, Jane. II. Title.
    TX907.3.F6B37 2008
    647.95759—dc22

                                                        2008017229

Printed in the United States of America

10 9 8 7 6 5 4 3 2 1

To my mother and late father, for making memorable meals a priority.

—*Nancy Barber*

With love and gratitude to my husband, Gary Bolding.

—*Jane Bolding*

Contents

Acknowledgments

It's impossible to do a project like this without help from lots of people. Bonnie Tensen, the third Gourmette, inspired and amused us throughout the project, and we still wish she were on the cover with us. Without Andy Dehnart's technical assistance, we might still be scribbling drafts in notebooks and adding expenses on an abacus. Special thanks to Bob Hishon and Janet Martinez for helping us through the legal labyrinths and to Dom Rodi for taking photos. A big thank-you to Karen Kaivola, without whose sage advice we might never have continued this project, and to Mary Norris and GPP for recognizing the value of the book in the first place. Thanks also to all the Floridians, diners, workers, and owners who took the time to share their stories during our research.

A number of people joined us on the road to help eat and critique. Many also contributed valuable information about the restaurants in their area: Honorary Gourmettes include Angie Aboutanos, Fran and Dan Arnold, Nancy Arnold, John Barber, Nancy Barber Sr., Elvin Bale, Gloria Bale, Nita Bale, Grady Ballenger, Jessica Bohan, Michael Bolding, Gary Bolding, Ellie Branch, Steve Branch, Karen Cole, Pat Curtis, Andy Dehnart, Susan Dupree, Beth Gannon, Bernie and Dorie Garnett, Mafalda Giovannetti, Suzy Hammer, John Hanson, Katie Hunter, Tyler Hunter, Karen Kaivola, Marie LaTulip, Greg McCann, Betsy Miller, Jim Moran, Bonnie Morgan, Jeanine Morton, Lissa Munroe, Priscilla Myers, Jim O'Toole, Frank Perrino, Francoise Plantey, Lynn Polke, Jan Porges, Tim Radis, Phyllis and John Schrock, Bonnie and Adam Seidon, Dan Stetson, Suzy Taylor, Bonnie Tensen, June Tensen, Paul Wallace, Eli Witek, and Rusty and Terri Witek. Lots more folks didn't get to eat with us but provided local expertise on various sections of Florida cuisine. Restaurant Scouts include Marian Almaroth, Steve Aimone, Renee and Tony Alivento, Dan and Jory Arnold, Patrick Arnold, John Barnhill, Mary Ann Becker, Pat and Homer Bodiford, Bobby Branch, Todd and Rosalie Carpenter, Ann Jerome Croce, Roberta and Greg Favis, Denise Hall, Tim Hammer, Eugene Huskey, Linda and Darrell Langley, Rebecca Sexton Larson, Bob Leaman, Patti Lockenbach, Shirley Lockenbach, Janet Martinez, Rodney May, Craig Miller, Nancy's Stetson students, John Pearson, Greg Porges, Harold and Karen Rifas, Ricky Sills, Andrew and Shelley Sessions, June and Bob Sitler, Steve and Cathy Soud, Gary and Treesa Soud, Volusia County Master Gardeners, and Wayne Wincey.

Nancy would like to thank all the family, friends, and strangers who listened to her complain far too much about eating far too much, especially David Bartlett, Daniel Bodiford, and Penny Taylor. Jane sends love and gratitude to her children, Ashley and Michael, for their encouragement and support. Thanks also to her family (Mary Ann and Kent Davidson, all the Abbotts, Woods, and Frames) and friends who have shared good meals and good times, especially her Wednesday and Thursday Night Book Clubs, Little Rock Tribe, Christmas Dinner Gang. If we've left anyone out, thanks to them too.

Introduction

Most folks don't think of Florida as a culinary destination, maybe because people are so focused on theme parks, beaches, and golf, or maybe because all they see is prepackaged fast food and generic chains. That's just the Florida marketed by slick travel companies and greedy developers. The Gourmettes know the truth: The gateway to the real Florida is the state's local restaurants—not the chains at interstate exits or the corporate eateries built in and around theme parks, but the restaurants just a little off the beaten path. The problem is, you need an insider to show you the way, a local who can take you where the locals go and show you a Florida you'll never find in the usual tourist books. We aim to bring you the real Florida through great destination restaurants with plenty of character, community, and killer food. We want to show you where to find the right barbecue pits, tandoor ovens, Cuban sandwich presses, and breakfast griddles. We know where to locate the best grouper sandwich, the most succulent smothered pork chops, the sweetest Apalachicola oysters, and the best grilled hot dogs. We've sat with the Amish snowbirds at Yoder's, the nudists at Como Nudist Resort, the superwealthy at Ta-boo, and the migrant strawberry workers at Monterrey Grill. There's so much to see in Florida that the normal guidebooks don't show. The Gourmettes will help you find it.

Our mission is twofold: help tourists get a sense of the real Florida and help outstanding independent restaurants stay busier than they already are. As Gourmettes, we consider ourselves ambassadors of good eating. We've searched the state's back roads within 10 miles, give or take a few, on either side of the four major interstates, 95, 75, 10, and 4, to come up with the best possible places to please the palate and give a sense of local color. Our goal is to make these fun-to-dine-at places easy to find. How many times have you driven on an interstate about lunchtime, hungry for great food, but not wanting to take time out of the trip to figure out where you might find it? The answers are all here.

We've given you precise directions for how and when to find these places, including exit numbers, mileage figures, street addresses, and the usual operating hours and days off. Sometimes, though, independent restaurants take funny vacations— maybe Erlene made the state bowling finals or the Hopkins are having a private family reunion at the restaurant—so it's always good to call ahead and make sure a place is open before you drive there. Most times they will be. When an establishment can be reached from one or more of the interstates, we provide a cross reference to the place's full write-up following our directions. When identifying local roads, we use SR for State Road and CR for County Road.

We hope you'll enjoy our write-ups so much that you won't just want to go to these restaurants, you'll want to eat there with us. For the Gourmettes, this is all fun. We're culinary detectives who like to interview, research, and road-trip to find the best restaurants in the state, and we have a riotous good time along the way. We were both raised in the South in families that knew how to eat. In keeping with our heritage of Southern hospitality, we want you to enjoy the very best trip possible in the Sunshine State, and that means rubbing elbows with locals, trying out the good stuff we eat. In the process, you can help support and preserve an important part of American culinary culture and keep the corporate chains from quickly usurping our mealtimes.

Follow along with us as we eat kangaroo for the first time in Jacksonville, make our own pancakes tableside in DeLeon Springs, munch Cuban sandwiches in Little Havana, and savor soul food where the NBA stars hang out in Orlando. Don't let Disney fool you; Florida is a feast of culinary pleasures, and we want to tell you about them all.

—The Gourmettes

Price Guide

$ = Under $5
$$ = $6–15
$$$ = $16–25
$$$$ = $26 or more

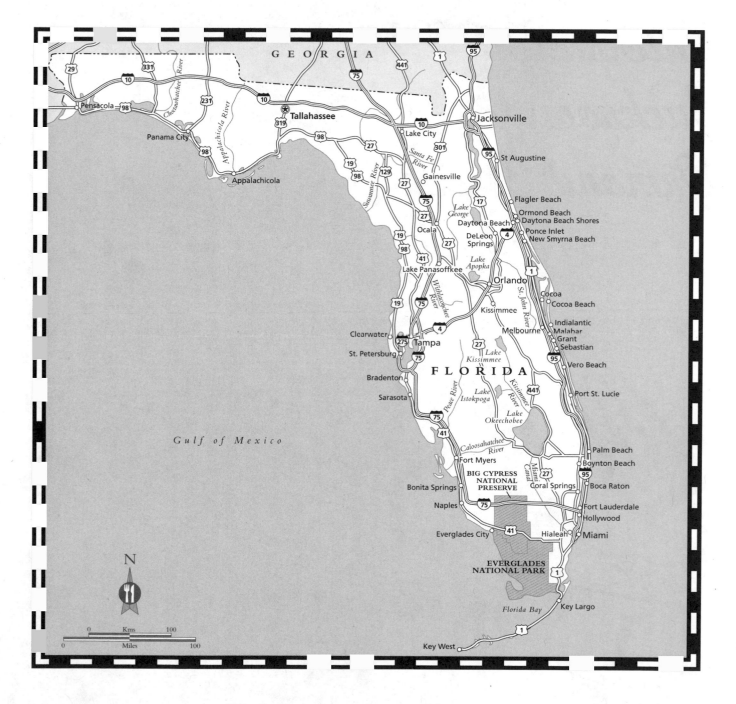

Interstate 95
Jacksonville to Ormond Beach

1

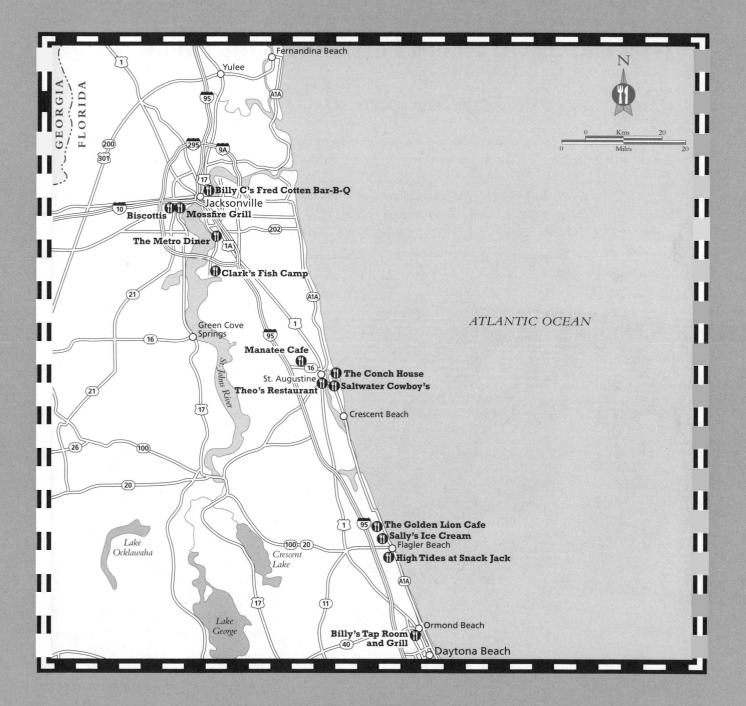

GEORGIA
FLORIDA

N

0 — Kms — 20
0 — Miles — 20

1

Fernandina Beach

Yulee

95

A1A

200
301

295

9A

17

10

Billy C's Fred Cotten Bar-B-Q

Jacksonville

Biscottis   **Mossfire Grill**

202

The Metro Diner

1A

Clark's Fish Camp

21

A1A

1

Green Cove
Springs

16

95

St. Johns River

Manatee Cafe

16

St. Augustine   **The Conch House**

Theo's Restaurant   **Saltwater Cowboy's**

21

17

Crescent Beach

26

100

Lake
Ocklawaha

20

ATLANTIC OCEAN

Crescent
Lake

1

95

The Golden Lion Cafe

100 20

Sally's Ice Cream

Flagler Beach

High Tides at Snack Jack

A1A

17

11

Ormond Beach

Lake
George

**Billy's Tap Room
and Grill**

40

Daytona Beach

I-95 Exit 354A: Where Pork and Politics Meet

Billy C's Fred Cotten Bar-B-Q

2623 Main Street, Jacksonville; 904-356-8274. Open Monday through Thursday 10:30 a.m. to 3:30 p.m., Friday and Saturday 10:30 a.m. to 8:00 p.m. Closed Sunday. $–$$

From I-95: Take exit 354A—US 1/Martin Luther King Jr. Parkway/FL-15 South (.6 mile). Follow the US 1 exit toward US 17/Main Street (.1 mile). Stay straight on US 1/FL-15/West 20th Street Expressway (.1 mile). Turn right onto North Main Street/US 17/FL-5 (.2 mile). Bar-B-Q will be on your left.

Willie Willis, Janice Starks, and Johnnie Brown

There's something sacred about walking into a barbecue joint as venerable as Billy C's Fred Cotten Bar-B-Q. The cinderblock building and barbecue secrets are as old as WWII, when Fred Cotten brought his sauce, pit skills, and entrepreneurial flare to the historic Springfield section of Jacksonville. A portrait of Mr. Cotten himself hangs on the back wall as if he's still overseeing the place.

We love the dark brown paneling, wooden booths, and Mason-jar lighting fixtures, and as usual, we go for the counter seats so we can chat with the employees and the locals. The guy sitting next to us cut Fred Cotten's lawn when he was a kid, and Willie Willis, the colorful pit-master, seems happy to talk about barbecue and Jacksonville politics, both of which have been brokered here since 1945.

When we ask Willie what's best on the menu, he says, "How my supposed to decide what's better? The ribs are tender, the chicken's juicy, and the pork is good. We serve home-style cooking and we keep it simple. In the last seven years, all we've added is sausage, turkey, baked beans, banana pudding, and corn. Everything else on the menu is the same as it was in 1945."

Willie's hitting a hot point here, one that's hinted at in the place's multiple names. We didn't understand it until we returned to the restaurant several weeks later and got to talk to others who work there, including Billy C. himself, also known as Billy Cowart, a former tax accountant who got his start cooking for his National Guard buddies. Billy bought the business at the start of the new millennium from Fred Cotten's son, who's got his own joint, Cotten's BBQ, across the river. The two got into a run-in when Billy tried to change the name of the restaurant.

Johnnie Brown, who's worked here since 1989, says Fred's poltergeist comes out if anyone tries to change the things Fred started. "I hold all the secrets to this place," Johnnie tells us. "I started out washing dishes, and now I'm the manager. All the ideas, from the sauce to the meat—they're Fred Cotten's." Anyone tries to change things? "Fred won't have it," Johnnie says mysteriously.

It's true enough that the basics—the secret sauce, a thin mixture of vinegar, mustard, salt, and seasoning salt; the fall-off-the-bone ribs; the moist, smoky chicken; and the savory pulled pork—may be just the same as when Fred started the place. And Willie didn't lie: they're all good. On the other hand, Billy Cowart has made some excellent additions to the menu, including homemade sausage, mixed from the rib trimmings minus the fat and gristle. Billy C.

and his wife, Angela, pack the spicy sausage themselves. He also added the best banana pudding Nancy has ever had, creamy and light with Vanilla Wafers still fresh and crunchy, and delicious deep-fried corn, which the menu calls "grilled." All three additions are fitting complements to Fred's original menu, which is probably why we didn't see Fred's poltergeist, even though we were looking.

Don't let the grim brown concrete building deter you. Billy C's Fred Cotten Bar-B-Q plays host to some of Jacksonville's biggest politicos and local power brokers. Al Gore even ate here in 1988. The barbecue, old and new, is worth the visit. And who knows? You might even catch a glimpse of Fred's poltergeist, up in a corner by a Mason-jar light fixture.

I–95 Exit 351C or 351A: Big City Bistro Charm

Biscottis

3556 St. Johns Avenue, Jacksonville; 904-387-2060; www.biscottis.net. Open Monday through Thursday 10:30 a.m. to 10:00 p.m., Friday 10:30 a.m. to midnight, Saturday 8:00 a.m. to midnight, and Sunday 8:00 a.m. to 9:00 p.m. $$–$$$

From I-95 South: Take exit 351C—Margaret Street (.5 mile). Turn right onto Park Street (.8 mile), left onto King Street (.2 mile), and right onto St. Johns Avenue (1 mile). Biscottis will be on your left.

From I-95 North: Take exit 351A toward Park Street. Turn left onto Park Street (1.1 mile), left onto King Street (.2 mile), and right onto St. Johns Avenue (1 mile). Biscottis will be on your left.

(See the write-up in Chapter 8, page 193.)

I–95 Exit 351C or 351A: Southwestern Fire

Mossfire Grill

1537 Margaret Street, Jacksonville; 904-355-4434; www.mossfire.com. Open Monday through Thursday and Saturday 11:00 a.m. to 10:00 p.m., Friday 11:00 a.m. to 11:00 p.m., and Sunday 11:00 a.m. to 9:00 p.m. $$–$$$

From I-95 South: Take exit 351C and merge onto Margaret Street (.5 mile). Mossfire will be on your left.

From I-95 North: Take exit 351A toward Park Street. Turn left onto Park Street (.3 mile) and left onto Margaret Street (less than .1 mile). Mossfire will be on your left.

(See the write-up in Chapter 8, page 195.)

I-95 Exit 348 or 347: Yo, Check Out This Diner!

The Metro Diner

3302 Hendricks Avenue, Jacksonville; 904-398-3701; www.metrodinerjax.com. Open daily 7:00 a.m. to 2:30 p.m. $$

From I-95 South: Take exit 348—US 1/FL-5/Philips Highway. Make a slight right onto St. Augustine Road (less than .1 mile). Turn right onto River Oaks Road (.3 mile) and then left onto Hendricks Avenue/FL-13 (.5 mile). The Metro Diner will be on your right.

From I-95 North: Take exit 347—Emerson Street/US 1/FL-126. Turn left (west) onto Emerson Street (1.5 miles). Turn right onto Hendricks Avenue/FL-13 North (.5 mile). Get in the left lane and make a U-turn at Inwood Terrace. The Metro Diner will be on your right.

Who would have thought that a banana surplus could result in something so sublime? The Metro Diner is home to the most amazing French toast we've ever encountered: a concoction called "Yo Hala on the Square." Owner Mark Divoli orders in bulk and found that he was never using up all the bananas in a case, so he commissioned his chef to come up with a recipe to use the extras. Thus began the masterpiece: thick hallah bread slices are stuffed with bananas sautéed in Frangelico—a hazelnut liqueur with flower and berry essences—and mixed with cream cheese, then dipped in egg batter and grilled

Mark Divoli and the heavenly Yo Hala

before being smothered in a blueberry/strawberry compote and dusted with powdered sugar. You can also add maple syrup, the real deal. Some might consider this overkill, but it's actually fabulous. The first weekend it was on the specials blackboard, one woman came up to Mark and said, "That is just simply the best thing I've ever put in my mouth. You must put it on the menu." Lucky for us all, they did.

But the Yo Hala isn't the only great item on the menu at The Metro Diner. In fact, it's hard to find anything on the menu that's not excellent. When Mark took over in 2000, he looked at every dish and asked, "How can I make this item better?" Now, for example, they hand cut their rib eyes, and they use imported tomatoes from Italy. All the changes meant upgrades to an already good menu.

You can have breakfast all day except for the pancakes and French toast, which they stop serving at 11:00 a.m. Monday through Friday; weekends you're OK. The eggs Benedict are some of the best we've had, and the crab cake Benedict, the grilled cheese and ham (or bacon) breakfast sandwich, and the other French toasts are all great choices. Hash browns can be given "a kick"—for 50 or 75 cents they'll add onions, peppers, jalapeños, bacon, tomatoes, mush-

rooms, sausage, ham, chili, or the works for $4.50 more. Nancy added mushrooms and onions and got enough hash browns to feed an offensive line.

For lunch, try the fish sandwich, fried, grilled, or blackened. We got ours fried, and the golden crusted fish, moist and flaky, hung off the ends of a toasted, open-faced bun. The platter was so full that the *homemade* potato chips had to be served on their own dish. The meatloaf and mashed red-skinned potatoes are like your mama used to make (if she was a good cook).

It's not just the food that makes The Metro Diner special, though; it's also the people. "We're a family who loves to feed people," said Mark. "When I saw the open kitchen, I knew I could cook and be a part of the customer base that comes in here. We've built this business by being with the customers." Mark's parents own the business with him and his wife, Brooklynn. Mark's dad, John, is getting the new catering kitchen up and running, and Mark's mom, Sandi, greets and seats people on the weekends. Even Mark's 3 ½-year-old-daughter, London, keeps up the hospitality by sitting at tables with guests she doesn't even know.

Lots of the customers are regulars, though, like the Weavers, who own the Jacksonville Jaguars. "I have people who walk in the door," said Mark, "and I could tell you what time it is without looking at my watch." Locals come to The Metro Diner for simple reasons: delicious food in a friendly atmosphere. You can't go wrong. It's the kind of place where you need our directions, but not really our advice . . . except, don't miss the Yo Hala.

Yo Hala on the Square

2 slices of halla bread, cut 1-inch thick
2 sliced bananas, ½-inch thick
½ cup of brown sugar
1 Tablespoon of Frangelico nut liqueur
4 ounces of softened cream cheese
eggs
spices (nutmeg, cinnamon, pumpkin)

Sauté bananas, brown sugar, and Frangelico nut liqueur for 5 minutes on low heat; set aside. Put cream cheese in a bowl to soften, and then fold in your sautéed stuffing mixture in the bowl. Let this chill for at least an hour in the refrigerator. Get 1 slice of bread and spread on 1 inch of the mixture. Then add the other slice of bread on top. It should look like a sandwich.

Cut your sandwich in half on a biased angle. Dredge the sandwich in a French toast mixture (egg and spices—nutmeg, cinnamon, and pumpkin). Place it on the grill and brown the entire sandwich halves, top, bottom, all sides of the triangle cut.

Stack and layer your sandwich on your plate, pour a strawberry/blueberry compote on top, then sprinkle powered sugar on top of that.

Strawberry/Blueberry Compote

Heat up 1 cup blueberries, ½ cup brown sugar, and ¼ cup white wine. Cook out the alcohol and thicken the mixture with a slurry (cornstarch and water). Once thick, add and fold in 8 whole strawberries.

—Courtesy of Mark Divoli, The Metro Diner

I-95 Exit 337 or 335: Savoring the Taste of Down Under

Clark's Fish Camp

12903 Hood Landing Road, Jacksonville; 904-268-3474; www.clarksfishcamp.com. Open Monday through Thursday 4:30 p.m. to 9:30 p.m., Friday 4:30 p.m. to 10:00 p.m., Saturday 11:30 a.m. to 10:00 p.m., and Sunday 11:30 a.m. to 9:00 p.m. $$–$$$

From I-95 South: Take exit 337—I-295 north toward Orange Park (2.8 miles) to exit 3, Old St. Augustine Road. Keep left at fork, following signs for Old St. Augustine Road south (.4 mile). Turn left onto St. Augustine Road (.9 mile). Turn right onto Hood Landing Road (1.6 miles) and Clark's will be on your left.

From I-95 North: Take exit 335—St. Augustine Road west (3.5 miles). Turn left onto Sparkman Road (.3 mile) and then left onto Hood Landing Road (1.1 miles). Clark's will be on your left.

Hemingway went on hunting safaris. Peter Hill Beard went on photography safaris. The Gourmettes? We go on eating safaris. One of the best places around for this sort of adventure is Clark's Fish Camp, located on Julington Creek. Their "Call of the Wild" appetizers include antelope, buffalo, venison, rabbit, ostrich, gator (tail or sausage), turtle, quail, frog legs, smoked eel, snake ("Don't order the snake. It's all bone," our server told us), and our personal favorite—*fried kangaroo*! Now, we know what you're thinking, Skippy? Fried? Served up for an entree? No, we just got the appetizer portion, but kangaroo is delicious. Not anything like chicken. Not like any

other meat we've ever tried. The grilled antelope (thin, tender, and medium rare) and fried ostrich are also delicious, all served with a sesame ginger sauce.

If stalking the menu for game isn't your idea of fun, don't despair. The offerings are extensive, with plenty of more recognizable seafood—good shrimp, scallops, oysters, and soft-shell crab—and the popular prime rib: Jack's Cut—three pounds for the serious eaters; Joan's Cut for those a bit less hungry. Jack and Joan Peoples bought the Fish Camp in 1974 when it was just a bait and tackle shop. They wanted to give up the pressure of their corporate jobs: Jack was an executive for a food broker and Joan had worked at Barnett Bank for fifteen years. When they discovered they "couldn't make a living out of crickets and renting boats for $3 a day," they added an oyster bar and some other items. "It seemed like food was what the people wanted," said Joan. Isn't it always?

Besides all the exotic eating opportunities, you feel like you're in the wild, with stuffed animals of all sorts lurking in every nook and cranny. Joan says it all got started when they bought an opossum holding a beer can in Franklin, North Carolina. "Everyone thought he was so cute that we bought a skunk—and then things just got out of hand." The place is a taxidermist's Noah's ark, with lifelike critters all over: lion, tiger, deer, bear, giraffe, rhino, koala, raccoon. Outside, they've got a giant artificial alligator among cypress knees and a largemouth bass mail box. Inside, any place there's not a stuffed animal, there's a fish plate. Joan has more than 500 plates with fish on them displayed on the walls of the restaurant, and

she has another 500 or so at home. The Peoples have moved about as far away from Corporate America as you can imagine.

In the phone book, their slogan is "Where the locals eat," which is true. You'll always find plenty of locals at Clark's. It's also nicknamed "The Peoples' Place," a pun on the name of the owners and the populist atmosphere of the restaurant, where folks are friendly and conversation is easy. On one of our visits, when a guy came up to the bar, the bartender said, "What'll you have? A swift kick in the butt?" We looked up at her. "Oh, don't worry, he's a regular," she said and winked. When Jane got caught eyeing a basket of fried pickles down the bar, their owner, Greg, a hairdresser in town, offered to let us try some. We gladly munched on a couple. Good stuff.

To close a meal, pass on the chiffon key lime pie, but if you get a chance to try their special of deep-fried cheesecake with raspberry sauce and whipped cream, don't miss it. Mostly, though, don't miss perhaps your only chance in Florida to try kangaroo.

I-95 Exit 318: To Your Health!

Manatee Cafe

525 State Road 16, Westgate Plaza, St. Augustine; 904-826-0210; www.manateecafe.com. Open Monday through Saturday 8:00 a.m. to 4:00 p.m., Sunday 8:00 a.m. to 3:00 p.m. $–$$

From I-95: Take exit 318—SR 16 east toward St. Augustine (4.1 miles). Manatee Cafe will be in the Westgate Plaza on your right.

Have you ever eaten manatee? Don't worry, we haven't either. Clark's kangaroo appetizer had you worried, though, didn't it? This cafe gets its name from what's on its walls (representative twentieth-century manatee art with the odd mermaid or dolphin thrown in for good measure), not what's on its plates. The Manatee Cafe isn't your usual Gourmettes' dining experience, mostly because it's, well, healthy. It's always good to occasionally stray from our comfort zones, though, and besides, we've got lots of vegetarian friends and a couple of vegan acquaintances. We wanted to make sure that they and readers of their ilk have some options in Florida too.

So, if you find yourself flying down I-95 in serious need of a wheat grass shot or a tofu Reuben or a spelt waffle or even nutritional yeast dressing for your salad, this is the place to go. If you happen to be traveling with a carnivore, there's also turkey or chicken salad, chicken pita sandwiches, and real scrambled eggs. The bad news is that the restaurant has moved from its original funky location north of Castillo de San Marcos, the old fort in St. Augustine, to a less inspiring spot in a strip mall. The good news

is that now it's a lot closer to the interstate. A veggie burger made with black beans, oats, rice, vegetables, and spelt flour is now only 3.9 miles off your beaten path. Holy carrot juice!

The Manatee originally opened in 1994 as a juice bar. To satisfy some hungry customers, current owner Cheryl Crosley, classically trained in French cuisine, started experimenting with healthy meals, which led to a real kitchen with real cooking going on. According to Cheryl, the cafe sort of "created itself." There wasn't and still isn't much of a plan, it just evolves. That's lucky for the local faithful who pack the place at breakfast and lunch, and lucky for you if you're looking for a healthy alternative to fast food.

The Manatee didn't entice us to start eating healthy all the time, but what a pleasure it was to have a healthy break! The breakfast burrito loaded with vegetables and scrambled tofu was awfully good, but we'd go back to our comfort zone of scrambled eggs instead of tofu next time. The veggie omelet was a little bland, but the accompanying hummus, rich and smooth, made up for it with its heavy garlic. We love chips and hummus as a side option with breakfast. The spelt pancake, served with a medley of fruit or nuts and bananas was . . . well, we suspect those who regularly enjoy spelt, that nutty grain known as *farro* in Italy and *dinkle* in Germany, would find it irresistible.

A vegan cream of broccoli soup was surprisingly delicious. Jane's always amazed when she finds any vegan thing delicious. The tabbouleh was heavy on

the garlic, but tasty, and so was the pizza: pita bread loaded with lots of fresh cauliflower, tomatoes, sprouts, onions, and sweet potato. Nancy *loves* sweet potatoes, and she felt she might live forever after so many fresh veggies at one sitting.

Besides the menu items—all "prepared using pure filtered water and, when available, certified organic-grown fruits, vegetables, grains, legumes, herbs, spices, and coffees"—Cheryl also runs a small market at the front of the restaurant, where you can stock-up on healthy snacks and vitamins for the road. No more need for that bag of Snickers and M & M's to keep you going.

I-95 Exit 318 or 311: Stalking Estelle

Theo's Restaurant

169 King Street, St. Augustine; 904-824-5022. Open Monday through Friday 6:30 a.m. to 3:00 p.m., Saturday 6:30 a.m. to noon. Closed Sunday. $

From I-95 South: Take exit 318—SR 16 east toward St. Augustine (5.3 miles). Turn right onto North Ponce De Leon Boulevard (1.9 miles) and left onto West King Street (.1 mile). Theo's will be on your right.

From I-95 North: Take exit 311—SR 207 east (4.8 miles). Turn left onto US 1 (about 1 mile) and then right onto King Street (.1 mile). Theo's will be on your right.

We stalked Estelle, Theo's co-owner, for weeks. She didn't want to talk to us, didn't want to meet us, didn't want to answer our questions, and she still doesn't want us to print her last name. We're friendly Southerners. We couldn't imagine someone not wanting to talk to us. Finally we took a posse of eaters up to St. Augustine for lunch, and Jane cornered Estelle when she ventured outside the kitchen into the dining room. Jane is originally from Arkansas, and she is not to be denied. We suspect Estelle's in the witness protection program, although she denies it and maintains she's just "weird." Perhaps she had a bad experience with writers in a past life. No need to worry about the Gourmettes, however. We love Theo's! So does our posse. We enjoy hobnobbing with the St. Augustine muckety-mucks and hoi-polloi under a ceiling of hanging flotsam: old buoys, crab pots, channel markers, fishing nets, rudders, and other bits washed up by the sea. The original restaurant spent years in the historic part of the city before moving some blocks away in 1993 to their current location. The old St. Augustine fishing and boating photos continue the nautical decor.

As engaging as it is, atmosphere is secondary here. Mike, the other co-owner, and Estelle may be secretive, but they turn out some great food, much of it starting with homemade buns and pita bread, made daily from (secret) recipes handed down from Mike's grandmother Yia Yia (not her real name). The breakfast sandwich, for example, starts with a toasted homemade bun that looks like a hamburger bun but tastes like it was made from scratch by the loving hands of a Greek grandmother. It's crunchy and light, and melts in your mouth. The egg, cheese, and ham, bacon, or sausage are a tasty middle, but the bread is the star. The Greek omelet is filled to bursting with

If you're looking for sweet instead of spicy, Theo's also serves giant homemade cinnamon buns for breakfast, and occasionally for lunch if any are available so long. Ask for them warm. They're guaranteed to give your blood sugar a run for its money, and even Nancy, the sweetest Gourmette tooth, scrapes off some of the abundant icing before savoring each bite.

You'll also enjoy the lunch sandwiches, which are served on the same homemade buns, although we'd skip the burgers. The hot dogs are outstanding, but the best thing for lunch, by far, may be the gyros. These "Greek" sandwiches, which likely as not originated in New York, are the real deal and not to be missed if you're a gyro fan. Plus, at the end of lunch, your friendly server always brings a free chocolate chip cookie.

As long as Mike and Estelle stay hidden from whoever's looking for them, you should have great breakfast/lunch possibilities in St. Augustine for years to come.

gyro meat and a generous sprinkle of feta over the top. Mike cooks up the gyro lamb meat himself, and even Jane, who's not a gyro meat fan, loved it. The hash browns are good, and Minorcan Datil Pepper Hot Sauce is always served up as one of your condiment possibilities. This is hot sauce for those who've always wanted to be hot sauce eaters but never had the iron stomachs for it, so Nancy especially loves it. In other words, the Minorcan Datil Pepper Hot Sauce is long on flavor, short on hot. The Minorcans arrived in St. Augustine in 1777—they *walked* there from New Smyrna after tiring of indentured servitude to Dr. Andrew Turnbull for nine years in the New World—toting along the seeds of their precious datil pepper, which is now a St. Augustine specialty. When you see "Minorcan" on a menu, the dish almost always includes the delicious datil pepper.

I-95 Exit 318 or 311: Castaway World

The Conch House

57 Comares Avenue, St. Augustine; 904-824-2046; www.conch-house.com. Open Sunday through Thursday 11:00 a.m. to 9:00 p.m., Friday and Saturday 11:00 a.m. to 10:00 p.m. $$–$$$

From I-95 South: Take exit 318—SR 16 east toward St. Augustine (5.3 miles). Turn right onto US 1/Ponce de Leon Boulevard (1.2 miles), left onto West Castillo Drive (.3 mile), and right onto South Castillo Drive/FL-A1A (.5 mile). Then turn left, staying on FL-A1A, onto the Bridge of Lions (.3 mile). Stay straight on Alcazar Street as FL-A1A veers a little to the right (.4 mile) and turn right onto Comares Avenue (.1 mile). The Conch House will be on your left.

From I-95 North: Take exit 311—SR 201 east (4.8 miles). Turn left onto US 1 (about 1 mile) and then right onto King Street/CR 214 toward downtown (.7 mile). Take a left onto Avenida Menendez and then a slight right onto FL-A1A and the Bridge of Lions (.3 mile). Stay straight on Alcazar Street as FL-A1A veers a little to the right (.4 mile) and turn right onto Comares Avenue (.1 mile). The Conch House will be on your left.

If the castaways from Gilligan's Island decided to combine their efforts to open a business on the mainland after their rescue, The Conch House might be it. The motel and marina were built in 1946, but the separate restaurant got its start on stilts at the end of a dock in 1984. The small decagonal building, which is now the Conch House Lounge, was designed and built by Jimmy Ponce Jr. and David Ponce, who claim to be members of the oldest documented family in the nation. St. Augustine is the oldest city in the nation, but that's as far as we can verify. The building was modeled after the Capo Bath House that was in the bay near the Castillo de San Marcos and burned down in 1914 after many years of use by men on one high tide and women on the other. The current lounge has a nautical decor, with anchors, thick ropes, and portholes for windows, the kind of spot where Jack Sparrow and his mates might gather. A spiral staircase winds up to a small private room with a round table and a semicircular bench, the perfect place to bring your six favorite friends and plan a conspiracy.

The first restaurant on the dock was such a success that a few years later the Ponces decided to turn that into a lounge and add a much larger restaurant between the motel and the marina. This time the

it doesn't get much better than this. Until your food arrives: maybe the plump, succulent oysters still tasting of the sea, having been quickly fried in a light batter. Even Jane, who holds as an article of faith that oysters need to be dredged in cornmeal before being fried, loved them. Nancy claims that cornmeal more often than not tends to overpower the oyster flavor and texture. In any case, most of your fried oysters in Florida will be made without cornmeal, so Jane will complain a lot, but not about these fried oysters. The island shrimp sandwich is also a great choice, as are the conch fritters, the crab salad, the blackened mahi, and anything with the Minorcan barbecue sauce. You might also try one of the two most popular items on the menu: butter rhum scallops or sesame tuna. All the seafood served here is caught by local fisherman, and it's guaranteed to be the freshest in town.

The Conch House is also famous for hosting the "Great Chowder Debate" every fall, where local restaurants vie to see who has the best chowder in town. The debate got started in the early 1980s when the chef wanted to add New England Clam Chowder to the menu and the Southerners didn't think that

architecture was based on chickee huts, a design by the Seminole tribe involving a wooden frame and lots of palm fronds. With the help of Seminoles and 8,500 palm fronds, The Conch House began to take its current shape. There's now a large two-story "chickee hut," enclosed with multiple rooms, a smaller enclosed chickee hut bar, and a number of tiny private open chickee huts. If you're lucky, you'll get seated in your own private chickee hut overlooking the marina located on Salt Run, which flows into the Intracoastal Waterway.

While you're sitting in your own private chickee hut, smelling the salt air, reading the romantic graffiti carved on the support beams, defending yourself from the easily discouraged seagulls, and watching the yacht traffic with a cool breeze blowing through your hair, you can think about how great Florida is—

would go over very well. So, he got a few restaurants together for a Chowder Cook-Off, and today upwards of 3,000 guests show up to try a variety of different styles of chowder, any of which Southerners now eat with relish. The Conch House's own Minorcan conch chowder is a strong contender, with lots of green peppers, onions, conch, tomatoes, potatoes, and celery.

As if the architecture, food, and view weren't enough, The Conch House is also known for its live music and live alligators. There's live music year-round on the weekends, and during the summer, 1,500 to 2,000 guests show up for Reggae Sundays each week. Oh, and don't forget to stop by the live alligator exhibit on the back end of the property. The St. Augustine Alligator Farm supplies the restaurant with young gators that live at The Conch House until they outgrow it and trade places with more youngsters (gators, that is).

I-95 Exit 298: A Taste of Cracker Life

Saltwater Cowboy's

299 Dondanville Road, St. Augustine; 904-471-2332; www.saltwatercowboys.com. Open year-round Wednesday and Thursday 5:00 to 9:00 p.m., Friday and Saturday 5:00 to 10:00 p.m., and Sunday 5:00 to 9:00 p.m. Open Monday and Tuesday 5:00 to 9:00 p.m. during summer; closed Monday and Tuesday during winter. $$$

From I-95: Take exit 298—US 1 toward St. Augustine (7 miles). Turn right onto FL- 206 (3.8 miles), left onto FL-A1A North (3.2 miles), and left onto Dondanville Road. Cowboy's will be at the end of the road on the left.

If you're looking for a sense of old Florida, before all the rich folks arrived by train or car in the 1920s, back when pioneers were roughing it, eating off the land and fending off bears and alligators and mosquitoes, you might try Saltwater Cowboy's. Howard "Cowboy" Dondanville built the restaurant in the style of a turn-of-the-century fish camp in 1963 among the salt marshes of the Intracoastal Waterway. The building, which has been added onto since then, has old wooden floors, a tin roof, handmade willow twig furniture, plenty of driftwood art, and a swamp of stuffed raccoons, wild cats, buzzards, opossums, and the like to watch you eat. Lace curtains suggest that Cowboy's wife or grandma wanted to pay lip service to a feminine touch, but this restaurant isn't about "pretty." Skins of gators and snakes hang on the walls, and there's a wall of old black-and-white photos of bear killers, cockfighters, and gator wrestlers across the hall from the bathrooms.

The baby-back ribs and fried shrimp are the most popular items on the menu, but if you're feeling adventurous, you might try the "Florida Cracker Combo," an appetizer of frog legs, cooter (soft-shell turtle), and alligator tail. We weren't all that impressed with the cooter, but the frog and gator were tasty. The Oysters Dondanville, served on the half shell with garlic, butter, vermouth, and scallions, were rich and delicious. All the seafood is delivered fresh every day, and if you can't decide, go for the combination platter—shrimp, scallops, deviled crab, and fish (mahi-mahi when we were there), served fried or broiled or (best of all) blackened if you can talk your server into calling in chits with the chef. Nancy smiled big and begged. All entrees are served with garlic cheese bread and an unusual house salad of varied greens, raisins, apple slices, walnuts, red onions, celery, radishes, and a creamy apple vinaigrette house dressing.

No question about it, Saltwater Cowboy's is "cheesy" and rustic, but it's got a beautiful view of the sunset, and you're bound to see some wildlife outside while you're waiting for a table. They accept no reservations, so people often wait for tables, especially on weekends. Pick up a margarita at the bar window, sit back in a primitive chair, look out over the marsh, and think about what Florida must've been like when the first settlers arrived.

I-95 Exit 284: A Deck with a View

The Golden Lion Cafe

500 North Oceanshore Boulevard/FL-A1A, Flagler Beach; 386-439-3004; www.goldenlioncafe.com. Open daily 11:00 a.m. to 10:30 p.m. $$

From I-95: Take exit 284—SR 100 east toward Flagler Beach (3.5 miles). Turn left onto North Oceanshore Boulevard/FL-A1A (.1 mile). Golden Lion will be on your left, just past Sally's Ice Cream.

We have yet to find a better view than the rooftop deck at The Golden Lion. To the east you've got the gorgeous expanse of beach (north or south, depending on which way you're facing) and to the west, if you plan your visit at sunset, you've got the pinks, purples, and oranges of the setting sun. Throw in a boat drink and a Golden Lion burger topped with onion rings, barbecue sauce, bacon, and cheese, and Florida is tough to beat. As a bonus, I-95 exit 284 is the closest exit to the beach off an interstate anywhere in Florida (3.5 miles), and for an extra ¹⁄₁₀ of a mile, you can be at The Golden Lion.

Fortunately for all of us, in the early 1990s, Tony and Carolyn Marlow decided to give up a casino life in the Caribbean and buy a tiny beat Italian sandwich shop that had gone belly up in Flagler Beach. First they changed the name of the restaurant to The Golden Lion, the same name of the pub in Central London that Tony's parents had run. Then they added an international beer selection. Then they had to figure out what to serve. Fish 'n Chips seemed an obvious choice. Tony jokes that he went "from blackjack chips to fish 'n chips." He consulted an American policeman on vacation from Ohio for a batter recipe (no kidding), and they were off and running.

At first, not many folks traveled north of SR 100 in Flagler. The activity was concentrated to the south.

But then the people who understand good beer started showing up, then people fell in love with the fish and chips (turned out the Ohio cop knew his fish batter) and burgers and fish sandwiches and crab cake sandwiches, and then they added on the deck upstairs and an extra dining room and outdoor seating, and—voila!—a Gourmette destination was born!

Besides the view, the food, and the drinks, which Tony says he always wanted to be ancillary to the food, they also have live music on the weekends. During the slow winter season, they have a single acoustic entertainer on Friday and Saturday nights. Once the clocks spring ahead, the "summer" season officially starts, and there's live acoustic music on Fridays and Sundays, and reggae on Saturdays. "We've never tried to go too loud," says Tony. He likes to keep the setting relaxed. In fact, during one Bike Week (traditionally the rowdiest week of the year for any-

place serving alcohol within easy biking of Daytona), the Marlows hired a string quartet to play. "It was a killer," says Tony, laughing. "Everyone else had rock and roll, and I had a string quartet. You gotta have fun." The crowd of bikers in their leather chaps clapped politely and enjoyed themselves all the same.

This section of FL-A1A is also part of a 72-mile stretch that has recently been designated a "national scenic byway" (one of only three in Florida). It's called the A1A Scenic & Historic Coastal Byway, and it starts at Ponte Vedra Beach outside of Jacksonville to the north and extends south to the Flagler/Volusia County line. So once you make it to The Golden Lion, you may want to avoid the interstate for a while longer and drive along the beach. Kick back, in the car or out; the views are great.

Meals Worth Stopping for in *Florida*

I-95 Exit 284: Location, Location, Location

High Tides at Snack Jack

2805 South Oceanshore Boulevard/FL-A1A, Flagler Beach; 386-439-3344; www.snackjacks.com. Open daily 11:00 a.m. to 10:00 p.m. NO CREDIT CARDS, and the use of ATM cards incurs an extra $1.25 charge. $$

From I-95: Take exit 284—SR 100 east toward Flagler Beach (3.5 miles). Turn right onto South Oceanshore Boulevard/FL-A1A (2.7 miles). Snack Jack will be on the left.

When we pull into the sandy parking area of Snack Jack's, as the locals call it, in the Mini Cooper, good-looking boys in orange safety vests open each of our doors for us. The Gourmettes take flip-flopped steps out, Jane hands the keys to the cute boy on her side, and we head past NASCAR posters and mounted surfboards, through the outdoor deck, past the bar and the middle-aged beach bum playing "The Piano Man" on the guitar, and reach our destination: the back-porch eating area, which hangs right over the sand and gives us views of the Atlantic, in an area where we might even see whales. Jane's seen them twice over the years. On this stretch of FL-A1A, most buildings, residential and commercial, are across the two-lane road from the beach, and that's one of the reasons it's part of a "national scenic byway," because you can drive right next to the beach. Snack Jack's is one of the few buildings right on the sand.

This longtime hangout for surfers was built in 1950, and it's been called Snack Jack's for decades.

Gail Holt and Karol Mowery bought the place in 1995 and changed the name to High Tides at Snack Jack, which is very difficult to remember in its entirety. The new owners held onto the joint's funky, beachside atmosphere: The walls are covered with

signs like SURFER GIRL CROSSING, and BUS TO BOSTON MARATHON (huh?), license plates from Michigan to Aruba, and an assortment of patches, mostly from law-enforcement and rescue groups. Any problems in the area, you know where these folks hang out. The signs on the bathrooms read DUDES and DUDETTES. There's often live music, and check your calendars for the monthly "Full Moon Party." We'd hang out here even if they didn't serve food. It's one of those places that almost forces you to slow down, relax, and enjoy the world. The weather doesn't really matter. They can lower glass windows on the porch if it's raining. Unfortunately, there's a screen between you and the sea when it's nice, but you can always choose to sit on the outside deck for a totally clear view.

When you're ordering, the shrimp are a good choice. The peel-and-eat are tasty, and the fried are okay; the drunken with the "flaming sauce" will leave your mouth burning if you're a hot sauce wimp like Nancy. If you're in the mood for fish, we'd say skip the catch of the day, which is always snook, and go for the southwest tuna sandwich. Also, the wings— served raging, flaming, barbeque, or chicken (aren't they all chicken?)—are excellent.

Mostly, though, hit Snack Jack's for the location, location, location . . . and the valet parking.

We All Scream . . .

If you're in the mood for a great dessert in Flagler Beach, **Sally's Ice Cream**, in the Pepto-Bismol-pink concrete-block building draped in white Christmas lights, has been an institution there for more than twenty years. Ed Ruhs serves up killer s'cream, some from his own recipes. The soft serve (twenty-seven flavors) is billed as "the best you've ever had," but we've never had it because we adore the hard-pack (twenty-eight flavors) so much. Jane loves the Black Raspberry Haze the most, and Nancy loves the bodacious Heath sundae with caramel, chocolate, heath bits, and whipped cream over vanilla ice cream. Oh, baby! The fresh peach ice cream, available only in summer, is awfully tasty too. The only problem is that Ed enjoys doing strictly his "own thing," which means he opens and closes when he feels like it. He's especially likely to close if it's cold or rainy, so give him a jingle before you go, or drop by and see if he's open after a trip to The Golden Lion next door. Great ice cream with a view of the ocean is worth screamin' for . . . .

➡ 401 North Oceanshore Boulevard/FL-A1A, Flagler Beach; 386-439-4408. Hours and days flexible and closed some winter months, which is a nice way of saying Ed opens when he likes. $

➡ From I-95: Take exit 284 — SR 100 east toward Flagler Beach (3.5 miles). Turn left onto North Oceanshore Boulevard/FL-A1A (less than .1 mile). Sally's will be on your left.

I-95 Exit 268: Tap into Old-School Charm

Billy's Tap Room and Grill

58 East Granada Boulevard, Ormond Beach; 386-672-1910; www.billys-tap.com. Open Monday through Friday 11:30 a.m. to 10:00 p.m., Saturday 4:30 to 10:00 p.m. Closed Sunday. $$–$$$

From I-95: Take exit 268—SR 40 east toward Ormond Beach (5 miles). Billy's will be on your right in a strip of shops.

If you like old school, you'll love Billy's Tap Room and Grill. Everything about it is old school: the building, the menu, the service, and the clientele. Unlike Clark's Fish Camp or Saltwater Cowboy's, Billy's is old school in the rich not the roughin' it Florida tradition. John D. Rockefeller's old house, The Casements, is practically right next door to Billy's current location. Supposedly, Rockefeller asked his doctor where the healthiest place to live in the world was, and the doctor recommended Ormond Beach. So he ended up next to Billy's.

Billy's got its start in 1922 as a tearoom in the historic Ormond Hotel, which opened for the rich and famous each year from the Sunday after Halloween until Easter Sunday. (Today, the front window of Billy's has a sign that says WELCOME WINTER LOCALS. Snowbirds remain a constant.) In 1926 Billy MacDonald bought the current building and slowly turned it from a tearoom and gift shop into a speakeasy and then into a full-blown pub by 1937. General Manager Brad Disch tells about Billy's oldest son,

Maria Reisch and Brad Disch oversee the bartender's
Bloody Mary

Frank MacDonald, explaining that during Prohibition, you could step on a particular button in the bar, and doors would open to reveal slot machines and a stock of bootleg whiskey and homemade beer. Billy's has seen plenty of raucous good times, including during World War II when the WACS staying at local hotels apparently packed the place, but after the war Billy's started focusing more on food.

These days, Billy's still serves up plenty of drinks from behind the original solid maple bar, but the restaurant is more staid and upstanding, with the local Rotary and Daughters of the American Revolution meeting regularly in the banquet rooms, and plenty of regulars stopping by for their favorite meals. "If you call ahead on Monday, they'll save one of the meatloafs for you," we hear a bartender tell a local who is worried about getting there early enough for the special. Some folks even drive up from Orlando for a meal here. The interior is cool and dim with dark mahogany paneling, and lots of black-and-white photos of historic Ormond Beach and historic sports figures. It has a clubby feel, but the friendly atmosphere means it won't take long for you to feel like you belong to the club.

For dessert, the key lime pie is excellent: a traditional sweet/tart filling topped by meringue and served on a plain, not graham-cracker, pie crust. And the bread pudding has a killer whiskey butter sauce.

Old school though it is, they give youngsters a reason to show up, too, with a children's menu that includes barbecued baby-back ribs as well as the standard favorites (chicken fingers, etc.). Each kid's meal comes with a free mini brownie sundae for dessert. Old school tastes pretty good.

Most important, though, the food is consistently good. The Maryland-style crab cakes and grouper (served twenty-four different ways—ask for "The Famous Fish List" and count 'em) are both tasty. The scallops and shrimp are also good, and they cut up your calamari to order. The seafood is fresh and you pay for it. As usual, we'd avoid the tilapia, unless you like your fish tasteless and inoffensive. We call tilapia the "tofu of the sea," but without the flavor-absorption ability. Red-meat options include beef, lamb, veal, and pork, and there's a special "twilight menu" (read early-bird specials) from 3:00 to 5:30 p.m. Monday through Friday and 4:30 to 5:30 p.m. on Saturday. Jackie's Wedge Salad, a delicious dish of iceberg lettuce, crumbled Gorgonzola, bacon, chopped tomatoes, and homemade ranch dressing, sent Jane swooning back to her childhood. Speaking of blue, the blue sirloin burger is great, and so are the vegetable and mashed potato side dishes for any of the entrees.

Interstate 95
Daytona Beach
to Malabar

2

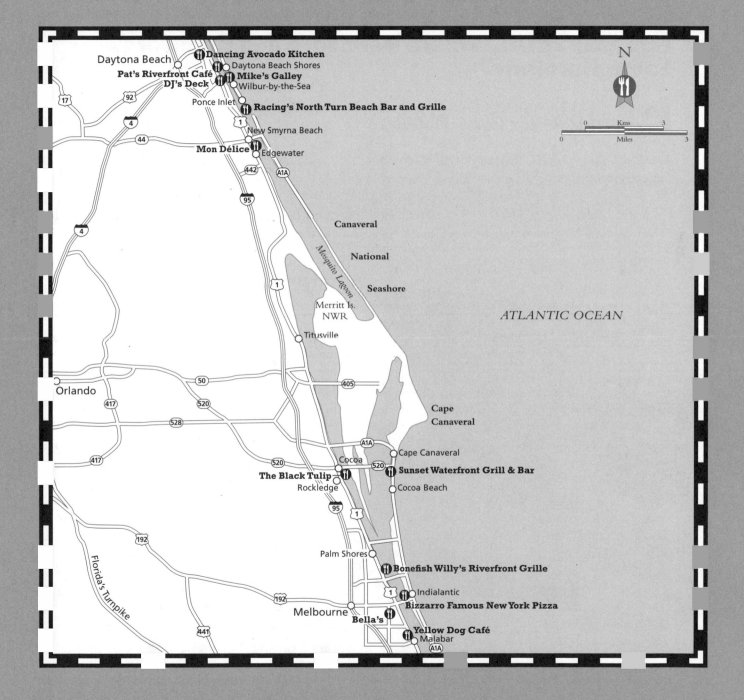

N

Daytona Beach

Dancing Avocado Kitchen
Daytona Beach Shores
Pat's Riverfront Café
Mike's Galley
DJ's Deck
Wilbur-by-the-Sea
Ponce Inlet
Racing's North Turn Beach Bar and Grille
New Smyrna Beach
Mon Délice
Edgewater

17
92
4
44
442
A1A
95
1

Canaveral

National

Mosquito Lagoon

Seashore

Merritt Is.
NWR

Titusville

Orlando

50

ATLANTIC OCEAN

405

417
520
528
417

Cape
Canaveral

A1A
Cape Canaveral
Cocoa
520
Sunset Waterfront Grill & Bar
The Black Tulip
Rockledge
Cocoa Beach
95
1

192

Palm Shores
Bonefish Willy's Riverfront Grille

417

Florida's Turnpike

192

1
Indialantic
Bizzarro Famous New York Pizza
Melbourne
Bella's
441
Yellow Dog Café
Malabar
A1A

Kms 0 3
Miles 0 3

I-95 Exit 261A: "Where Herbivore and Carnivore Eat in Harmony"

Dancing Avocado Kitchen

110 South Beach Street, Daytona Beach; 386-947-2022; www.avacadokitchen.net. Open Monday through Saturday 8:00 a.m. to 4:00 p.m. Closed Sunday. $$

From I-95: Take exit 261A—US 92/International Speedway Boulevard east toward Daytona Beach (5.3 miles). Make a right onto Beach Street, and the Avocado Kitchen will be on your right.

Mario Stemberger of the Dancing Avocado

The Dancing Avocado Kitchen looks like the brainchild of a transplanted California hippie, but owner Mario Stemberger is a native Daytonian. So is his wife, and so are his five homeschooled kids. There's lots of mosaic work with stones that say things like LOVE, PEACE, and FRIENDSHIP on them, a giant tie-dye square on the ceiling, funky signs, chalk drawings on the brick walls, and specific instructions: "hippies use side door." Mario cares about healthy food, and there is no smoking allowed, indoors or out. "Our customers just live longer" is one of the DAK's mottos—there are many. He cares about recycling but doesn't mind drinking. Check out the wide array of imported and domestic beers. He also cares about customer satisfaction. He stopped by our table, not knowing who we were, asked us how our meal was, and thanked us for coming, struggling for parking (not that bad really), and settling for a "small piece of real estate." (We got a tiny two-top, the last table in the place at lunchtime.)

The place is littered with avocado art. In fact, DAK is the biggest consumer of avocados in Volusia County. And the mascot costume that Mario drags out and makes one of his kids wear at local festivals? You guessed it, a giant avocado. You can get avocado omelets (a favorite of Jane's), avocado melts, and guacamole in burritos, quesadillas, or about anything else you like on the menu.

Breakfasts are excellent. Omelets and burritos set the standard and come in many guises. The Iguana veggie—assortment depends on the season—is a particularly delicious option. "Big Belgium Waffles" are thrown in for good measure. Be sure to check out the granola syrup! Whole wheat bread is delivered every morning from a local bakery and toasted up for your breakfast pleasure.

Before you start thinking this is a spot for only the health nuts among us, consider the "Dave Burger," named in honor of Daytona Beach's building inspector, who forced the installation of a grease trap as large as the one in a local steak house for what was then intended to be a vegetarian restaurant. In order to pay for the trap, Mario put the burger on the menu and kept count of the number sold until the grease trap was paid off: 1,700 burgers. For fun, they've kept dubious track of total burger sales up on the wall: 81,945 when we were last there. Besides burgers, you can get sausage, turkey, ham, and bacon at breakfast, and chicken and steak (tenderloin cuts) for lunch. The place lives up to the motto on the menu: "Where herbivore and carnivore eat in harmony." And if you need more calories, try the "Tater Chunks," deep-fried potatoes . . . baked with cheese.

Almost everything we've had at DAK is good. We like the "Fire Cracker Shrimp Burrito" with black beans, rice, lettuce, diced tomato, jack cheese, guacamole, and homemade salsa—mild or hot, you can't go wrong. The burgers are good, and the "Fire and Ice Cucumber Salad" is a great complement, all hot and cold at the same time. Our favorite thing of all, though, is the "Sweet Fried Plantains" dusted with salt, cinnamon, and sugar. The salty-sweet tastes dance in your mouth with the crispy-soft texture. Yum. Also, on your way out, don't forget to pick up one of the homemade cookies or muffins at the counter where you pay.

Mario's goal is "to help people find a pathway to healthy eating," and the Gourmettes are ready to follow him wherever he leads. One of the official DAK T-shirts says, "Carpe diem. Choose wisely, each man's life is but a breath." Nancy will choose another order of the plantains, please.

I-95 Exit 256: Escape Under the Bridge

DJ's Deck

79 Dunlawton Avenue, Port Orange; 386-760-2277. Open Sunday through Thursday 11:00 a.m. to 10:00 p.m., Friday and Saturday 11:00 a.m. to 11:00 p.m. $$

From I-95: Take exit 256—FL-421 east (which becomes Dunlawton Avenue/FL-A1A) toward Port Orange (4.9 miles) and make an almost U-turn to your left to go down under the bridge. DJ's will be on your right.

*N*ow *this* is a proper food chain: The shrimp at DJ's Deck start out scooting around in the ocean. Then one of several shrimp boats J.C. Freeman owns gathers up the shrimp and brings it to King's Seafood, which is at the marina under the Dunlawton Bridge. A giant load of it is immediately delivered to J.C.'s daughter, Kim Graham, and her husband, David Graham, who own DJ's Deck, right next door to King's Seafood. They grill it or fry it or boil it, and then it ends up in a red basket on your picnic table of choice under a tiki-esque thatched roof or an umbrella right by the Intracoastal Waterway, and—voila!—into your mouth. That is why the shrimp at DJ's Deck is so fresh and tasty. The family has eliminated the middle man.

Shrimp isn't the only delectable option, though.

Jill Talk

Things can get pretty fishy in Florida. Just ask Al Gore. That's why it helps to arm yourself with at least a rudimentary knowledge of the state's most popular fish. Remember the first rule: the fresher, the better. Here's a Gourmettes' primer to get you prepped for your next piscatorial escapade:

Catfish—A Southern favorite, the farm-raised versions are mild, but the wild ones hold back a bit of river mud in their taste. The flesh is white, firm, flaky, and low in fat. Order them pan- or deep-fried.

Cobia—This big ole fighting fish, a favorite of sport fishermen, is flaky, white, and succulent. It has plenty of fat content, grills up great, and reminds us of mahi-mahi.

Flounder — This flat fish swims on one side and wears both its eyes on the other. It's a dainty fish with a delicate texture and mild taste. It doesn't hold up on the grill.

Grouper — We love this meaty fish, which is firm enough to stand up to any kind of cooking method you want. Its mild flavor and lean, flaky texture compliment all sorts of radical and traditional sauces. It's getting expensive, though, and harder to find fresh.

Mackerel — The Europeans eat it more than we do, but plenty of tasty mackerel are caught just off the Florida coast. These fish have firm, dark flesh that's fatty and full flavored, again not a good choice for those who don't like their fish to taste like fish. An excellent choice, however, for those looking to up their Omega-3 oils. It's also great smoked.

Mahi-mahi — They don't call it dolphin because people might get it confused with Flipper and miss out on this moist, firm, flaky fish with a rather strong but pleasant flavor. Not for the faint-of-heart fish eaters.

Mullet — Smoke it, baby. Nuff said.

Pompano — Another pugnacious sport fish, pompano has a unique sweet flavor that matches up well with high spice and tropical fruits.

Red Snapper — A Gourmettes' favorite, this mild, delicate white fish is low in fat and firm. It goes great with almonds and plenty of butter (so much for the low fat).

Salmon — This most versatile of fish comes in all sorts of makes and models. It's high in fat and has plenty of distinctive salmon taste. Eat it any way you can.

Swordfish — Not a Gourmettes' favorite, this is another of those fishy fish. Its meaty, grayish flesh is firm and high in fat. Get it grilled or, better yet, order another kind of fish altogether.

Tilapia — People have been farm raising these fish at least as far back as 2500 B.C. Egypt. It's mild with white or pinkish flesh and can be prepared just about any way you like. We call it the "tofu of the sea," only it doesn't absorb as much flavor as tofu. It's about as bland as fish gets.

Tuna — Our favorite, tuna runs the gamut from the pale pink or white albacore tuna that our moms turned into potato-chip-topped casseroles all the way up to the deep ruby red sushi-grade yellowfin tuna that restaurants all over the state have made a staple. The darker the "beefy" meat, the stronger the flavor. The stronger the flavor, the better — as long as it's plenty fresh!

Danish had an illicit international affair with a Mexican fried ice cream, this would be their illegitimate offspring." Good stuff.

Whatever you decide to get, you'll order at the bar window and then a friendly server will find your picnic table when the food is ready. DJ's also has tables inside in case of bad weather, but otherwise, outside is the place to be. The servers are always attentive and helpful. David says that they ask them "to be professional and to have fun. We call it professional fun." It works—efficiency and great food in a laid-back, fun environment. The place is so laid-back, they don't even have railings between the deck and the water. Watch your two-year-olds. Otherwise, it's a family friendly place with a kids' menu where young and old congregate to "chill" and eat well. And if you get the chance, the sunsets are often spectacular with silhouettes of boats set against a dramatic backdrop of purples, pinks, oranges, and reds.

The blackened mixed grill with teriyaki-marinated basa fish, scallops, and shrimp is a great bet, as is the fried basa sandwich, which will feed a family of four. Basa is technically in the Vietnamese catfish family, but it's sometimes sold under the grouper name (if your "grouper" sandwich is cheap, chances are it's really basa) and doesn't taste at all like American catfish. Basa is a good grouper substitute at a fraction of the price. Try the homemade chowder-gumbo with shrimp, fish, okra, celery, tomatoes, and onions. The hush puppies are sweet with onions and red peppers. Nancy loves them; Jane doesn't like her hush puppies sweet. The shark bites with Tiger Sauce—homemade horseradish and mayo—are also good, and we like the beer-battered fries as well. Any of the meals go great with a cold draft or bottled beer. For dessert, try the fried cheesecake, which our friend Bonnie, an erstwhile Gourmette, describes this way: "If a cheese

34

I-95 Exit 256: The Secret's Out

Pat's Riverfront Café (at Seven Seas Marina)

3300 South Peninsula Drive, Port Orange; 386-756-8070. Open daily 7:00 a.m. to 2:00 p.m. $–$$

From I-95: Take exit 256—SR 421 east (which becomes FL-A1A North/Dunlawton Avenue) toward Port Orange (4.9 miles) and turn left onto South Peninsula Drive/FL-421 (.4 mile). Pat's Riverfront Café will be on your left around the back of Seven Seas Marina.

Pat's advertises itself as "Daytona's Best Kept Secret"—not for long now that the Gourmettes have found it. We wouldn't have known about it except that we showed up to eat at Mike's Galley on a sluggish Tuesday, Mike's "swing day"—he opens or not depending on his mood when he rolls out of bed. This morning was apparently rough for him. We asked about second choices at the Beach Quarters Resort, and the desk clerk sent us to Pat's, which is hidden behind the Seven Seas Marina. Just drive into the giant boatyard with half-worked-on boats all over the place, keep going past the big warehouse, past the sign that says NO CARS until you're almost to the docks, and there's Pat's. It's a true dive, a hole-in-the-wall restaurant that sits next to the Intracoastal Waterway and attracts the nautical types, local yokels, and slumming yuppies.

Pat, *the* Pat of Pat's Riverfront Café, learned to cook on the job . . . not something you expect or hope to find going on in a restaurant. But that

Some of Pat's kitchen crew

happened a long time ago, more than twenty years, when Pat first started working at the cafe. She'd hired on as a waitress, but the then–owner/manager would disappear, leaving hungry customers who talked Pat through the cooking, promising to eat whatever she produced. They did, and still do. Soon Pat took over the place, hired other waitresses and cooks, and turned out thousands of home-cooked meals. Most of the staff has been there almost as long as Pat—unheard of in the restaurant business. One server has been there since 1991, and there's only one newcomer, an old-timer's son's girlfriend. How does Pat manage to keep people working for her so long? She just grins and says, "Pay them well." The staff claims it's the feeling of being part of a family. They even look like family, all the servers being blonde and middle-aged, and most wearing tank-top T-shirts. Pat considered closing after the hurricanes of 2004, but she realized she had too many people depending on her.

The customers, many of whom are regulars with as much time in as the staff, also are treated like family. At the table next to ours, the wife had gotten there on time while her husband, who was meeting her, was stuck in traffic. She ordered for both and was served. When he showed up, Pat came out with his foot-long hot dog—which looked mighty good, by the way—with "you're late" written in mustard on the bun. Seeing the dog immediately made Jane regret her tasty but healthy choice of a turkey sandwich.

Pat's has your usual diner lunch options, like meat loaf and mashed potatoes, hamburgers, and grilled cheese, but our favorite meal at Pat's is breakfast. The Full Sail Omelet, with onions, black olives, mushrooms, tomatoes, and what they call hot peppers but are really banana peppers, is outstanding. We tried to figure out why we hadn't been eating banana peppers in our omelets all our lives. The seafood omelet used imitation crab, fish of some sort, and tiny shrimp, all of which were once frozen, and yet it managed to work. The funky-chunky hollandaise sauce served on top works too, even if it ain't pretty. The home fries, grilled with onions, are the perfect accompaniment. The ham on the eggs Benedict is thick and delicious. The Cajun sausage is tasty, but it wasn't Cajun; maybe kielbasa that happened to be made in Louisiana? Bread is not Pat's thing, so we'd recommend staying away from anything that falls under that broad category: e.g., French toast or biscuits. We're not counting the blueberry pancakes in that warning, though; they're pretty scrumptious.

The kitchen—SLAVE QUARTERS says the sign—is open to the dining room so we could watch our cook. Late-twentieth-century American beer art is well represented—MGD, Bud, and Bud Light especially—and joke signs abound, such as IF YOU WANT SOMETHING, LIFT YOUR HANDS OVER YOUR HEAD AND WAVE FRANTICALLY. The car photos scattered on the walls are Pat's collection (the actual cars, not the photos).

Sunday mornings are particularly crowded, but you won't mind too much as you sit out on picnic tables under the palms and oaks, by the marina and water, and wait for someone to poke her nose out the door and yell, "Nancy!" "Jane!" Almost like Mom.

I-95 Exit 256: Size Doesn't Matter at Mike's

Mike's Galley (inside the Beach Quarter Resort)

3711 South Atlantic Avenue, Daytona Beach Shores; 386-767-3119, ext. 104. Open Wednesday through Sunday 7:00 a.m. to 1:00 p.m. and sometimes Tuesday 7:00 a.m. to 1:00 p.m. Closed Monday and sometimes Tuesday. It might be worth calling ahead to make sure Mike is up and running. $–$$

From I-95: Take exit 256—SR 421 (which becomes FL-A1A North/Dunlawton Avenue) east toward Port Orange (5.1 miles). Turn right onto South Atlantic Avenue/CR 4075 (.4 mile) and Mike's Galley will be on your left inside the Beach Quarter Resort.

You'd never find Mike's Galley without us. A galley pretty much describes the size of this converted efficiency, a corner unit overlooking the beach, with no dishwasher other than Mike and a small apartment-size refrigerator. Mike's is a tiny place with big food. The recipes are his mom's, and he gives her "110 percent of the credit." Mike doesn't advertise (he has a small sign out front that you can read only if you're heading north on FL-A1A) because he barely has room to fit the people who've lucked onto the restaurant. Five tables inside and five tables on the L-shaped balcony outside, mostly two-tops, are all he has to offer, but it's worth the wait if you find a line, which is more likely on weekends or during one of the prime Daytona tourist weeks— Bike Week, Speed Week, Spring Break, etc.

Home-baked breads and pastries highlight the menu. Get the toasted cinnamon bread with whatever else you order. We had intended to recommend the place mostly for breakfast, but it's great for lunch as well. Why not eat breakfast and then walk, run, or swim on the beach below and come back for lunch? We've done it. Hey, no sacrifice is too great for our readers!

At breakfast, the mix-in's—scrambled omelet concoctions—are primo, with lots of fresh ingredients to choose from. Any of the egg-and-breakfast-meat combos are good, though. The real dilemma is whether to order the home fries—crunchy on the outside, tender on the inside, grilled with onions and seasoning—or the potato pancakes, which are also crunchy on the outside and tender on the inside with plenty of onions. Giving up either is a loss, so we recommend trying both. The regular pancakes with chocolate chips, blueberries, or pecans are also tasty, as is the French toast.

For lunch, the club sandwich with thickly sliced, home-cooked turkey and ham and home-baked toasted bread would surely ruin all the other club sandwiches you'll ever have in your life except for the American cheese that usually comes with it. Ask for Swiss and you'll have a club nonpareil. The burgers are also good, as are the fries and the quiche and the cinnamon buns and the sticky buns. We love it all. We ordered so many different things at Mike's one day, trying to find something subpar, that our server, Lori Graham, the only employee, got more and more amused with us. "Anything else?" she'd smirk again and again, and we'd keep finding something. Finally, we gave up. "We would have ordered more," Jane told her, "but I'm on Weight Watchers, and I've used up my points for the month."

When we finally waddled out, Lori was on her break, eating at a table near the door. "Ladies," she told us, shielding her ham sandwich as we walked past, "leave my food alone."

Mike is chief cook and bottle washer

Meals Worth Stopping for in *Florida*

I-95 Exit 256: A Good Excuse for a Pit Stop

Racing's North Turn Beach Bar and Grille

4511 South Atlantic Avenue, Ponce Inlet; 386-322-3258; www.racingsnorthturn.com. Open daily 11:00 a.m. to 11:00 p.m. $$–$$$

From I-95: Take exit 256—SR 421 east (which will become Dunlawton Avenue/FL-A1A North) toward Port Orange (5.1 miles) and turn right onto South Atlantic Avenue/CR 4075 (3.2 miles). Racing's North Turn will be on your left, and they have parking on your right.

In the earliest days of stock car racing, folks who had honed their driving skills outrunning the law during Prohibition made their way to Daytona Beach for a go at the beach track, so named because one straightaway was on the beach, and the other was on FL-A1A. As the track evolved and the popularity of the sport grew, a restaurant was built in the 1950s just north of the north-turn grandstands. Through a number of incarnations, the restaurant is still there, and it's known, appropriately enough, as Racing's North Turn these days.

Walter and Rhonda Glasnak bought the place in 1998 and are particularly interested in the racing history of the building, which was named a historical landmark during Race Week of 2007. They have all sorts of racing memorabilia around the place, and if you're lucky, you might even run into a driver while you're there. Manager Lars Bienemann says that "Ray Fox, who has a shrimp salad sandwich named after him, and Russ Truelove, who has a prime rib sand-

wich named after him, love to sit and tell stories and sign autographs." Russ flipped his car six times when downshifting from 130 mph on the North Turn in 1956, so we bet he's got special memories of sand and sky from about 100 yards away from the restaurant.

We've never run into Ray or Russ, literally or figu-

George Ephren Sr., early stock-car legend

ratively (although we hear great things about Ray's shrimp salad), but one day at the North Turn, we were lucky enough to meet up with George Ephren Sr., who stopped by the restaurant with his family for a build-your-own ½ lb. burger. In 1936 George raced a yellow Ford Roadster (#33) to third place in the first stock car race on the Daytona Beach Road Course against Bill France, Sr., and Lee Petty, Richard's dad. "I won $17.50 and had to go to Bill France's bar to pick up the money," George recalled. "The way it used to be, you took care of your own car and you raced against rum runners. I had to be my own pitman. Took off bumpers, headlights, fenders. Used to take 200 lbs. of sand and strap it in the rumble seat to keep weight over the rear wheel," which held the car down. He'd even drive his race car down from his home in Jacksonville. "If you could run a car 100 mph, you had a good car," said George. "I ran mine

120." George ran one more race in Daytona, and then settled down to a stint in the military and a career as a machinist and a postal worker. Now he just comes to Daytona for the burgers.

When NASCAR was formed in 1948, the Beach Road Course hosted the first event. Daytona International Speedway took over the Daytona races when it was built in 1959, and NASCAR has never been the same.

It's easy to get sidetracked on racing history at the North Turn and forget about two arguably more important factors: killer food and the great deck that sits right over the sand. For appetizers, we love the bacon-wrapped sea scallops—best either of us has ever had. They manage to keep the scallop sweet and moist while getting the bacon crisp. The baked mushrooms stuffed with crabmeat and cream cheese and smothered with cheddar cheese are awfully good, too, especially if you're a major cheese fan. Nancy ordered them for a taste and couldn't stop eating them. The fried fish Reuben with slaw and provolone in place of sauerkraut and Swiss is pretty darn good, too, although the "Mad Marion" Melt, grilled or blackened basa smothered with provolone and grilled onions on rye, is even better.

If you're a race fan, this is the place for you. If you couldn't care less about racing, but you love sitting on a deck at the beach, watching the waves and eating good food with the sea breezes in your hair, this is the place for you too. Or if you just like sitting at a sports bar, drinking, eating, and watching your favorite game, this is the place for you too. Racing's North Turn has everything but fancy.

I-95 Exit 249: Bon Appetit!

Mon Délice

557 3rd Avenue, New Smyrna Beach; 386-427-6555. Open daily 8:00 a.m. to 6:00 p.m. $–$$

From I-95: Take exit 249—FL-44 east toward New Smyrna Beach. FL-44 becomes East 3rd Avenue after you cross the causeway (5.9 miles). Mon Délice will be on your right.

*I*f you grew up in Central Florida, as Nancy did, your beach of choice was probably New Smyrna Beach, what some affectionately call "Orlando East." And if you spent any time at all in New Smyrna, then you probably know about Mon Délice, a *boulangerie* that's been an institution there since a French couple opened the place in 1976 and started changing the way Floridians think about croissants and baguettes. Nancy has fond memories of Mon Délice as a child, and it's even better under the "new" ownership that bought it in 1992, Serge and Pamela Sorese.

Serge grew up in the French Riviera, where his father and two uncles all had restaurants. He has baked and cooked all his life. He moved to Florida after he met his future wife, who was from the Orlando area. "All my wife's family could talk about was going to the Mon Délice Bakery in New Smyrna. I went for the first time in 1989 and fell in love with it." Serge didn't like the big city anyway and preferred small seacoast towns, so a few years later, he went to the owners of Mon Délice, sat down in their kitchen over a bottle of red wine, and negotiated the purchase. "The whole thing was settled in four hours," said Serge, "the European way with no paperwork or lawyers. We got the lawyers involved *after* we had it all worked out." The transition was a smooth one, and the place continued to be a true French bakery, even down to the way they package your delicacies.

A true French bakery means that this is not your typical Gourmette recommendation. There are no tables or chairs for dining inside, not even a picnic table outside. But you are just down a few blocks from one of Florida's nicer beaches, and it's tough to find a better dining spot than that. You can choose from a very limited assortment of submarine sandwiches and a much wider assortment of French pastries. While the Gourmettes think an assortment of pastries is a perfectly acceptable breakfast, lunch, or dinner option, we realize there may be some traditionalists among you. The sandwiches are served on one of the best baguettes you'll find in Florida. The salami is a Gourmette favorite, layered with provolone, dressed with vinaigrette, and pressed. The crunchy exterior meets up with a delightful oozy interior. As for the pastries, Nancy's a big fan of the *pain au chocolat* (chocolate croissant) as well as any of the other croissants and also what the French call *mille feuille* (a thousand leaves) and the Americans call a Napoleon, alternating layers of paper-thin pastry and cream, topped with vanilla icing, drizzled with chocolate streaks, and then combed. Jane likes to stick with the fabulously moist and rich coconut macaroons unless she's seduced by a custard-filled éclair. The whipped cream–filled éclair just doesn't drip down your chin in the same way the custard one does.

Serge tells us that very often he sees the same people three times in a day. "The customers come in first in the morning when they get their coffee and croissant before they head to the beach. Then they come back between 11:00 and 2:30 for a sub. Then I see them again at the end of the day when they stop by to get some pastries for the family at home." We can hardly think of a better day!

I-95 Exit 201: Old World Charm

The Black Tulip

207 Brevard Avenue, Cocoa; 321-631-1133. Open Tuesday through Saturday 11:30 a.m. to 2:00 p.m. and 5:30 to 9:00 p.m. Closed Sunday and Monday. $$–$$$

From I-95: Take exit 201—SR 520/King Street east toward Cocoa (4.2 miles) and turn right onto Brevard Avenue/CR 515 South. Black Tulip will be on your right.

According to owner Daniel Colzani, there are people who've been coming to The Black Tulip for a quarter of a century who have never had anything but "the duck," in other words, the "Tulip Crisp Roast Duckling, a crisp Long Island duck, double roasted and covered with a not-too-sweet sauce made of apples, cashews, and red wine." Mm-mmmm.

When Daniel was flying once, a man across the aisle learned Daniel was the owner of The Black Tulip. He jumped up, hugged Daniel, and yelled out to the rest of the passengers, "Oh, my God! This man cooks the best duck I've ever eaten." They bought each other drinks all the way to Brazil.

That's the kind of passion Daniel's cooking inspires. Although the duck has a cult following, there are lots of other reasons to visit The Black Tulip. Only 4.2 miles off the interstate, the Tulip is an upscale but relaxing respite from the hassle of the freeway. You can dine inside or out on real tablecloths

with real food, real service, and jazz on speakers in the background, assuming no one is playing live on the baby grand piano. For lunch the value is hard to beat, with lots of great salad, soup, and entree options for less than $10. You can order your salads small or large, and the tasty black bean soup is Daniel's mom's recipe. Try the Fresh Crab Cake, as big as a saucer and made with minced vegetables and spices that give it an unusual and delightful flavor. The "Brutus" salad is a hearty mix of romaine, bacon, Parmesan cheese, mushrooms, tomatoes, and homemade croutons. The Avocado Ritz Platter, shrimp salad in a light orangey dressing served in half an avocado, is another good choice and comes with fresh fruit and a Russian potato salad. The escargot on a bed of creamed spinach and topped with hollandaise and grated Parmesan are rich and satisfying too.

Don't be scared off by the fancy sound of the place, though; at lunch folks come dressed in shorts and tennis shoes as well as business attire. At dinner the prices go up but are still reasonable, and the place becomes more romantic with candles and soft music. Even then, there's no dress code, and Florida casual prevails.

If you're there for dinner and looking for something other than duck, you might try the Veal Oscar topped with Florida blue crab, fresh asparagus, and hollandaise; the grouper with crab stuffing, wrapped in pastry; or the Baked Mahi-Mahi Caprice, filets topped with sliced bananas, baked, and then finished with lemon sauce. There's plenty to choose from with duck, veal, chicken, steak, pork, fish, and pasta all on the menu.

Desserts are delicious too. Nancy especially loves the perfect traditional key lime pie, which is much harder to find in Florida than we realized. We've been eating key lime pie all across the state, and although it's relatively easy to make, very few restaurants manage do a good job, despite most of them trying. Jane is a big fan of the Brazilian Flan, also a recipe from Daniel's mother.

Daniel describes Cocoa as "paradise," and we think that during or after a long day of driving, you might find The Black Tulip a small slice of paradise.

Meals Worth Stopping for in *Florida*

I-95 Exit 201: Over the Causeways to Island Time

Sunset Waterfront Grill & Bar

500 West Cocoa Beach Causeway, Cocoa Beach; 321-783-8485; www.sunsetwaterfrontcafeandbar.com. Open daily 11:00 a.m. to 10:00 p.m. $$–$$$

From I-95: Take exit 201—SR 520/King Street east toward Cocoa (11.1 miles). Sunset Waterfront Grill will be on your right just over the Banana River Bridge, the third bridge you'll cross.

*T*he first time we went to the Sunset Waterfront Grill & Bar—or the Sunset Café as it's sometimes known—it was at the end of a long sad day of Gourmetting: We'd been foiled at three restaurants for which we'd had high expectations. People think it's all "glam" being a Gourmette, getting to eat and eat and eat in exotic locales, but they don't realize how disappointing most of the places we eat are. Some days are better than others. This one was rough. Anyway, on a whim we decided to try the Sunset Waterfront one Saturday afternoon about four-thirty. We sidled up to the bar, ordered a beer, listened to the guy playing guitar and singing "Take It Easy," looked out onto the expansive Banana River and saw dolphins making graceful arcs above the water, and—poof—our worries were gone. Our bartender told us the dolphins are here often, manatees and turtles sometimes, too. Like those machines that suck smoke out of the air, the Sunset Café somehow sucks the stress right out of you and leaves you with a peaceful, easy feeling. And yes, it happened before the beer had a chance to kick in. Truth is, we hadn't even tried the food, and this place was "in."

That afternoon we had the bacon-wrapped scallops appetizer and a dozen oysters, which were acceptable, but we'd be "forced" to come back several more times to try various dishes on the menu . . . and

The Ragtime Rascals in action

hear the Ragtime Rascals . . . and watch a sunset. But we're getting ahead of ourselves.

We admit that the Sunset is a little farther from the interstate than you might like to venture (11.1 miles), but the drive is past the quaint historic downtown Cocoa, and over several bridges that give you gorgeous views of the rivers that help separate Cocoa Beach from the mainland. If you've got a little extra time, it's worth the drive. The Sunset has live music every day of the week that starts about 6:00 p.m. on weeknights, but earlier on weekends. Happy Hour with drink specials and free hors d'oeuvres is from 4:00 to 6:00 p.m. Friday through Wednesday. There's no Happy Hour on Thursday afternoon because the Ragtime Rascals play from 2:00 to 5:00 p.m. for the wildest group of seniors we've seen outside The Villages. They laugh, flirt, dance, and form conga lines,

but apparently they don't drink much and have been known to eat too many of the free hors d'oeuvres, so no more freebies on Thursdays.

Back to the food: Our favorite things are the oyster po' boy, perfectly cooked oysters—in batter, much to Jane's dismay—served open-faced on buttered toasted French bread, and a gigantic dessert of beer-battered deep-fried apple slices with ice cream, caramel sauce, cinnamon, and whipped cream. We're getting hungry as we write. They make all their own desserts except the chocolate cake, which happened to be the favorite dessert of two of the bartenders. The shrimp and scallops were also good.

But the main thing is the peaceful, easy feeling. One time when we were there we saw dolphins being chased by pelicans, both after the same fish. Obviously, it makes sense to plan your visit to include sunset if possible. As the red orb touches down on the opposite side of the river, the restaurant operations stop, the folks without views of the water head out to the dock, and everyone pauses till the last rays have sunk below the horizon. On a clear day, it's worth the 22-mile round-trip.

Meals Worth Stopping for in *Florida*

I-95 Exit 183: "To Fish or not to Fish? What a Stupid Question."

Bonefish Willy's Riverfront Grille

2459 Pineapple Avenue, Melbourne; 321-253-8888; www.bonefishwillys.com. Open Monday through Saturday 11:00 a.m. to 10:00 p.m., Sunday 11:00 a.m. to 9:00 p.m. $$–$$$

From I-95: Take exit 183—FL-518/Eau Galle Boulevard east toward Melbourne (4.7 miles). Turn left onto US 1/FL-5/Harbour City Boulevard (1.2 miles), right onto Cliff Creek Drive (.1 mile), and left onto Pineapple Avenue. Bonefish Willy's will be on your right.

The original Bonefish Willy used to guide Ernest Hemingway in the Bahamas when Papa was in search of . . . you guessed it . . . bonefish, one of the toughest and best fighting sport fish around. Papa would have been happy to have spent a leisurely dinner at Bonefish Willy's Riverfront Grille after a tough day on the flats. The Gourmettes are ready for a leisurely dinner there anytime.

The setting seduces you first, the 1918-ish cottage—dim and cool and nautical—that leads you out to the recently expanded deck and outdoor bar where you can sit and face the Indian River. On one trip we saw a dolphin, a flock of seagulls, two brown pelicans, and a great blue heron all squabbling over the same school of fish. Nights, the deck and outside tiki bar (beer and wine only) are lit by a romantic combination of tiki torches, rope lights, and large red-and-white Christmas lights. Outdoor heaters keep things warm on cool nights, and sometimes they've got live music outside—a steel drum player one night when we were there. "I always feel like I'm in the Keys here," says co-owner Terry Holt. "No matter how frustrated I get, I can walk out on the deck and feel totally different." He's right. We feel different too.

The second, more surprising thing that seduces you is the food. Some restaurants that have gorgeous real estate let the scenery pull the customers in and figure the clientele will settle for whatever they get. Not Bonefish Willy's. Here, co-owners Tina Quinn (an exacting connoisseur of food—one of those people who can taste a dish and tell you all the ingredients in it and what changes should be made) and Terry Holt are committed to quality food. "So many places get all this stuff from Sysco Foods," says Terry. "Everything here's made from scratch." And it's fresh.

Our first time there, we tried "Willy's Combo Platter" to start things off. The outstanding Oysters Willy were served on the half shell and topped with spinach, onion, andouille sausage, and cheddar-jack cheese, and the crab cake was great—mostly crab, juicy inside with a crisp outside, and served with a creamy remoulade sauce. The coconut shrimp that came with the platter were a bit overdone. We also tried the conch fritters, which were amazing when topped with the tomato-pineapple salsa that came with them. The black bean soup was delicious but we liked the gumbo even better. It was loaded with goodies—fish, shrimp, and andouille sausage—and was served with warm French bread topped with butter, Parmesan cheese, and herbs. Mmmmmmm. The snapper in asparagus curry sauce was spicy and delicious, with a great veggie side: red beans, corn, celery, and onions combined in a red sauce. For dessert, Jane likes the key lime pie, chiffon type, very light, but we'd recommend the peanut butter chocolate pie even more.

For lunch, the sandwiches, burritos, and the like are accompanied by a side of island pasta salad, a garlicky combination of rotini, and chunks of cucumber, onion, and tomato. Nancy loves the "Grouper Willy," with grilled fresh grouper on pumpernickel with pineapple coleslaw, cheddar-jack cheese and remoulade. It's tasty, but Jane thinks it might even be better without the cheese. The oyster po' boys are also delicious with their beer-battered, Cajun-seasoned freshly shucked oysters.

Hemingway would've loved this place.

Meals Worth Stopping for in *Florida*

I-95 Exit 180: Attitude Is Everything

Bizzarro Famous New York Pizza

4 Wavecrest Avenue, Indialantic; 321-724-4799. Open Monday through Thursday 11:00 a.m. to 9:00 p.m., Friday and Saturday 11:00 a.m. to 11:00 p.m., and Sunday noon to 9:00 p.m. $–$$

From I-95: Take exit 180—US 192/FL-500 east (8.7 miles). Turn left onto FL-A1A/Miramar Avenue and in less than .1 mile turn right onto Wavecrest Avenue. Bizzarro's will be on your right.

If Florida's Southern hospitality starts wearing on you, all those strangers smiling and telling you to "Have a great day!". . . if you find yourself longing to be bullied in that New York/New Jersey way, we've got a place for you: "The Original Bizzarro Famous New York Pizza." Here's a typical scenario: The Gourmettes walk in, and the guy behind the pizza counter says, "What do you want?" all mean-like.

Nancy says, "Just a minute." Gourmettes never order quickly. There's too much to take in on a new menu, this one on the wall above.

"Hurry up!" he yells at her. Then a minute or two later, when she's ready to order, he ignores her, punishing her for being so slow. She starts to try to order with the guy behind the cash register, but he barely shakes his head and cocks it toward the guy who was formerly grilling her about what she wanted. "I just take your money," says the cash-register guy.

Finally the first guy decides she's been punished enough and takes her order for two slices. Then the cash-register guy says, "To drink?"

"I can order drinks from you?" Nancy asks.

"I guess."

If you were raised in the South and had never met anyone like these guys, you'd probably assume they

The surliest pizza makers in Florida

crust, fresh sauce, plentiful cheese, and generous toppings. Almost makes you forget you're eating pizza in Florida. They advertise "Home of the World's Largest Slices." Hyperbole, no doubt, but the slices are plenty big and delicious. The calamari, too, is worth ordering, with its light batter and fresh marinara dipping sauce.

The king of attitude here is Francesco, who started this business in 1988. Along the central eastern coast of Florida, you're liable to find any number of Bizzarro's Pizzas, and you might start wondering if the Gourmettes have gone to the dark side and started supporting big chain restaurants. Here's the scoop: those other Bizzarro's were probably started and sold by Peter Bizzarro, Francesco's brother, or they're owned by someone else in the family. Francesco is one of seven children who moved to Brooklyn from Naples, Italy, when Francesco was ten. Lots of them moved to Florida somewhere along the way.

Whereas Francesco settled down and devoted himself to "The Original" Bizzarro Famous New York Pizza, Peter has been spreading the family name far and wide by starting pizza joints and then selling them. Some of them, and some other Bizzarro's started by other members of the family, are really good; some maybe not so much, but we decided that since Francesco has been faithful to this one original pizza place for so long and the pizza is so good and the setting—a surfer hangout across a small road from the beach—is so great that this Bizzarro's is "in." You're on your own at any of the others.

were at least rude, maybe sadistic. Of course, this is merely flavor, scenery. Scratch the surface (as we did after several visits) and these guys are puppy dogs, all wanting their picture in the book and sweet as can be. At Bizzarro's, the attitude is part of the ambience. You get it for free with any purchase. "That's what they're here for," owner Francesco Bizzarro says, "to give you a hard time. Makes it worth the trip."

Even if you don't feel heartened by the attitude, it's worth the trip just for the pizza with its thin crispy

Meals Worth Stopping for in *Florida*

I-95 Exit 180: Delizioso!

Bella's

1904 Municipal Lane, Melbourne; 321-723-5001. Open for lunch Monday through Friday 11:30 a.m. to 2:30 p.m. Open for dinner Monday through Thursday 5:00 to 9:00 p.m., Friday and Saturday 5:00 to 10:00 p.m. Closed Sunday. $$–$$$

From I-95: Take exit 180—US 192/FL-500 east toward Melbourne (6.1 miles). Turn right onto Municipal Lane, and Bella's will be on your right.

"It started with a blind date," explains Chef Frank Demolfetta. The Gourmettes are suckers for stories that start like this. Bella Forster chimes in, "Some good parties and good cooking later" they decided to go into business together. Frank is a third-generation Italian chef and was selling wholesale Italian food before teaming up with Bella. "My heart is in the kitchen," he says. They looked all over Melbourne and finally found a place in 1998—half of what Bella's is today. The restaurant immediately took off, and they've expanded to twice their original size and are often packed. Frank takes care of the kitchen, and Bella takes care of the dining room and books. A troupe of family members from both sides chips in and helps out with various duties.

Why do so many locals return again and again to this little Italian restaurant in Melbourne's downtown? They come back for Bella's Salad with fresh greens, lots of Gorgonzola and Romano, an excellent olive salad, artichokes, red onions, and tomatoes, all dressed with their signature Italian dressing. The mini is large enough to share for a starter. They come back for the knots of fresh bread, served hot and

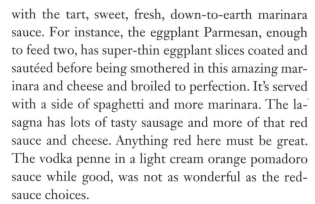

with the tart, sweet, fresh, down-to-earth marinara sauce. For instance, the eggplant Parmesan, enough to feed two, has super-thin eggplant slices coated and sautéed before being smothered in this amazing marinara and cheese and broiled to perfection. It's served with a side of spaghetti and more marinara. The lasagna has lots of tasty sausage and more of that red sauce and cheese. Anything red here must be great. The vodka penne in a light cream orange pomadoro sauce while good, was not as wonderful as the red-sauce choices.

Then there's the pizza, with a crust that's thin and crisp in the center of the pie while the outside edges are crisp with a softer inside. It's all covered with more great red sauce, bubbling cheese, and fresh toppings (homemade meatballs, zucchini, proscuitto, fresh mozzarella, whole mushrooms, broccoli, eggplant, plus all the usual options). They warn you that the pizzas are hand tossed and might take thirty to forty minutes. It's worth every minute.

The second time we went, the same chirpy, accommodating hostess showed us to our table, but our official server was "in the weeds" (restaurant lingo for "way busy") and not very happy to play the Gourmettes' parlor game of "what do you like better, X or Y?" "What are your favorites?" etc. "Look, it's all good," she said, exasperated. And as off-putting as her answer was, she's right. It is all good, and lots of it is great. Frank knows his Italian cooking, and the place almost feels like a large Italian home from which you leave satisfied and well cared for.

Frank Demolfetta and Bella Forster

dripping in garlic butter. They come back for the friendly hostess who acted like our long, lost servant, cheerfully attending to our every need on our first visit. They come back for the rich, cheesy pasta e fagiole. But most of all they come back for anything made

I-95 Exit 173: A Doghouse You'll Want to Be In

Yellow Dog Café

905 US 1, Malabar; 321-956-3334; www.yellowdogcafe.net. Open for lunch Tuesday through Sunday 11:30 a.m. to 2:30 p.m. Open for dinner Sunday and Tuesday through Thursday 5:00 to 9:00 p.m., Friday and Saturday 5:00 to 10:00 p.m. Outdoor Dog Bar open Tuesday through Sunday 11:30 a.m. to closing. Closed Monday. $–$$$$

From I-95: Take exit 173—SR 514/Malabar Road East (4.2 miles) until it dead-ends into US 1. Turn left onto US 1 (.6 mile) and Yellow Dog will be on your right, riverside.

Nancy, who was born without the requisite dog-loving gene, can't understand why anyone would pick a yellow dog as a name and decorating motif for a restaurant, but Jane, who owns two yellow dogs herself, liked the place even before she saw it. This little shack on the Indian River in Malabar has yellow-dog photos and art everywhere, with an occasional non-yellow dog thrown in who must have friends in high places.

As it turns out, Nancy and Stuart Borton, the owners who named the restaurant, don't have a yellow dog; in fact, they don't have any dogs at all because Stuart is allergic to them. But they do have friends who have a yellow dog, and they did buy a German shepherd named Tinio, who's not yellow, to donate to the Brevard County Sheriff Department. Stuart, who had restaurants in Australia for many years, likes to tell a story about a dingo there who saved his life in the Outback, but that's just apocryphal.

Nancy Borton is serious about dogs, though, so serious that she's planning "Dog Day Afternoons" on the new 3,000 square-foot split-level deck they've just constructed. A woman who lives in the area and owns "the third ugliest dog in the world" is helping her out with dog activities, which will go along with dog menus. We're not making this stuff up.

The story here isn't really about dogs, though. The story is about spectacular food in a great old river shack built in the late 1940s. A number of restaurants and bars that mostly catered to the fishing community have called this place home, but Yellow Dog, which opened in 1998, targets a trendier clientele. The Bortons describe the fare as "comfort food with a flair," but we'd put the emphasis on flair. Maybe it's "comfort food" if you were raised a Bush or a Kennedy.

On our first visit, we arrived early for lunch, and as a server led us to our table, we passed a line of employees—we're not sure why they were in a line—who each greeted us and smiled. When we reached our table, Jane's son, Michael, said, "You know, I really do feel welcome." And so did we. That must be the comfort part of the meal.

For lunch or dinner, don't miss starting off with one of the soups. Our server let us try a sample of the crab bisque, and it was so rich, delicate, and delicious that we ordered the chicken curry soup as well. We liked it almost as much as the bisque. The creamy curry didn't overpower the chicken, carrots, celery, and onions. We cleaned the cup with the warm soft herb bread that accompanies the meals.

The soups only portended the good things to come. "The Lady Dog" (a perfectly grilled Portobello mushroom with roasted red peppers, artichoke hearts, spinach, and Havarti, served on focaccia bread) was delicious, as was the seafood pasta in a pesto cream sauce, as was "The Good Ole Dog" (an old-fashioned juicy burger), and "The Sloppy Dog" (shredded tenderloin with barbeque sauce, grilled onions, Portobello mushrooms, and Havarti), also served on focaccia bread. We haven't tried anything we didn't like.

For dinner, try the house favorite, Stuart's own onion-crusted chicken with a caramel citrus glaze, or perhaps the pecan-crusted mahi-mahi. The prices are hefty, but this is the kind of place that makes it worth dropping big bucks on an entree. The only outrageous prices on the menu were the soft drinks at more than $3 a pop.

Full dinners are only served inside, but if you'd just like to have a drink and some high-end, healthy bar food, don't forget the deck overlooking the water. No reservations are necessary for the deck, although you're best to call ahead if you want to have dinner inside, or if you and your pooch are looking to hit the deck on a "Dog Day Afternoon."

Interstate 95
Grant to Palm Beach

3

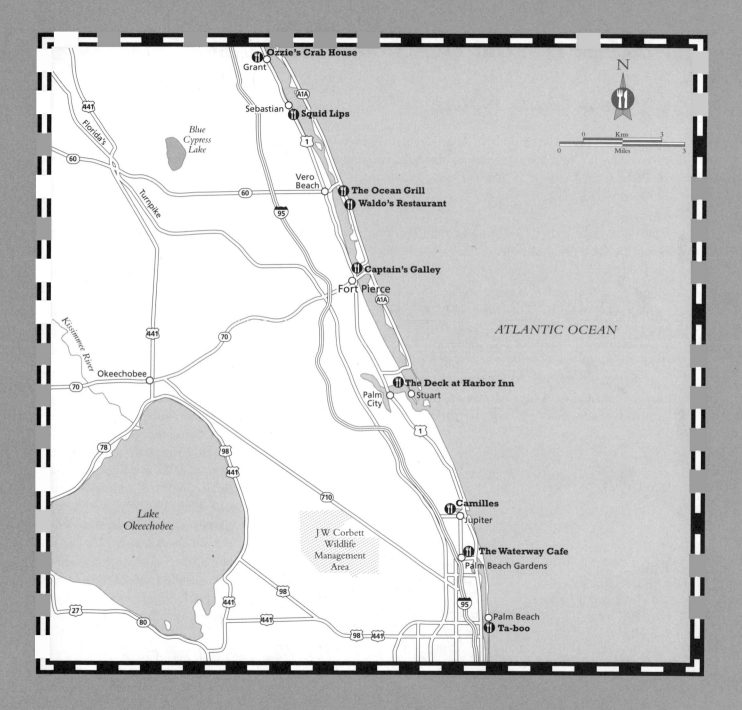

N

Ozzie's Crab House
Grant

A1A

Sebastian Squid Lips

1

Blue
Cypress
Lake

Florida's

441

Turnpike

60

60

95

Vero
Beach
The Ocean Grill
Waldo's Restaurant

Kissimmee River

441

70

Captain's Galley
Fort Pierce

A1A

ATLANTIC OCEAN

Okeechobee

70

78

98

441

710

The Deck at Harbor Inn
Palm City   Stuart

1

Lake
Okeechobee

J W Corbett
Wildlife
Management
Area

98

Camilles
Jupiter

The Waterway Cafe
Palm Beach Gardens

27

80

441

98 441

95

Palm Beach
Ta-boo

0   Kms   3
0   Miles   3

I-95 Exit 173: Old-Time Country and Crab

Ozzie's Crab House

6060 South US 1, Grant [*NOTE:* At press time, Ozzie's was undergoing renovation due to a fire. Please call information for their latest phone number and call ahead before visiting]. Open Sunday through Thursday 10:00 a.m. to 11:00 p.m. (they've been known to close early if slow), Friday and Saturday 11:00 a.m. to 11:00 p.m. $$–$$$

From I-95: Take exit 173—FL-514/Malabar Road east (4.2 miles) and turn right onto US 1 (6.6 miles). Ozzie's will be on your right.

At Ozzie's, the "tablecloths" arrive early in the morning as the paperboy makes his rounds. If the conversation lulls at your table, you can read about the local news while you're waiting for your crab, hammer, and pick. We stumbled into Ozzie's for the first time on a slow Monday night in Grant, known by some locals as "a quaint drinking village

with a slight fishing problem." We wandered past the long tables covered in daily rags, perfect spots for messy group feeds.

Blue crabs are king at Ozzie's, which has been here since 1966. The main dining room got a face-lift after Hurricanes Francis and Jeanne blew through in 2004, but the lounge and patio survived okay and managed to stay open during the renovation.

We sat at the bar and struck up a conversation with two locals who told us about the live music every night but Monday (drat!), either in the restaurant or the lounge or both. Officially, the music is billed as country/classic rock, but the local we talked to bragged about the old-time country. "It's like *Hee Haw* meets crab house," he explained, although he did mention an eighty-eight-year-old woman who sometimes takes the mic to sing raunchy songs that probably wouldn't have gotten past the FCC during

Hee Haw days. Rumor also has it that Minnie Pearl's cousin used to stop by for a song or two.

We were here for crabs, though, not country music, so we ordered the Neptune Platter: ½ lb. of king crab, ½ lb. snow crab, ½ lb. Dungeness crab, three Maryland-style (with Old Bay spice) crabs, three garlic crabs (with lots of the shelling work done for us), and six steamed shrimp. It's a feast made for sharing. First thing we asked for was coaching to refresh our memories on the best way to open up these puppies. A veteran from the kitchen came out and demonstrated the hammer movements and cracking necessary to get out as much juicy meat as possible. It's good to have to work for your supper. Plus it makes for communal fun. Plus, crabs sure taste good. Kings and snows and Dungenesses and Maryland style blues and garlic blues—there wasn't a crab in the bunch we didn't like. Local fishers catch the Florida blue crabs, which are available nearly all year-round, and they import the rest from various spots.

If you're dragged here by crab lovers but don't happen to care for the crustaceans, you'll have lots of other seafood possibilities (fresh fish, scallops, shrimp, oysters), or you can choose a porterhouse, sirloin, or New York strip steak. If you're looking for something lighter, they've got plenty of sandwiches, including burgers, fish, fried soft shell crab, crab salad, fresh lump crabmeat, and crab cake. There's a recurring theme here. You can also try the fried blue crab claws, garlic claws, or crab claw cocktail among other appetizers. The gumbo is dark brown and rich, with okra, green pepper, celery, and, you guessed it, crab, crab, and more crab.

Remember, though, that if you get hooked on the country music one night over in the lounge, you can order anything on the menu to eat except crabs. Only the dining room is set up for the messy stuff.

I-95 Exit 156: Good Eats and Good Views

Squid Lips

1660 Indian River Drive, Sebastian; 772-589-3828; www.squidlipsgrill.com. Open Sunday through Thursday 11:00 a.m. to 9:00 p.m., Friday and Saturday 11:00 a.m. to 10:00 p.m. $$–$$$

From I-95: Take exit 156–CR 512/Fellsmere Road east toward Sebastian (6.4 miles). Turn left onto US 1 North/FL-5 North (.7 mile), right onto Jefferson Street (less than .1 mile), and left onto Indian River Drive (.5 mile). Squid Lips will be on your right.

With a name like Squid Lips and Arlo Guthrie living just down the river, this place has a good start. Then when you arrive, the first thing you notice is that every seat in the house has a view of the water. The square building sits on pilings in the Indian River, has views on three sides, and looks out onto a marina. With a three-sided bar in the middle of the restaurant, it's looking even better. Sometimes, though, the proximity to water and great views gives restaurants the license to cut corners in the food area. Not so at Squid Lips.

General Manager Ben Bishop sets the tone: "We wanted to be known for the food. The atmosphere is just a bonus." He's managed to pull it off too. As Nancy's friend Angie says, "The food is classier than the atmosphere," and the Gourmettes *love* the atmosphere. The building got its start as one of the oldest fish houses in the area. The local fishermen would bring their fresh catches here before the fish got transported by railway to trucks waiting to deliver them to retailers. Ben keeps that old fish house tradition alive with all the major ocean varieties: grouper, mahi-mahi, tuna, and salmon.

The most popular sandwich is the Abaco fish sandwich, a mild white fish, hand battered with coconut in-house like everything else—nothing arrives

premade—fried, and topped with mango chutney and melted Swiss cheese. If that doesn't float your boat, you can get fish in all sorts of other ways: crunchy (mild fish dusted in seasoned flour and rolled in cornflakes), citrus (oak-grilled salmon marinated in homemade Italian citrus dressing), Parmesan, Thai, and lemon-caper, just to name a few. Squid Lips likes to take the basics and then give you lots of options; for example, with their homemade sauces, which include black-cherry-pepper, apricot-ginger-lime, and honey-lime.

Nancy's favorite item on the menu is the Cajun bacon-wrapped sea scallops that are grilled with the honey-lime sauce. The crab-stuffed shrimp are also delicious. Jane loved the shrimp po' boy, but you can also get one with fried oysters, crawfish, or calamari if you'd rather. You also might not be able to resist the coconut onion rings—mutantly huge onions, rolled in a coconut-rum batter and fried, then served with orange marmalade horseradish sauce. The kitchen is inventive, and the inventions we've tried largely work. Don't miss the drunken sweet potato, sauced with brown sugar, Myers dark Jamaican rum, and tropical spices. Yummy.

You needn't stick to seafood entrees, however. Squid Lips brings in premium Angus beef and cooks up a variety of chicken dishes as well as boneless pork loin that they finish over the oak wood grill and top with black-cherry-pepper sauce.

Ben is right: The food rules here. Squid Lips isn't just a pretty face on the water.

P. S. Sebastian is home to the original Squid Lips, but if you're looking for a location closer to the interstate, they've just opened a new Squid Lips just east of Exit 183 in Melbourne at 4052 West Eau Galle Boulevard; 321-259-3101.

The Ocean Grill

1050 Beachland Boulevard, Vero Beach; 772-231-5409; www.ocean-grill.com. Open for lunch Monday through Friday 11:30 a.m. to 2:00 p.m., for dinner Monday through Friday 5:45 to 10:00 p.m., Saturday and Sunday 5:00 to 9:00 p.m. $$–$$$$

From I-95: Take exit 147—FL-60 east (8.6 miles). Turn left onto Indian River Boulevard/CR 603 (.9 mile) and right onto Merril P. Barber Bridge/FL-60 (1.6 miles), which becomes Beachland Boulevard. The Ocean Grill will be on your right just before you drive onto the sand.

The Ocean Grill's motto is "where the unusual is commonplace." Indeed. Waldo Sexton died in 1967, but many of his odd artifacts grace the building his family still owns. Waldo, an early citrus and dairy pioneer with an idiosyncratic aesthetic sense, scavenged at various estate sales in Palm Beach and bought up all sorts of curious artifacts from the rich and famous. The Sexton homes, motels, and restaurants became showcases for these offbeat artistic assortments.

Waldo is long gone, but his treasures embody his spirit at the Ocean Grill, run by the Replogle family since 1965, despite four major hurricanes and two deadly nor'easters. Twice, storms took the dining-room floor out to sea, but each time it's been rebuilt.

Nancy has been coming here since the early 1990s before the installation of the 600-yard artificial reef. Back then, the water came up under the building at high tide, and in the bar, you felt like you were drinking on a yacht. Because of the reef, the tide rarely reaches the pilings nowadays, but at low tide, you can still catch a glimpse of the *Breconshire*, a steamship from London that sunk just off the shore in 1884, the year before Waldo's birth.

The Ocean Grill opened in 1941 with an open-air dance floor, but soon the biting insects convinced Waldo to cover it. During WWII, the Grill was a naval officer's club, and the Chicago mob allegedly operated it for a period after the war. Nowadays, the old dance floor is part of the dining room, but Waldo's artistic visions are still everywhere: lots of pecky-cypress paneling, the Sexton coat of arms by the back bar, an ornate bank window, whimsical light fixtures with different colored bulbs, lots of wrought iron and antique wooden doors (the man *loved* old doors), and paintings galore, even on the women's bathroom stalls.

Waldo claimed that the signature piece at the restaurant was the world's largest mahogany table cut from one solid piece of wood. The President of the Philippines once owned it. Waldo lied a lot, though. Fact or fiction, the majestic table seats twelve and looks like it awaits King Arthur and his knights. A gigantic wrought-iron light fixture watches over it. The leather and brass chairs are from The Everglades Club in Palm Beach. Truth and legend indelibly intertwine with Waldo and his stuff, so take these claims as you will.

At lunch or dinner, you're in for a culinary treat as well as a feast for the eyes. For lunch, the shrimp salad with capers, carrots, red pepper, and tomatoes is fresh and flavorful. The lobster roll, decadent and delicious, is full of large hunks of claw and tail meat on a toasted French roll. The club sandwich bulges with turkey, avocado, tomato, and lettuce, and the deviled baked crab comes with hunks of blue crab in a subtle spice. In the sides department, the creamed spinach was tasty, and Jane loved the coleslaw with purple and green cabbage, carrots, pineapple, apple, and celery seeds.

For dinner, we love the plump fried oysters, and the roast duckling and shrimp specials are house favorites. Choose also from steaks, pork chops, chicken, and more seafood options. Waldo's beach world and killer food make the 11-mile drive worthwhile.

Waldo's Gone Corporate

This is only a partial entry because Waldo has once again led us into corruption, and now we're not only telling you about a spot that's more than 10 miles from the interstate, but we're also telling you about a place that's owned by (gasp!) a corporation. We won't give much free publicity, and we like the food much better at The Ocean Grill anyway, but in case you get bitten by the Waldo bug, you might want to walk down the beach after lunch at The Ocean Grill and check out **Waldo's Restaurant** and bar in the Driftwood Resort. Waldo built the resort in many stages from plans in his head and more stuff he had salvaged. He would verbally explain things to the carpenters or draw diagrams in the sand. Much of the Driftwood looks just a bit off-kilter, like parts of it aren't quite at the right angles, but that's all part of the charm, and you'll see lots of Waldo's treasures, especially part of his bell collection from ships, missions, fire houses, churches, trains, animals, and farms. Back in the old days, if they liked you, everybody would ring a bell as you departed the motel. If they didn't, you left in relative silence.

Waldo used to give tours of the place and tell stories about the various objets d'art. Legend has it that one day a woman enjoyed his tour so much that she tagged along again for a later one. Waldo told different stories about the same artifacts. The woman challenged him on his facts. "I'd rather be a liar than a bore," he explained. We'd rather be a little corrupt than not tell you about another part of what's left of Waldo's World.

The Sechuan Palace at 1965 43rd Avenue in Melbourne is also a Waldo's haunt, his old "Turf Club," where he gave aspiring artists a showplace, but which has the least of Waldo's World left clinging to it. Once you get hooked by the old man's legend, though, it's hard not to check out what he left us.

➡ 3150 Ocean Drive, Vero Beach; 772-231-7091; www.thedriftwood.com. Open Sunday through Thursday 11:00 a.m. to 9:00 p.m., Friday and Saturday 11:00 a.m. to 10:00 p.m. $$–$$$

➡ From I-95: Take exit 147 — SR 60 east toward Vero (8.6 miles). Turn left onto Indian River Boulevard/CR 603 North (.9 mile), right onto FL-60/Merril P. Barber Bridge (1.6 miles), and right onto Ocean Drive (.1 mile). Waldo's will be on the left, in the Driftwood Resort. Look for on-street parking.

Meals Worth Stopping for in *Florida*

I-95 Exit 131A: Friendly Attack of the Killer Pancakes

Captain's Galley

825 North Indian River Drive, Ft. Pierce; 772-466-8495. Open Tuesday through Saturday 7:00 a.m. to 2:00 p.m., Sunday 7:00 a.m. to 12:30 p.m. (breakfast only). Closed Monday. $–$$

From I-95: Take exit 131A—Orange Avenue/FL-68 east (4.5 miles) and turn left onto US 1/FL-5 North (.5 mile). Then turn right onto Seaway Drive/FL-A1A/Avenue F (.1 mile) and left onto North Indian River Drive (less than .1 mile). Captain's Galley will be on your left.

WELCOME TO CAPTAIN'S GALLEY, STRANGER BUT ONCE, says the driftwood sign over the entrance to this spacious diner located across the street from the Intracoastal Waterway. The owner's aunt, Marie Hogya, and head server Kathy Bender set the hospitality bar high for the "Galley Girls," who serve locals and snowbirds alike. The harried waitresses scurry back and forth with a kind word for the newbies or a smart remark for the regulars.

A restaurant doesn't make it on friendly service alone, though, and Captain's Galley has the food to back up its amiable ambience, especially for breakfast. The first time there, Nancy ordered the breakfast special that included two eggs, bacon or sausage, pancakes, biscuit or toast, and home fries or grits. She spent a little extra and got her pancake with pecans and whipped cream. Money well spent. The pancakes here are darn-near perfect and especially tasty when filled with other goodies. They're king of the menu

for good reason: Owner Dennis Horvath has the homemade mix specially ground to order at a mill in North Carolina and shipped down regularly to feed the hoard of hungry eaters who pass through the Captain's Galley. Banana pancakes are Dennis's favorite, but it's hard to imagine that they're better than the pecan ones. The pancakes and equally delicious waffles come plain or with a variety of flavorful add-ons, including apples, blueberries, bananas, and strawberries. Go with the pecans!

Dennis was raised in a restaurant-owning family in Ohio. His parents bought a well-known franchise that shall remain nameless, but Dennis saw the light, and he opened up his own independent restaurant in 1985. "I wanted to do it my own way. Why pay somebody else for an idea you already had?" he says. Two years later he moved into the much larger building that still houses the Captain's Galley.

For those who want to branch out beyond the pecan pancakes, the overstuffed omelets and eggs Benedict and Florentine are also outstanding. Many of the breakfast favorites come in half portions too, so you can mix and match if you're so inclined or eat like a sparrow. It's hard to go wrong here for breakfast, but French toast may be the best thing to skip.

For lunch, Captain's Galley is famous for their crunchy grouper sandwiches, made with almonds and cornflakes in the batter. This was the first restaurant in the area to serve it. Now, even though you can get a crunchy grouper elsewhere, lots of folks still drive far to get the Captain's version. "They say it's just not the same other places," says Marie.

Meals Worth Stopping for in *Florida*

I-95 Exit 101: Here's the Meat; There's the Fire

The Deck at Harbor Inn

306 Northwest North River Drive, Stuart; 772-692-1200. Open for lunch Wednesday through Saturday noon to 4:00 p.m. Open for dinner Wednesday through Saturday 5:00 to 9:30 p.m. and Sunday 5:00 to 8:00 p.m. Closed Monday and Tuesday. $–$$$

From I-95: Take exit 101—FL-76/Southwest Kenner Highway east (5.6 miles) and turn left (north) onto Southwest Federal Highway/US 1/FL-5 (.6 mile). Just before the bridge turn right onto Southwest Joan Jefferson Way (less than .1 mile) and make an immediate left onto Southwest Albany Avenue (less than .1 mile). Turn left onto South Dixie Highway/CR 707/CR A1A/Old Dixie Highway (.7 mile) and left again onto Northwest Fern Street (less than .1 mile), which curves right and becomes Northwest North River Drive (less than .1 mile). The restaurant will be in the part of the Harbor Inn that's on your left. Pull into the inn parking lot, park in the restaurant spots, and walk between the buildings to find the restaurant.

On our first trip to The Deck, it took us a while to find it and a few minutes to get oriented once there. We'd just purchased a raw bratwurst and bun that we'd get to cook ourselves on the grill that takes up most of one wall of the dining room. A lovely woman who'd been a long-standing member of the Daughters of the American Revolution (it's amazing the things you find out about people over a flame) and who had had a boat at the marina here for sixteen years suggested that we slice our bratwurst's spine before grilling so that it all got cooked. We weren't really worried about cooking a bratwurst, but we weren't totally sure about the protocol at the grill. Not waiting for us to figure it out, she just

Cindy Picos, Ruth Clark, and Steve Tetro

took the bratwurst from us and started the grilling process herself. "You should grill the bun, too," she said, pointing to an open spot on the grill. "You can always tell the newcomers," she said. "They're sort of looking around, trying to figure things out. Chips are over in the Charles Chips can, sauerkraut's in the Crock-Pot, mustard's on the salad bar." And then our Fairy God Griller was gone. We finished grilling and sat outside on the deck overlooking the marina, pairing the bratwurst with an excellent crab Caesar salad with real crab and homemade dressing.

"I don't wanna leave," said Nancy.

"You don't want to go to the next restaurant?" asked Jane.

"I don't want to go anywhere. I just want to sleep here on this wooden bench with the water lapping up against the shore and the breeze blowing past my face, and I want to wake up to someone offering me a place to live on their boat that's permanently docked here."

It's *that* kind of place. We were on shaky ground for two minutes and were ready to live here forever in half an hour. Unfortunately, we had more restaurants to find, so we couldn't stay. When we returned the second time, we sat at the bar under the giant cypress-root chandelier festooned with an assortment of baseball caps. The original owner had pulled the enormous root out of local Peck's Lake.

"Everything's good," said the bartender/server when we asked our usual opening question. "I've

Meals Worth Stopping for in *Florida*

worked here two years and never had a complaint."

"That's because you carry a gun," teased the talkative guy from Philadelphia sitting next to us. It's a friendly bunch.

"A lot of people say this is like Cheers," continued the bartender. "Everybody knows everybody. We usually ask for people's first names on their order, and that's how we get to know people. 'As The Deck Turns' we call it." Insults and flirtations zinged around the three-sided bar, but it's the kind of place where a single female would feel comfortable hanging out.

The place clearly has its share of frequently told tales, including the ones about the folks who cook their own meat (steaks, dogs, bratwursts, and burgers): for example, the people who put cheese on the top of their burger and then flip it over on the grill or the folks who forget to take the Saran Wrap off their steak before grilling. "Then there's the subset of stories about Lord Seabury, who showed up wearing one white glove, a tux jacket, shorts, and no shoes. When filling out the application to dock his yacht, he answered the emergency contact question with "The Lord." Yep, this place has no shortage of characters.

The Deck has been here since 1977 when Norman Lay decided he wanted a hot dog stand on the water. As it flourished, he began to add a few more things to the menu. By the time Steve Tetro and his wife Ruth Clark bought The Deck in 1997, Norman was up to dogs, tuna sandwiches, and burgers for lunch and New York strips, filets, and chopped steaks for dinner.

Steve and Ruth have added lots more seafood, salads, soups, and sandwiches, including excellent crab cakes with lots of fresh blue crab and a great balance of spice and bread crumbs. The classic New Zealand mussels are huge and tender, and the linguini with white clam sauce is full of chopped clams and garlic and comes with a trip to the salad bar, which is filled with lots of fresh goodies, including marinated artichoke hearts and a great blue cheese dressing.

Whether you eat at the bar, in the dining room, or out on the deck, give this quaint spot a try, and you too may find that you never want to leave.

I-95 Exit 87A: Thin-Crust Chicago Pizza?

Camilles

711 West Indiantown Road, Jupiter; 561-743-1157. Open Monday through Saturday 11:00 a.m. to 10:00 p.m., Sunday 4:00 to 9:00 p.m. $–$$

From I-95: Take exit 87A—FL-706/Indiantown Road east toward Jupiter (3.1 miles). Make a U-turn at Philadelphia Drive (just past the miniature lighthouse on your left) and head west on Indiantown Road/FL-706 (.1 mile). Camilles will be on your right in the corner of an L-shaped strip mall.

One of Nancy's students from Jupiter recommended Camilles, and when we found out it advertised "Thin-crust Chicago pizza . . ." we smirked at each other. We knew all about the deep-dish and stuffed Chicago pizzas, but *thin*-crust? We didn't have high hopes for the place, but we couldn't resist seeing what this oxymoronic "thin-crust Chicago pizza" was like.

Were we ever glad we did! Haughtiness and ignorance make a terrible combination, and the Gourmettes were promptly put in our places by the half-wheat/half-white crispy crust, almost like a thick cracker, loaded with fresh delicious toppings and cut into squares. Our server explained about the crust: "We can't make calzones or anything else with this. It's just for pizza. It's better for you, too, because of the whole wheat flour." Some folks who need lives apparently get upset about the square cut of the 'za, so if you want it cut in a pie shape, you can ask for it that way ahead of time. At lunch, you can get a special "2 slices and a soda" deal for $4.99, and those slices will automatically be cut in pie shape. This gets so confusing. It's best not to get too caught up in all the fuss over pizza shapes; instead, simply enjoy the

pizza. Upon further study, we found that Chicago indeed has a fine tradition of thin-crust pizza, the more demure sibling of the flaky mega-crust big brothers. Camilles, however, is one of the very few places you can find thin-crust Chicago pizza in Florida.

At Camilles, co-owner Bobby McConnell told us that they try to use the freshest ingredients, they use the most expensive cheese, and they even get their sausage delivered twice a week from a butcher who uses their own recipe to mix up the meat. We loved it, and the meatballs too. Although they aren't homemade, Bobby explained that they tried fifty different meatballs from the vendor before they found ones they liked.

They're also especially proud of their Steak and Cheese sub. "A lot of people say it's the best in South Florida," Bobby boasts. He and his sister, Shirl, and Jason Daly had worked at the restaurant for eleven years before eighty-year-old owner Ken Camille decided he'd had enough of the business. "This place feels like home to us," said Bobby. "We hated to see it close down." So they decided to buy the business in 2006, renovate the space with sports TVs and a saltwater aquarium, revamp the menu with beer and wine and more upscale ingredients, and now they have people lined up out the door every night. Major League first baseman Sean Casey drops by frequently during the off-season, and Johnny Depp's dad is a regular too.

We learned not to be too quick to pigeonhole a great city's pizza. Now we're on the lookout for a joint that serves deep-dish New York pizza. Let us know if you find one.

I-95 Exit 79A/B: Boat Party

The Waterway Cafe

2300 PGA Boulevard, Palm Beach Gardens; 561-694-1700; www.waterwaycafe.com. Open for lunch Saturday and Sunday 11:30 a.m. to 4:00 p.m. and dinner Monday through Thursday 4:00 to 10:00 p.m., Friday through Sunday 4:00 to 11:00 p.m. Bar menu available Monday through Thursday until 10:45 p.m., Friday through Sunday until 11:45 p.m. $$–$$$

From I-95: Take exit 79A/B—FL-786 east (2.2 miles). Waterway Cafe will be on your right just before the drawbridge.

The Waterway Cafe is, so far, the best singles joint in the book, but don't let that dissuade you if you've already got a mate in the car with you. But then again, during the tourist season or not, it's also a place likely to have many senior citizens like Jane (Nancy will pay for that remark), so don't let the party-atmosphere dissuade you. It's a laid-back waterfront party in any case. The "Sunday Night Dance Party" with its reggae band is probably the wildest it gets.

At lunch you can join area business people and get quickly in and out or you can linger for a leisurely lunch under turn-of-the-century Ivy League crew boats suspended from the ceiling. When the weather is good, the windows come off and it's an open-air restaurant. In inclement weather, it's temperate and dry and still has great views of the Intracoastal Waterway. You can also choose to sit on what they claim to be "Florida's only floating boat bar," a round bar out in the waterway, connected by a wooden walkway to the main restaurant. They also have another tiki bar and outdoor seating. You'll find a place you like somewhere.

The cafe is just south of the PGA Boulevard Bridge, an old drawbridge that's being phased out by a new improved bridge. Jane romanticizes drawbridges because she doesn't have much experience with them, while Nancy, who spent chunks of her wayward youth with grandparents in Ft. Lauderdale, detests them because they always seem to break down or go up just as you get to them. Here at the cafe, they have a popular boat drink called Broken Bridge, named after the drawbridge because it was so often broken. With vodka, gin, rum, triple sec, and Southern Comfort in this orange juice/grenadine mixture, you'll be broken too if you drink many of these.

In addition to being the best singles joint, The Waterway Cafe also has the best happy hour we've found in the state thus far. We suspect the two are related. From 4:00 to 6:30 p.m. Monday through Thursday and from 3:00 to 6:30 p.m. on Friday, you can enjoy half-price drinks, beer, and wine, and choose from a wondrously cheap happy hour menu, featuring turkey burgers with sweet potato fries (excellent), brick-oven pizzas, marinated chicken breast sandwiches with fries, conch fritters, artichoke-crab dip, and more. You just can't go wrong.

We especially liked a local organic beer they have on tap called Monk's Trunk, which has an aftertaste—call us crazy—that reminds us of wine. The Friday happy hour we were there, the party was just cranking up when we left. Acoustic music was starting up in the dining room, two six-sided bars in the main restaurant plus two bars outside were full, and five women in cowboy hats holding shots were just beginning a night that they would be talking about for years. We were sorry to have to head back to the interstate.

The Cafe starts you off with warm rosemary rolls with honey butter. Yum. The Thai chicken pizza with peanut/ginger/sesame marinated chicken with green onions, bean sprouts, carrots, cilantro, peanuts, and mozzarella was a great blend of tastes, and the seafood stir-fry with fresh mahi-mahi, salmon, scallops, shrimp, and oriental vegetables was a feast of freshness. The menu is so extensive that, like the seating, there's something for everyone. The Waterway *fra Diavlo* (fresh fish, scallops, shrimp in a spicy marinara over linguini) is another favorite, as is the tropical mustard-glazed salmon, grilled and basted in a pineapple Dijon glaze.

The place was built in 1986 and has survived this long not just because of their amazing view, but also because of their commitment to good food and friendly service, and a cranking party on Sunday nights.

I-95 Exit 70: Lifestyles of the Rich and Famous

Ta-boo

221 Worth Avenue, Palm Beach; 561-835-3500; www.taboorestaurant.com. Open for lunch daily 11:30 a.m. to 5:00 p.m., and for dinner Sunday through Thursday 5:00 to 10:00 p.m., Friday and Saturday 5:00 to 11:00 p.m. Late-night menu available Friday and Saturday until midnight. $$–$$$$

From I-95: Take exit 70—FL-704/Okeechobee Boulevard. Follow FL-704 east over the Intracoastal Waterway to the second light after the bridge (2.7 miles). Turn right onto South County Road (.2 mile), go to the second light, and turn right onto Worth Avenue. Ta-boo will be halfway down the block on your right.

You could come here for the legends—the invention of the Bloody Mary, the place where Joe Kennedy and Gloria Swanson barricaded themselves in the ladies bathroom all night, the story about the German submarine captain who came ashore during WWII to eat here. Then again, you could come here for the celebrity watching—you might catch a peek of Deepak Chopra, Jimmy Buffett, Donald Trump, who knows? Or, you could come here for the dynamite food—affordable at lunch, less so at dinner. But we really think that you should come to Ta-boo because it's an extreme end of the Florida lifestyle, a chance to brush elbows with old and new money and see how the other .2 percent live. We like to show you the lows and the highs, and it's as important to have a feel for the legacy of the super-rich in Florida as it is to eat at rural diners in North Florida or fisher's hangouts along the coast or Cuban mainstays in South Florida. It's all part of the hodgepodge that makes up this great, if complicated and quirky, state.

On our first trip to Ta-boo, we sat at the cool, dark bar, just down from a regular, Mr. B. He was talking to our bartenders, A. J. and Ian. (The names have been changed to protect the wealthy and sycophantic.) They had a big discussion about another regular, Edward, who had had an incident with Susan, another bartender. Edward and Mr. B. were regulars for lunch, part of the gang. But one day Edward tried to save two seats at the bar for friends who were joining him and—horror of horrors—Susan gave the seats away to two women looking for places at the nearly full bar. Edward quit coming to Ta-boo for a while, but, needing the restaurant more than his pride, he had just showed up the night before and talked to A.J. Now, apparently Edward was going to start coming in again for lunch, but only on days when Susan wasn't working.

"We'll probably never see those two women again either," lamented Ian.

"But Edward ate here *every day*," chimed in Mr. B., incredulous.

"Yeah, we try to remember that," said Ian. "Sometimes I forget."

"How can you forget something like that?" said A.J., shaking his head.

All three were quite indignant, and we hope that order has been restored in the Palm Beach universe by the time you read this—at least on the days when Susan isn't working.

Here in Palm Beach, sycophancy is taken to new levels. And why not? The menu prices are high and the potential for exorbitant tips even higher. We overheard a venture capitalist talking to his banking guru about a potential deal with the man coming to meet them: "Either his idea is revolutionary with the possibility of great residuals or . . . ." and then he started whispering. Drat!

We'd have to say, though, that all the food we had was worth the price. We loved the spicy crab stack, a round tower of layered baby greens, mango, succulent crab, roasted red pepper, and mashed avocado, surrounded by alternating pools of remoulade and a spicy dressing that will light a small fire in your mouth. The grilled chicken, sun-dried tomato, and goat cheese salad on a bed of mixed greens was huge, and the goat cheese arrived in giant rounds. The portobello pizza with Gorgonzola and caramelized onions was also delicious, and so was the pistachio-crusted salmon on a mixed-green Greek salad. For dessert the chocolate mousse, gigantic and light with a thick Oreo crust, was delightful.

We also had to try the Bloody Mary, since it was supposedly invented here. It certainly tasted like the sea—a bit like an oyster when you drench it in cocktail sauce. We missed the olive and celery accoutrements and like the spicier versions better, but it's always good to go back to the roots of something.

At night, when the lights are dim and the candles lit, the place becomes much more romantic, less power brokering. (Although perhaps romance is just another form of power brokering.) During the week, they have a piano player in the evenings, and on Friday and Saturday nights, they clear off the room with the wooden floor across from the bar, and a DJ keeps the party going until the early morning hours. Taboo is a place to see and be seen, but also a great spot to further your sociological study of the Sunshine State.

Interstate 95
Boynton Beach to Miami

4

N

Kms
0   20

Miles
0   20

Boynton Beach
**Two Georges
Waterfront Grill**

Delray Beach

Boca Raton

Cap's Place
Lighthouse Point
Pompano Beach **Calypso**
Lauderdale-by-the-Sea
Thai Spice **Country Ham N' Eggs**
Greek Islands Taverna

Fort Lauderdale

Dania Beach
Jaxson's Ice Cream Parlor & Restaurant
Le Tub
Hollywood

ATLANTIC
OCEAN

Hialeah

Garcia's Seafood Grille & Fish Market
Versailles
Miami

Key Biscayne

Biscayne
Bay

Everglades
National
Park

Kendall

▲ Biscayne National Park

I-95 Exit 57: A George for All Seasons

Two Georges Waterfront Grille

728 Casa Loma Boulevard, Boynton Beach; 561-736-2717; www.twogeorgesrestaurant.com. Open daily 11:00 a.m. to 10:30 p.m. $$–$$$

From I-95: Take exit 57—FL-804/Boynton Beach Boulevard/Northwest 2nd Avenue East (.9 mile). Turn right onto US 1 South/North Federal Highway/FL-5 South (.1 mile) and left onto East Ocean Avenue (.1 mile). Then turn left onto Southeast 6th Street (less than .1 mile) and right onto Casa Loma Boulevard (less than .1 mile). Look for a parking place or valet parking ahead on the left.

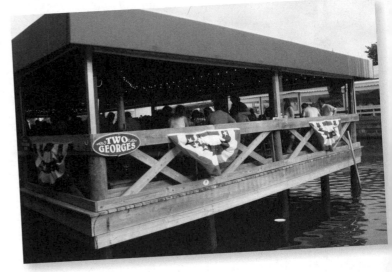

The name conveys the multiple personalities of this place well. The first time the Gourmettes stopped here, just to get a feel for the place, it was a Friday afternoon. We made our way along the docks, past the charter boat crews cleaning the day's catch, past the sunburned fisherfolk talking about the ones that got away, and, naturally, we gravitated to the first bar we found, which turned out to be the South Deck.

The rectangular bar sat under a giant fiberglass shark hanging in the middle of an open-air room full of tables and people. From one side of the room, you could look across a narrow canal to Banana Boat, another restaurant and bar about twenty years younger than Two Georges, which had its half-century anniversary in 2007. The people-watching, in this bar or across to that one, was first-rate. That's not to say that all the people we were watching were first-rate, but there were many to watch in various stages of inebriation. It would be fair to say that we were a bit out of our element. "Loud music meat market" comes to mind as a description. Also, with fifteen TVs and

sports flags all over, if you're looking for a rowdy place to watch a ballgame, this would be a good spot. We only lasted for one drink, but upon touring the rest of the premises, we discovered that this was the wild George's room.

The laid-back George's room, called the Tiki Hut, was only separated by the width of a dock, and it was attached to outdoor seating on the relatively quiet East Deck, which overlooks the Intracoastal Waterway. Although the Tiki Hut looked a heckuva lot like the South Deck, down to the giant shark hanging over the bar (it was a hammerhead in the Tiki Hut), the vibe was totally different. As soon as we stepped into it, we knew, this was a George a Gourmette could love. The laid-back George had built a Tiki Hut with more of an island feel, while the wild George's South Deck felt more like a South Florida sports bar (the Tiki Hut only had two TVs).

All this talk of the Georges is, of course, just Gourmette fantasizing. The truth is that both father and son George Culvers are no longer around, and Steve Scaggs owns the place now. The part we like is a newly built add-on and has a saltwater aquarium under the giant shark.

It also has servers who manage to stay incredibly honest, helpful, and attentive, even though they were "in the weeds" almost the whole time we were there. It's a popular place. Expect to wait. Free valet parking is the way to go, and they only take reservations for parties of eight or more, and then only during June through January.

As for the food, it's not hip or nouveau, but the seafood's fresh and the burgers are big and juicy. Our favorite meal is the Crab Norfolk. Jane swears that they needed an extra George just to keep busy picking crab for the Norfolk, a large pile of fresh, succulent crab, floating in a pool of nutty brown butter. At Ozzie's you'd spend an hour getting out this much crab, which can be lots of fun, but sometimes you're in the mood to be pampered.

The conch fritters are the biggest selling appetizer, oddly shaped and more the consistency of deviled crab than the hush puppy texture you often get. Everything on the fried platter—shrimp, scallops, clams, and fish—was lightly battered, fresh, and delicious.

The desserts were okay. The key lime pie is best if you feel in need of something sweet, but you won't miss much if you opt out.

In the laid-back Tiki Hut, our server explained the South Deck to us: "That's for the big local boozers. Also there's a juke box over there, so the music is harder. This side the music is piped in." There's something for everyone at Two Georges.

I-95 Exit 38 or 38A: Florida's Rumrunning, Gambling Past

Cap's Place

2765 Northeast 28th Court, Lighthouse Point; 954-941-0418; www.capsplace.com. Open January through April Sunday through Thursday 5:30 to 9:45 p.m., Friday and Saturday 5:30 to 10:45 p.m. Open May through December Sunday and Tuesday through Thursday 5:30 to 9:45 p.m., Friday and Saturday 5:30 to 10:45 p.m. Closed Monday. $$$–$$$$

From I-95: Take exit 38 (from south) or 38A (from north). Head east on Copans Road (2 miles) and turn left onto US 1/North Federal Highway (2 blocks). Turn right/east onto Northeast 24th Street/Lighthouse Drive. Now you are on a curvy road that winds through a residential area for about 1 mile. The road changes names several times. Just watch closely for the white and green directional signs (all fairly low) that say Cap's Place or Yacht Basin. When you get there, the dock will be on your left. Cap's has reserved parking by the dock, and there's also public parking in the immediate area. Just be sure not to park in reserved parking areas.

The only way to get to Cap's Place—unless you snag a special pass because of a disability or you know or are someone who lives on Cap's Island—is to take the short free ferry over from a Lighthouse Point dock. When you hear you have to take a ferry to Cap's, you may initially imagine something like Gilligan's Island, but Cap's Island is more exclusive than remote. You'll cruise past multimillion dollar homes with giant yachts, and just when you've decided you'd be happy to settle in for a three-hour cruise, you'll be at the late Cap Knight's dock. (You can actually see it from where you board the ferry.)

In the middle of this gated island, developed to the hilt with designer mansions, boats, and cars, are a series of blue-gray, low-ceilinged, flat-roofed shacks. One building is actually a converted barge that was used to haul material for Henry Flagler's railroad. This is where you'll be dining tonight. The island is a metaphor for the way high-rent developers bear down, trying to squeeze out the character and history of old Florida, where a guy like Cap Knight, rum-runner, casino operator, and restaurateur, could carve out a marginally honest living. Cap opened his place under the name "Club Unique" in 1928.

Cap's Place is legendary. In 1942, Winston Churchill and Franklin Roosevelt held secret war talks in nearby Hillsboro Beach at the home of Secretary of State Edward R. Stettinius. Stettinius asked Cap to cater the talks, and the two legendary politicians actually dined at Cap's Place one of the nights. Legend has it that Cap served them in his customary bib overalls. Our first time there, we sat in the same booth as the Secret Service officers did who had been guarding Bill Clinton on his visit to Cap's just a month before. Celebrities have flocked to Cap's Place for years. Anyone who was anyone in the Mob has been here, and Meyer Lansky used to be a regular—collections runs or just visiting? Seems that answer depends on who you ask. George Harrison and Casey Stengel also dined here (not together—and there's no indication that either had ties to the Mob).

The celebrities still show up, but the gambling days are long gone. So are the endangered turtle eggs used to make pancakes until Cap's arrest in 1962 at ninety-two years of age. And so is Cap Knight, who died in 1964, the year Nancy was born. The ghosts of a former time are still there, though—the rum-running, roulette-spinning spirit of the old days.

After you give your name at the hostess stand (reservations are recommended, but they always set aside tables for walk-ins), head back to the shack next door and have a drink at the dark bar made of Everglades' bamboo and wood from old ships. But don't have too many or you may lose your footing on the uneven floorboards when you head back to the dining room. A cautionary sign on the dock also pleads: WARNING UNEVEN DOCK. DO NOT WEAR HIGH HEEL SHOES.

Assuming you make it to the dining room, fresh fish is king. "We've got an eighty-year-old fisherman who brings in the fresh catch every day in an ice chest or on a gaff. If it's too big, it's on the gaff," our server

Jo told us. We ordered the tuna with black- and white-crusted sesame seeds in a ginger sauce and the wahoo with lemon caper sauce. First, though, we ordered a crab cake appetizer and found a new leader in the best-crab cake-in-Florida category. Jo claims it's the best crab cake on the planet, but we're unwilling to go that far. Nancy's mother, a crab cake aficionado, says it's the best she's ever had. It's definitely the most like Maryland's version—crab, crab, and more crab, with just enough seasoning and other stuff to hold it together. Delicious. So was the fish when it arrived. The sauces were perfect complements, and neither overpowered the fish. On our next visit, we tried the pompano almandine special, which wasn't as good, but the bacon-wrapped scallops in a lemon cream sauce sure were. Jo was a spectacular server during round one, but our second time there, the service was friendly but slow and inefficient. It's a crapshoot, we guess.

Make sure you try the famous hearts-of-palm salad, crisp, clean, and mildly spicy. It's unusual if not amazing. The "sweet potatoes mashed" are rich and cinnamon-y—a wonderful side dish. The desserts we tried—the key lime pie and the Reese's peanut butter pie—were both good, but not as good as the crab cakes.

From I-95, Cap's Place is no easy-off, easy-on restaurant. It's more of a destination experience. If you've got the time and the money (entrees run in the $20s and $30s) and you want to "Enjoy Florida—Like It Used to Be!" check it out.

I-95 Exit 36A or 36: A New Kind of Barbecue

Calypso

460 South Cypress Road, Pompano Beach; 954-942-1633; www.calypsorestaurant.com. Open Monday through Friday 11:00 a.m. to 10:00 p.m. Closed Saturday and Sunday. $$–$$$

From I-95 South: Take exit 36A to merge onto West Atlantic Boulevard/FL-814-E. Go east on West Atlantic Boulevard/FL-814-E (1.2 miles). Turn right onto South Cypress Road (.5 mile). Calypso will be in the strip mall near the Laundromat.

From I-95 North: Take exit 36 for East Atlantic Boulevard. Merge onto West Atlantic Boulevard and go east (.7 mile). Turn right onto South Cypress Road (.5 mile). Calypso will be in the strip mall near the Laundromat.

Sometimes the best things come in small strip malls next to Chinese takeout, coin Laundromats, and consignment shops. Don't be dissuaded by the view from the parking lot. Step into Calypso and be transported by the reggae music and kitschy island decor: seahorse art, parrot curtains, a Foster's Beer surfboard, and a big blackboard listing all the fresh fish and specials. A sign after our Gourmettes' hearts says GOOD FOOD IS NOT FAST AND FAST FOOD IS NOT GOOD. Indeed. Take a deep breath, forget about the South Florida traffic, and enjoy the laid-back Caribbean feel.

The atmosphere, however, is just the first surprise in this little two-room bar/restaurant. The real gem, the tour de force, the most fantabulous thing of all is the West Indies Barbecue Shrimp. Every once in a

Mary Johnson serves up West Indies BBQ

great while, the Gourmettes happen upon a dish so sublime that we're transfixed and immediately start plotting to get the recipe. This appetizer puts New Orleans barbecue shrimp to shame. Depending on whether you order it as a small or large appetizer or an entree, you'll get four, six, or eight shrimp on top of toasted rounds, swimming in a dark brown, butter-based sauce loaded with spice. When the shrimp are gone, you'll want a to-go cup for the sauce. "You want to keep that, don't you?" our server asks while pointing to the sauce.

"Yeah, I left Jane to guard it while I went to the restroom," says Nancy.

The server nods knowingly. "I've almost gotten my hand taken off a couple of times when I tried to take it."

We just *had* to include the recipe in the book. Fortunately, the owners graciously agreed. Lori and Chuck Ternosky moved down from New Jersey and opened up Calypso with Jackie and Mike O'Neal in

1990. Jackie is British and Mike is from Barbados. The guys were the cooks and the women handled the front end until Lori and Chuck bought out the O'Neals in 2008. "We built this business on locals," explains Lori. "We didn't want to depend on tourists. We're busy all year-round." Calypso started out down the street and didn't move to its current location until 2000. In the old place, Lori says they knew the name of everyone who came through the door. The traffic is heavier and more diverse here in the new location, but they still serve mostly locals.

Once you've had the barbecue shrimp appetizer (and if you're not deathly allergic to shellfish, you certainly *should* have the barbecue shrimp), the menu has lots more to offer. The fish is fresh and delicious; the "roties," the Caribbean's answer to the burrito, are huge and filling, with your choice of chicken, lamb, dolphin, or shrimp; the "cutters," island for sandwiches, are served on Kaiser rolls with your choice of steak fries, pigeon peas and rice, black beans, potato salad, coleslaw, or salad; and the grilled conch (tenderized but still a bit chewy) is killer with the Caribbean marinade. If the curries aren't hot enough for you, dab on some Walker's Wood Plenty Hot Jamaican Fire Stick Pepper Sauce and heat things up a bit. Wash it all down with Jane's new favorite drink, pink grapefruit Ting soda.

If you miss a trip to Calypso, be sure to try out the barbecue shrimp recipe at home. It's now a staple at Nancy's Thanksgiving dinners.

Calypso's West Indies Barbecue Shrimp

4 to 5 large shrimp, peeled and deveined
⅓ cup Calypso Barbecue Sauce (see below)
4 Tablespoons cold sweet butter, cut into
   4 pieces
4–5 crostinis (thin slices of a small baguette,
toasted)

Calypso Barbecue Sauce

4 large peeled garlic cloves
¼ cup lemon juice
1 cup Worcestershire sauce
1 ½ teaspoons onion powder
1 ½ teaspoons garlic powder
2 teaspoons dried thyme
2 teaspoons dried oregano
1 teaspoon seasoned salt or to taste
¼ teaspoon hot sauce (Matouk's
   recommended) or to taste
1 teaspoon cracked black pepper
3 Tablespoons Better Than Bouillon Beef Base
2 teaspoons paprika

Several hours or even a day ahead of time, puree all ingredients in a blender or food processor and store in refrigerator. Makes about 1 ⅓ cups.

Heat up ⅓ cup sauce in saucepan. (Recipe can be doubled or tripled.) Sauté shrimp in sauce over medium heat about 3 minutes or until almost done (almost all pink), turning shrimp once. Reduce the heat to very low and begin stirring in butter just until it melts. At that point, the sauce is very delicate. Immediately pour half of sauce on each plate, put crostinis on plate, put a shrimp on each crostini, pour the rest of the sauce on top, and serve immediately

*—Courtesy of Calypso Restaurant
and Raw Bar, Pompano Beach, FL*

I-95 Exit 32: Tropical Fish and Killer Thai Food

Thai Spice

1514 East Commercial Boulevard, Ft. Lauderdale; 954-771-4535; www.thaispicefla.com. Open for lunch Monday through Friday 11:00 a.m. to 3:00 p.m. Open for dinner Sunday through Thursday 5:00 to 10:00 p.m., Friday and Saturday 5:00 to 11:00 p.m. $$–$$$

From I-95: Take exit 32—Commercial Boulevard/SR 870 east (1.5 miles). Thai Spice will be on your right in a strip mall.

Lots of restaurants in Florida have outdoor dining, and most of the time, when the weather is good, we'd recommend sitting outside. Not at Thai Spice, though. They have tables on a little sidewalk between the strip mall restaurant and a cramped parking lot on busy Commercial Boulevard. Inside, though, the whole world transforms. Dark, exotic, and romantic, the only light sources at dinner are the small chic lamps hanging over tables and a number of brightly lit saltwater aquariums with colorful sea creatures swimming around. They renovated several years ago, adding intimate booths, extra aquariums, a black ceiling, and an additional room. With jazz playing softly in the background, this is a great place to take a date or just a beautiful world to escape to for a while.

Owner/manager/chef Michael Tatton grew up around the restaurant business. His Thai-Filipino father was the maitre d' at the famed Mai Kai restaurant in Ft. Lauderdale for thirty-seven years, and it was there that Michael's father met his American wife, the woman who would become Michael's mother. Michael got his start cooking at his house when he was thirteen, and by 1988, at twenty years of age, he was already set to open his own restaurant, Thai Spice, which at that time was a little take-out/delivery place with an Oriental market. As the food got more and more popular, he phased out the market and expanded to include seating. Now he has 32 fulltime employees, and the place seats 135 people. Michael loves tropical aquariums, which is why the restaurant has so many. Small sharks are among the dwellers, and once, before leopard sharks were outlawed in tanks, a Florida lobster ate one of Michael's leopard sharks. You never know what you might see at Thai Spice. All this is very good news for travelers looking for great food in a dramatic atmosphere only 1.5 miles from the interstate.

Tall, sophisticated, and handsome, our host looks like he stepped out of a James Bond film to seat us.

He is quite solicitous of Nancy's grandmother, who's just gotten the cast off a broken wrist and is moving gingerly. Our server also manages to hit that odd mix of formal and friendly, and our busboy Peter may be the best in the world, attentive, outgoing, and adorable. How many times do you remember your busboy's name? Nancy's grandmother would've married him by the end of the meal.

Tempting aromas waft from nearby tables, and it's tough to choose from a menu where everything sounds so good and is. Try the spring rolls or grilled calamari to start. A hearty peanut dressing comes on all the fresh and crisp house salads. As for soups, the hot and sour soup is among the best Jane has ever had in Florida: lots of mushrooms, tofu, and other veggies, and not at all gelatinous like so many hot and sour soups seem to be. Nancy still likes their sweet and spicy Tom Yum Gai best, though, with chicken, coconut milk, mushrooms, fresh lemongrass, galangal, scallions, and lime juice.

The seafood medley (scallops, grouper, shrimp, and calamari) is spectacular in a red curry sauce and beautifully presented with edible flowers. You won't be disappointed choosing any of your favorite curry dishes and other traditional Thai food, but the menu has lots more to offer, including gourmet seafood dishes. You can't go wrong with any of the fresh fish. The yellowtail snapper with lemon-butter sauce was as good as you'd find in the best seafood restaurants.

Try also the stone crabs in season or the live Maine lobster, another aquarium dweller. The steak, believe it or not, is also a popular choice. It would have been great on its own, but it reached new heights with the spicy Thai dipping sauce.

For a very reasonably priced lunch or a delicious dinner that's also a good value, Thai Spice is the Gourmettes' favorite Thai restaurant in Florida. Michael wants people to think of Thai Spice as a fine-dining destination restaurant, and so do we.

I-95 Exit 32: Lazy Beach Breakfast

Country Ham N' Eggs

4405 El Mar Drive, Lauderdale-by-the-Sea; 954-776-1666; www.countryhameggs.com. Open daily 7:00 a.m. to 2:30 p.m. $$

From I-95: Take exit 32—Commercial Boulevard/FL-870 east (3.4 miles). Turn left onto El Mar Drive (.1 mile). Country Ham will be on your left. There's a metered parking lot across the side street or metered parallel parking on the street in front. Don't let your meter run out!

Restaurants near the beach in South Florida are not always known for their homey atmosphere, but Country Ham N' Eggs is an exception. This landmark restaurant has operated under the same name since 1968 in laid-back Lauderdale-by-the-Sea, a little village nestled between Ft. Lauderdale and Pompano Beach. Country Ham N' Eggs is located about a block from the beach and a half block off the main commercial intersection of a town that's mercifully managed to limit building height in order to retain some charm amid the shell shops, restaurants, and gift stores.

"We try to make it very comfortable—on a first-name basis," said owner Robert Minlionica, a transplant from Long Island who runs the restaurant with help from his wife, father, and three teenage daughters. The restaurant is small and quaint with indoor and outdoor patio seating. A framed picture of the "Rat Pack" graces the back wall. To our knowledge, none of the Rat Pack ever ate here, but Adam Sandler did, and his mother and mother-in-law are regulars.

The server immediately recognized Jane's coffee deprivation and kept the brew pouring until Jane could fully open her eyes and read the extensive menu. The problem with the menu is that too many things look good . . . and are: pancakes, eggs Benedict,

French toast, country ham and eggs (oddly enough), "rolled" omelets, breakfast sandwiches, country fried steak, and home fries that Jane's husband, Gary, raves about. "You get little pieces that are crunchy and bigger pieces that give you that meaty potato texture," he explains. You also get green peppers and onions, just barely caramelized. A killer side dish for any egg choice.

Nancy's favorite option is the "Jersey Shore," an artery-clogging concoction of scrambled eggs topped with peppers, onions, and bacon (or sausage or ham if you choose), then hash browns, then smothered with cheddar cheese and broiled until the cheese is bubbly. Jane is less a fan of smothering food in cheddar cheese, but Nancy still has dreams about the Jersey Shore.

If you've been out partying the night before and need a hair of the dog, mimosas, wine, and beer are available for your breakfast dining pleasure. Most folks were sticking to the old-school coffee, though. Maybe on Sundays it's different.

Breakfast is served all day, but if you're in the mood for lunch, try the half-pound Angus burger or one of the wraps served with french fries or, Nancy's favorite, the sweet potato fries.

When we were ready to pay up, Jane happened to be holding the check and her credit card. The owner's dad, playing the role of cashier, came along and swiped both to save her a trip to the counter. Just another instance of helpful service, but Jane did worry for a minute—who had she just given her credit card to? No worries at Country Ham N' Eggs except for the metered parking outside. Don't be a minute under-quartered. You have been warned. Aside from the meter police, Lauderdale-by-the-Sea is a lazy beach hamlet, sure to please if you eat at Country Ham N' Eggs.

I-95 Exit 32: Ask No Secrets, Tell No Lies

Greek Islands Taverna

3300 North Ocean Boulevard, Ft. Lauderdale; 954-565-5505; www.greekislandstaverna.com. Open daily 11:00 a.m. to 11:00 p.m. $$–$$$

From I-95: Take exit 32—Commercial Boulevard/SR 870 east (2.3 miles). Turn right onto North Federal Highway/US 1 (1.6 miles), left onto East Oakland Park Boulevard/FL-816 (1 mile), and left onto North Ocean Boulevard/FL-A1A (less than .1 mile). Greek Islands Taverna will be on your right.

We aren't sure what it is with Greek restaurants and secrecy, but while the owners and management of most places are delighted to tell us their stories, the only two Greek places so far in the book (Theo's Restaurant and Greek Islands Taverna) have both treated us like we were the IRS instead of enthusiastic eaters trying to give them free publicity.

When we first called up to introduce ourselves and the book and ask a few questions, we had to work our way through the defensive armor that insists we must be selling something or trying to screw the restaurant over in some way. People often have trouble acknowledging or accepting gifts, especially from strangers, especially in South Florida, especially, apparently, some owners of Greek restaurants on Florida's East Coast. Once the woman on the phone was semiconvinced that we weren't selling anything—and it took some doing—she divulged that she was the one to answer our questions.

We started out simple. When did the restaurant open? "January 1999." Then we asked who owned it, and she told us his name was Sam Kantzavelos. We suspect this is where she decided she'd been too forthcoming with us. On the back of the take-out menus, you will note, it says "For further information please contact Sam at 954-565-5505." Just Sam. Not Sam Kantzavelos.

So, the next logical question seemed to be, "He's Greek then. Was he born in Greece or here in the U.S.?"

Well, that set her off. "There's no reason for you to know that! I've read guidebooks. I know what they have in them about food and prices. This doesn't have anything to do with it." When Nancy patiently tried to explain that our guidebook was somewhat different, that we were interested in stories and histories as well as the bare facts, she said we'd have to talk to Sam if we wanted any more information. She'd have him call us. Great. Just what we wanted anyway, only, you guessed it: Sam didn't call us back.

Based on all this, we've decided to focus only on the food and service at Greek Islands Taverna, both of which are spectacular, which is the only reason the restaurant is still in the book after talking to the management. Remember to eat, drink, and be merry—just don't ask a lot of questions.

If you're here for dinner, you might well end up waiting in a line that snakes past a display case and the serving area, so you can whet your appetite with the look and aroma of all your favorite Greek delicacies. A sign has the specials in English on one side and in Greek on the other. (At least we think they're the specials in Greek.) Greek Island Taverna is the real thing. Maybe Sam was born in Greece. No need to worry about your own anonymity; the host won't ask your name (secrecy runs both ways apparently), just the number in your party, and he may ask it several times while he seats people on the fly as tables become open.

It's hard to know where to start recommending things: maybe the succulent lamb chops, five of them charbroiled with lemon, oregano, and olive oil, or maybe the *garides tou sotiri*, gigantic baked shrimp, butterflied and covered with Sotiri's Secret Sauce. (Did Sotiri start all this secrecy? We suspect it includes mustard, garlic, and olive oil. Beyond that . . . ?) The sweetbreads are also delicious, and the moussaka is just like your Uncle Adelphos used to make.

Don't forget to start things off with an appetizer, though. The *saganaki* (Kefalatori cheese flamed in brandy) really shouldn't be missed, and *pikilia* offers you an assortment of four traditional dips to eat with your pita bread or the white and wheat bread that come with your dinner. Try the custard pie, *galakto-boureko*, for dessert. It's dense custard, not too sweet, wrapped in phyllo dough glazed in honey and cinnamon.

We haven't had anything we didn't like at Greek Islands Taverna. As long as we keep getting to enjoy the food, drink, and crowded, lively atmosphere at G.I.T., Sam can keep his secrets.

I-95 Exit 22: Ice-Cream Happy Days

Jaxson's Ice Cream Parlor & Restaurant

128 South Federal Highway, Dania Beach; 954-923-4445; www.jaxsonsicecream.com. Open Sunday through Thursday 11:30 a.m. to 11:00 p.m., Friday and Saturday 11:30 a.m. to midnight. $–$$

From I-95: Take exit 22—Stirling Road/FL-848 east (1.1 miles) and turn left onto US 1/South Federal Highway (less than .1 mile). Jaxson's will be on your left in a strip mall.

In 1956, Monroe Udell started selling ice cream and candy at Jaxson's in Dania Beach. Somewhere along the way, he added sandwiches, salads, and the like, but nowadays, his biggest export is nostalgia. Nostalgia is the reason you might pay more than $10 for a Reuben sandwich or around $10 for a banana split.

You pay extra for the red-and-white striped awning, the used-to-be-penny candy room, and "one of the nation's largest collections of rural American memorabilia," including old bikes, farm implements, photos, and many, many license plates. We think the extra money is worth the treat, at least when you're buying the ice-cream concoctions. Jane is nostalgic for a time when she never needed to count calories, when "butterfat" was not a bad word, and when she'd never heard of, or at least had never thought about, cholesterol. When she hits Jaxson's, she returns to that time. She has to, in order to guiltlessly consume the rich, homemade ice cream. Even a small is a large here, and the servers are used to providing to-go con-

"The Kitchen Sink" caps off a birthday party.

tainers. Nancy's eighty-nine-year-old, ninety-pound grandmother who hardly eats sweets managed to put a hurting on a hot fudge sundae made with peppermint ice cream. She had less to take home than any of us. Nancy, herself, was especially happy with the treasure room of kids' candy and the chocolate malted shakes.

When Udell moved down from the northeast in the 50s, he brought along lots of family recipes, and today, they still use many of those recipes as they make all the ice cream and all the toppings on the premises with lots of fresh dairy cream, butter, chocolate, fruit, and nuts. We especially like his vanilla ice cream smothered in one of the homemade toppings like hot fudge or hot butterscotch (which, according to our server, is the same thing as the hot caramel they advertise). The marshmallow topping didn't have as much oomph as the others. If you're inclined toward fruit toppings, try strawberry, cherry-pineapple, black raspberry, blueberry, or peach. If shakes and sundaes aren't your thing, you might try a "continental waffle" served with Vermont maple syrup or topped with ice cream. Or indulge further into nostalgia and get an ice-cream float or an ice-cream soda. The menu has more than enough ideas to spark your childhood ice-cream fantasies.

If you're really adventurous and in a group of four or more, you might try "The Kitchen Sink." For $10.95 a person, the kitchen staff will concoct a unique ice-cream extravaganza from their many choices of flavors and toppings and serve it up in a faux kitchen sink so that you can all dig in.

Jaxson's offers lots more than frozen treats, though.

If you dine inside, you'll be treated to complimentary popcorn, popped in one of the old-style poppers set up near the servers' station. Then you can choose from a variety of salads; hot and cold deli sandwiches; "Mile-Long" hot dogs; wraps; and even real steak, chicken, or shrimp dinners. Clearly, you don't have to make a meal out of the ice cream. We think it's a good idea, though.

If you just want a quick ice-cream cone or cup, you can always order from the outdoor window, and you can get a smaller version of ice cream for a more reasonable price. There might even be some street entertainers playing music along the strip mall. Yes, Jaxson's, too, is in a strip mall. Outside you'll remember that, but inside, decades will fade away.

I-95 Exit 21: Le Burger at Le Tub

Le Tub

1100 North Ocean Drive, Hollywood; 954-921-9425; www.theletub.com. Open daily 11:30 a.m. to 4:00 a.m. CASH ONLY. $$–$$$

From I-95: Take exit 21—Sheridan Street/FL-822 east (3.1 miles) and turn right onto North Ocean Drive/FL-A1A South (1.1 miles). Le Tub will be on your right.

Le Tub is a castaway bar with a burger problem. The problem all started when Oprah's friend Gayle King claimed it was the best burger in America, then *GQ*'s Alan Richman concurred, and the place has been a mob-scene ever since. The regulars here and even the owner, Russell Kohuth, apparently are not pleased. The servers all have major attitude, and the place only takes cash. There's an ATM in the restaurant next door, though.

Despite the struggles with fame, however, the place is vintage Gourmette. In the mid-1970s Russell transformed an old Sunoco gas station by hand into a Swiss Family Robinson–like outpost, using "flotsam, jetsam, and ocean-borne treasures all gathered daily over four years of daybreak jogging on Hollywood Beach." The place takes "multilevel" to a new level as you seem to move up or down about every six feet, which creates all sorts of nooks and crannies where you can end up eating on a picnic table, perhaps right next to the Intracoastal Waterway. The place is decorated primarily with brightly painted bathtubs and commodes and junglelike flora. You quickly forget you're right next to a busy section of FL-A1A and feel like you're off on some ill-tempered island. A couple of drinks, and it all becomes quite amusing. When Nancy asked for water, our server deadpanned, "Orange cooler."

"Orange cooler?"

it's a hot day in Hollywood, it'll be a hot day at Le Tub. Indoors is open-air with ceiling fans. Outdoors, you rely on Mother Nature's fans.

Still, though, the place is unlike any other in Florida, and on a beautiful day, you can sit out in the sun right on the water and toss extra french fries to the fish while drinking a margarita and feeding your face with ground sirloin as rare as you like. Bring your cash, patience, and smart-aleck retorts for the staff if you brave it.

The server looked annoyed and started making stiff-armed motions like she was directing an airplane to a gate, and Nancy noticed the plastic cups next to a big orange cooler on a nearby wooden stand. Serve yourself, apparently.

And the sirloin burgers, well, we don't think they're the best in America, but they're sure gigantic (thirteen ounces) and they start out with great meat, so they are pretty darn good. No fancy cheeses on top or bacon or mushrooms or anything. Just a basic giant-size burger. We wouldn't stray far from the burger on the menu, though.

So, it's true, we're only adding to their woes by letting even more people know about Le Tub, but we're keeping the write-up short with no photo, and we're letting people know about the problems—potentially a very long wait for a burger or sometimes a seat. If

I-95 Exit 3B: Where the Boys Are

Garcia's Seafood Grille & Fish Market

398 Northwest North River Drive, Miami; 305-375-0765. Open daily 11:00 a.m. to 9:30 p.m. $$–$$$

From I-95: Take exit 3B—Northwest 8th Street. Drive 4 blocks west on Northwest 8th Street, turn right onto Northwest 4th Street, and go 3 more blocks. Garcia's will be in front of you.

It's true that Garcia's has the ugliest waterfront view of any restaurants we've sent you to, but Jane says it doesn't matter because you won't be looking in that direction anyway since Garcia's has the best looking, sexiest, most flirtatious waiters of anyplace she's ever been. If sexy Cuban guys aren't your cup of *cafecito*, though, never fear. We've once again found our way to fresh seafood, this time with a Cuban flair.

You walk through the fish market first and get to check out just how fresh the seafood is as the fishmongers display the day's catch. To get to the tables, keep walking, either upstairs to a beautiful, old-world bar area, or outside to a deck with another bar and long wooden tables crammed in close to one another. On the deck, if you divert your eyes from the waiters, you look across the Miami River to a pink cargo warehouse with lots of big concrete pylons in front of it. There's an urban earthiness to it all, what with the weathered tables and the cracked and chipped underwater/over-water mural of Miami. Even the Miami scene depicted, with its high-rise buildings and giant ships coming in to port, isn't especially beautiful, although some manatees are thrown in to liven up the aesthetics. If you like your restaurants pristine, this probably isn't your kind of place, but if you end up here anyway, head upstairs, where it has the feel of a 1950s Havana bar.

They start you off with a fish spread-with-crackers *amuse bouche*. We ordered the ceviche *vuelva a la*

vida our first time there, and it was a decent, cheap version of the classic dish, with oysters and tiny shrimp in a soupy tomato cocktail. We'd check out the fish ceviche next time.

Garcia's dolphin sandwich is definitely worth ordering, fresh, tender, and flaky. All sandwiches and salads come with your choice of side dish: white or yellow rice, French fries, coleslaw, parsley potatoes, house or Caesar salad, sweet or green plantains. Sweet plantains and fresh fish is a great combination. If you're not a dolphin fan, try the snapper, grouper, or fried shrimp sandwiches—all fresh and tasty.

The regular menu is very basic, fresh seafood: jumbo shrimp, various fresh fish, grilled lobster, and conch steak. If it's stone crab season, you should give them a try. You're not likely to find them cheaper or fresher elsewhere. Also, for those who don't mind working to eat, try the whole yellowtail snapper, fried or grilled. "Fried is very nice," says the handsome server we ask about it. If you don't like seafood, there's not going to be much to make you happy here except the waiters.

The blackboard lists the day's specials, which tend to be a little more adventuresome than the menu. We tried a salmon in a mustard/tamarind swirl that set off little sparklers in the mouth. The fish was perfectly cooked and the spice in the mustard kept sparking with the sweet of the tamarind. That came with two sides and was an amazing value. Shrimp creole and shrimp and scallops in a spinach and lobster sauce were two of the other options.

For dessert, we asked our server if the key lime pie was good. He broke into a heavenly smile and said with absolute sincerity and enthusiasm, "Yes, it is the best in the world!" Of course we ordered it.

When we tried the key lime pie, Nancy said, "I bet he gets a lot of women in trouble." For us, fortunately, it was only key lime pie.

I-95 Exit 3A: It Ain't French

Versailles

3555 Southwest 8th Street, Miami; 305-444-0240. Open Sunday through Thursday 8:00 a.m. to 1:00 a.m., Friday 8:00 a.m. to 2:00 a.m., and Saturday 8:00 a.m. to 3:00 a.m. $–$$$

From I-95: Take exit 3A and merge onto FL-836 West/Dolphin Expressway (2.4 miles). Merge onto FL-9 South/Northwest 27th Avenue/Unity Boulevard (1.5 miles), and then turn right onto Southwest 8th Street/Tamiami Trail/US 41/FL-90 (.8 mile). Versailles will be on your right; there is parking next to the restaurant.

Jane describes Versailles as a cross between a multiroomed NYC coffee shop and Marie Antoinette's digs. Jane's husband, Gary, says it's like an "average-looking person who's got really elaborate makeup and hairstyling." However you describe it, it's a hybrid spot—the building, chairs, tables, and flooring are average, but the waiters wear white shirts and bow ties, chandeliers hang from the ceilings, and many, many mirrors proclaim over and over that this is Versailles. Don't let the French name or pseudo-decor fool you, though; this place is strictly Cuban, arguably the major Miami hub of Cuban food and power-broking right smack-dab in the middle of Little Havana. The servers speak little English, and it won't be the primary language when you eavesdrop either.

Really, it's three operations in one—a restaurant, a bakery, and a walk-up coffee window, plus the cigar shop, which we won't count. Since 1971, Versailles has been keeping this community caffeinated and

Meals Worth Stopping for in *Florida*

now serves more than 1,000 *cafecitos* a day. That's a lot of juice, and it helps explain why this place is always noisy and hopping, even into the early morning hours when the club crowd drops by looking for great grub at a reasonable price.

If it's your first time here, you might consider one of the Cuban samplers. We tried "The Classic," which comes with white rice, black beans, sweet plantains, delicious Picadillo (Cuban style hash, on the sweet side), succulent roast pork, the best ham croquette Jane's ever had, a good Cuban tamale, and boiled yuca (the root that gives us tapioca). You might not get excited about boiled yuca, and Nancy, even having tried this particular boiled yuca, wasn't especially excited although it was probably the best boiled yuca she's ever had. Jane, on the other hand, thought it was the most fabulous, delicious, to-die-for, best-I've-ever-eaten, didn't-know-it-could-be-this-good boiled yuca. Yep, that's right. Even though she's not usually crazy for yuca, she thinks the trip to Versailles would be worth it for the garlicky, gooey boiled yuca alone. Her husband, Gary, while not quite so ecstatic, concurred that this yuca was indeed something special. Nancy suspects that it's just the first time these folks have ever eaten boiled yuca that had any taste at all. Try it for yourself, though.

While Jane babbled on in her yuca euphoria, the Spanish baguette was transporting Nancy back to Europe, where she once fueled days of walking by eating great sandwiches on the cheap. Versailles' version has imported Serrano ham, Manchego cheese, and Cantinpalo chorizo pressed in a fresh Cuban mini-baguette. We both think that up to this point,

it's the best sandwich in Florida.

By the time dessert rolled around, Nancy and Gary were stuffed, but Jane gamely ordered Versailles custard, then had to use her knife to ward off the two thieves who wouldn't keep their spoons to themselves. Yellow custard tops a layer of moist sponge cake, and the whole thing gets a burnt sugar coating that you have to crack. Rarely has a dessert disappeared so quickly after a long day of eating.

Even if you're full at the end of the meal, though, you can still stop by the bakery and choose something for the road from among the many great pastry and small-sandwich options. The deli meats between two slices of Spanish tortilla looked particularly appealing, as did about fifty of the different pastries.

When you mention Cuban food in Miami, Versailles is the name on the tip of every tongue, but there's good reason for it. Don't let the crowds dissuade you. Versailles is a primo place to eat and people-watch.

Interstate 75
Lake City to Ocala

KEEP YOUR BEACH CLEAN

5

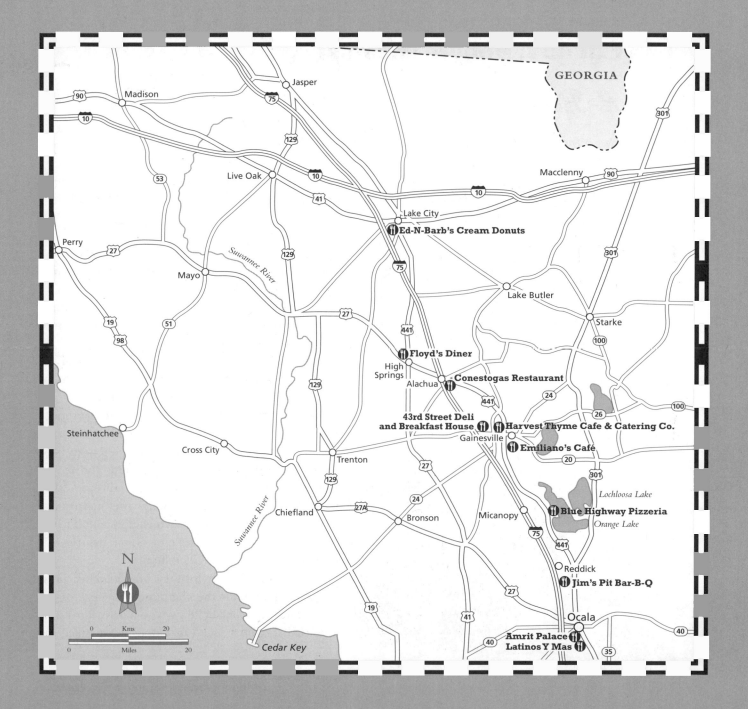

I-75 Exit 423: Donuts and Bust

Ed-N-Barb's Cream Donuts

567 Southwest Main Boulevard, Lake City; 386-752-1901. Open daily 5:30 a.m. to noon. $

From I-75: Take exit 423—FL-47 east toward Lake City (3.6 miles) and make a slight left as FL-47 becomes FL-41/FL-25 North/South 1st Street/Southwest Main Boulevard (.6 mile). Ed-N-Barb's will be in the old drive-in building on your right.

*E*d Collings is an unlikely looking donut meister. With long curly gray hair, a black Harley Davidson T-shirt and hat (both splattered with flour), and tattoos on his arms, he looks too tough to be a donut chef. Then again, you've got to be pretty tough to make donuts seven days a week. Ed's workday starts about midnight. His daughter works with him during the week, and his co-owner Barb works with him on the weekends.

Both Ed and Barb seemed tired when we arrived about noon. Barb is slow to smile, but when she does, her face lights up and her eyes sparkle. She said she tries to sleep from 4:30 to 10:30 p.m. to recharge for the long nights in the kitchen. Ed's a self-proclaimed sci-fi addict and sometimes that cuts into his snooze time. "Last night I was up till 9:30, but that's because it's the last ten episodes of *Stargate*." He's from New York, where he used to do body, paint, and fender work. When he arrived in Florida, however, "they wanted to pay me minimum wage after twenty-five years experience and all my own equipment." Thanks to Florida's lousy wage scale, a donut meister was born at the turn of the millennium.

You don't come here for their grandparently presence, though, or for the charming ambience of the white concrete block building with a drive-thru window (faded Monet and Van Gogh prints grace the

Meals Worth Stopping for in *Florida*

Barb knows donuts

varian cream, chocolate cream, strawberry cream, plus various éclairs and cannolis. The fruit-filled donuts are also plentiful and varied. Then there are the turnovers and the muffins and our favorite, the apple fritter, which is gigantic and filled with moist apple chunks and rivers of cinnamon and sugar.

Even better, these are the cheapest donuts, fritters, cinnamon rolls, éclairs, and turnovers we've seen in a long time. You can put a hurting on some baked goods here without eating into your Florida food budget. And anything that doesn't get bought by the end of the day is donated to the Suwanee Valley Rescue Mission to feed the homeless. Ed's not as tough as he looks.

walls inside); you come here for the great donuts. Nancy is an inveterate donut eater and white cream-filled are her favorites. She knew she'd like this place from the time she heard the name.

Jane is less enthused by donuts in general but Ed-N-Barb's has converted her, and on two occasions she was spotted wandering aimlessly around Lake City in a sugar-induced haze, her upper lip covered in powdered sugar, dots of Bavarian cream and black raspberry on her cheeks. She swears that the trans fats outlawed in New York have fled to Ed-N-Barb's, but still she can't help herself. Clearly, this is no health food stop, although you can get plain bagels or a ham, egg, and cheese croissant. Uh . . . those aren't quite health foods either. No matter, there are more important things in life than eating healthily, and cream donuts are one of them: white cream, Ba-

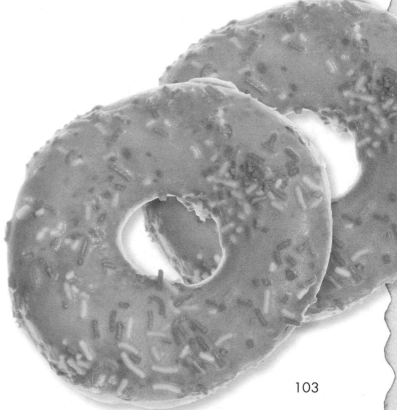

Meals Worth Stopping for in *Florida*

I-75 Exit 399: The Fifties Return

Floyd's Diner

615 Northwest Santa Fe Boulevard, High Springs; 386-454-5775; www.floydsdiner.com. Open Monday through Thursday 11:00 a.m. to 9:00 p.m., Friday 11:00 a.m. to 10:00 p.m., Saturday 10:00 a.m. to 10:00 p.m., and Sunday 10:00 a.m. to 9:00 p.m. $–$$$

From I-75: Take exit 399—US 441 North/FL-25 North and head northwest toward High Springs (around 6 miles). US 441 becomes Santa Fe Boulevard. Floyd's will be on your left.

When you're traveling, a lot of times it's hard to find a food stop that works for everyone, but Floyd's is about as close as you can get. First off, it's open for lunch and dinner seven days a week and brunch on the weekends. Next, the free Wurlitzer jukebox has favorites from the '50s, '60s, '70s, '80s, and '90s, and on Friday and Saturday nights, plus some Thursday nights, they have live music out on the patio. Finally, and most importantly, the menu is so extensive that it can please everyone in your minivan: the comfort-food folks, the vegetarians, the hip foodies, the big eaters, the light eaters, the sweet tooths, the picky children, and those in need of alcohol. Oh, yeah, and the family dog can join you on the patio if you like.

Floyd's is relatively new for a Gourmettes' stop. It only opened in 2002, but it looks a lot older than that, at least as far as style goes. It's a long, narrow traditional 1950s diner, down to the chrome and the antique cars out front.

If you make it there for brunch on Saturday or Sunday, you may have a wait, but it will likely be worth it. The omelets were cooked right with lots of goodies inside; the hash browns were decent. The fried eggs were perfect and the link sausage better than at most breakfast spots. It seemed, though, that the real pick of the day was the Carver cakes, a special that the man next to us had ordered that consisted of buttermilk pancakes smothered with cranberries and walnuts. They looked amazing and the guy confirmed that they were indeed as good as they looked, but he didn't offer us a bite. Drat!

When we returned for lunch, we tried one of "Alan's psychedelic big burgers," the six-ounce "classic" smothered in blue cheese (our choice among many toppings) on a toasted bun with lots of hot, crisp fries. The burger passed the test. We decided to forgo "The Smothered Motha," a half-pound burger with sautéed mushrooms, onions, and peppers and melted mozzarella. For vegetarians, there's a Boca

chicken), a chicken category (fried, parmesan, cordon bleu), a steak category (filet, sirloin, and strip), a pasta/rice category (veggie, jambalaya, Alfredo, paella, chicken/broccoli, shrimp scampi, eggplant with ravioli), a seafood category (Alaskan salmon, brook trout, tuna steak, fish 'n chips, and assorted fried creatures from the sea), a panini category, more sandwiches (Reuben, tuna salad, club, roast beef, hot dogs), and plenty of desserts (bread pudding, cheesecake, deep-dish seasonal pies, chocolate cake, and lots of choices from the ice-cream and soda fountain).

We ordered a chocolate malted shake with our lunch, and when it arrived, Nancy knew right away what was wrong by the dark color. A taste confirmed it.

"They made it with chocolate ice cream, didn't they?" asked Jane.

Horror of horrors, they did. Nancy quietly put it aside, hardly able to look at the sacrilege. When the

burger and a portobello sandwich.

From the comfort-food category, we tried "Thanksgiving Every Day," a hot roast turkey, open-faced sandwich with red mashed potatoes (skins on), an unusual and tasty apple-pear corn bread stuffing, and a large serving of corn. The portions in general tend to be large. The burger was better, but this will do if you're craving Thanksgiving fare. Also in this category, we could've had Salisbury steak, "Mike's Country Meatloaf," liver and onions, or a hot roast beef sandwich.

Lest you think we're exaggerating about the choices, there's also an appetizer category (barbecue chicken nachos looked incredible, but there's lots more, including coconut shrimp, calamari, soups, chicken tenders, and quesadillas), a "supersize salads" category (black-and-blue, chicken Caesar, chili taco, greens-fruit-pecans-blue cheese, and a house with

server came back, she asked if something was wrong with the shake.

"You made it with chocolate ice cream, didn't you?" Nancy gently accused.

The server nodded her head, baffled at what the problem was.

"You see," Jane explained, "we're used to it with vanilla ice cream and chocolate syrup."

"Oh, do you want me to make it like that?"

"Could you?" we piped up simultaneously, with hope rising to the surface.

"Sure."

And by golly, she did make another one, a *perfect* chocolate malted shake, made with vanilla ice cream just as it should be. It's not that we think a law should be passed that you *can't* make chocolate shakes with chocolate ice cream; it's only that we think there should be a law that you must prominently display a sign explaining your choice if you do so. The default should always be vanilla ice cream and usually is in Florida. In New York City, perhaps you need to order a "black and white" malt if you want it made with vanilla ice cream, but High Springs definitely ain't New York City. In any case, make sure you ask for vanilla ice cream if it matters to you as it does to us.

I-75 Exit 399: Round up the Young'ns and Head over for Some Vittles

Conestogas Restaurant

14920 Main Street, Alachua; 386-462-1294; www.conestogasalachua.com. Open Monday through Thursday 11:00 a.m. to 9:30 p.m., Friday and Saturday 11:00 a.m. to 10:00 p.m. Closed Sunday. $–$$$

From I-75: Take exit 399—US 444 east toward Alachua (1.4 miles) and turn right onto Northwest 140th Street/CR 235/CR 241/Main Street (.3 mile). Conestogas will be on your right. Additional parking is available in several city lots on the left.

On a Saturday night, the folks waiting for a table at Conestogas Restaurant stood or sat on benches, enjoying the Main Street view, listening to the soft rock piped into speakers above until the hostess would announce something like, "Six of clubs, your table is now ready. Six of clubs." We got an oversize king of diamonds when we put our name on the list, so we waited patiently, and it isn't long before we heard our card. (Apparently they never have more than fifty-two parties waiting.)

Rick Robertson christened this restaurant Conestogas when he opened it on the main drag in downtown Alachua in 1988 because Conestogas were giant wagons that played an integral part of the western expansion of the U.S. The Conestoga wagons were first developed in the early 18th century in the Conestoga Valley of Pennsylvania. For decades, they carried all

the things people thought they would need for a better life in the West. Likewise, Rick put all his money and some of his parents' money into this restaurant venture and hoped for a better life than the one he'd had for sixteen years working as a district manager for a corporate steak chain. The gamble paid off.

Conestogas is a family spot with better-than-family-spot food. They serve beer and wine, but not much of it by the looks of the tables around us and the cluelessness of the host who sat us and tried to take our drink orders. Our real server was great—knowledgeable and friendly, and we grilled her plenty. The warm honey-wheat bread was a good beginning, and we enjoyed our "Tenderfoot" filet mignon, even though it was served rare instead of medium rare. We were too hungry to send it back. We also liked "The Lariat Jumbo Shrimp" sautéed in garlic butter. We recommend the thin sweet potato fries as a side (of course!), although the home fries with green peppers and onions weren't bad either. The "Stogie Burgers" are excellent, apparently because they grind up scraps from their steaks to make the burger meat. The burgers arrive big and juicy with lots of whatever you order on top. If you're a light eater, you can also choose from a large array of entree salads.

If you're a superambitious eater, you can order "The Main Street Monster of a Burger," three sixteen-ounce stogie patties (for the math challenged, that's forty-eight ounces total—Yikes!) on a monster-size bun. It's only $19.99, and if you eat it all by yourself, along with your side dish of potato salad or "Garden of Eden" salad, you'll get a *free* key lime pie and a Conestogas T-shirt. Is that a deal or what!?

As you've undoubtedly discerned, the restaurant has an Old West feel to it, with menu names like "The Forty-Niner" (a mixed dish of sirloin tips, chicken tips, and sautéed shrimp) and nonsensical explanations including, "The miners dug deep, especially for the shrimp." It's a fun place, including the menu, atmosphere, and food. At lunch, we suspected we were the only nonlocals, nonregulars in the place, judging by the number of "Hellos" and "How are you's" called across the dining room and the amount of table hopping going on.

At the end of your lunch or dinner, you can choose from a big list of desserts. The New York cheesecake was perfectly acceptable, and Jane liked the French Silk pie pretty well. Or you can grab an ice cream for the road at Rick's ice-cream parlor and candy shop next door, whose cash register coincidentally doubles as the one for Conestogas. Because the servers don't take up your bill, you have to traipse through the candy/ice-cream shop with your kids in tow (or Nancy, who's just as bad when it comes to candy) in order to pay your bill. A clever marketing ploy to extract more from your pocketbook, and Nancy naturally succumbed, leaving with rubber chickens, Jelly Bellies, and candy cigarettes.

I-75 Exit 387: Brunch with the Locals

43rd Street Deli and Breakfast House

4401 Northwest 25th Place, Gainesville; 352-373-2927. Open Monday through Saturday 7:00 a.m. to 3:00 p.m., Sunday 8:00 a.m. to 2:00 p.m. $–$$

From I-75: Take exit 387—FL-26/West Newberry Road east toward Gainesville (1.1 miles). Turn left onto Northwest 8th Avenue/CR 338 (.6 mile), left onto CR 2053 (1.1 miles), left onto Northwest 25th Place (less than .1 mile), and left onto 43rd Street (less than .1 mile). The deli will be just behind Zaxby's in the strip mall.

*T*he original 43rd Street Deli and Breakfast House doesn't have a lot of bells and whistles. You might have trouble finding it even when you arrive at the strip mall it's in because there's no sign on the roof area, just a thin, orange neon sign in the window announcing its name. It's a neighborhood destination, though, and the neighbors all know where it is. The customers often include University of Florida faculty and staff, and the place stays busy. No extra signage necessary.

For breakfast, served till 11:00 a.m. Monday through Friday and till 2:00 p.m. on Saturday and Sunday, the sweet potato pancakes are outrageously good. We also tried the sweet potato waffle, and it was good too, but overcooked. The sweet potato fare is only on the specials list, but they keep the same specials most weekends. Another special, the "Popeye Benedict" (English muffin, tomato, spinach, poached egg, and hollandaise) was outstanding, and so was their regular Benedict. For those who like their lives orderly, they have plenty of omelets to choose from, and then they have lots of scrambles for those who don't mind everything thrown in all together, for example, the Greek scramble with tomatoes, onions, black olives, pepperoncini, and feta cheese. Jane's only complaint about it was that the plentiful bite-size ingredients should have been cut in half. Picky, picky.

They also do bagels of various kinds with all the traditional deli toppings, and something called "Belly Busters," which consists of potatoes, topped with cheese, topped with two eggs any style, then topped with whatever extras you want: bacon, ham, onions, peppers, mushrooms, etc. Belly buster indeed.

If you're like Jane in the morning and always on the lookout for a real cup of coffee, you'll be interested to know that 43rd Street uses Sweetwater Organic Coffee, "a 100 percent organic- and shade-grown, gourmet, fair-trade-certified coffee-roasting company" that's also based in Gainesville. It passed Jane's test on a sleepy Sunday morning.

Service at 43rd Street tends to run from competent to exceptionally friendly, depending on which college student gets assigned to your table and how much sleep he or she has had the night before. We had one peppy server who was waiting tables to earn beer money for the pubs in Ireland after she graduated from UF. Industrious girl. Usually the service is quick, although at prime times you may have to wait for a table.

At lunch, the fish Reuben is the best we've ever had. None of this coleslaw-Swiss-and-tartar-sauce stuff. This is the real Reuben . . . uh, except for the *one* substitution: grilled grouper, sauerkraut, Swiss cheese, and Thousand Island dressing, grilled on rye.

The traditional Cuban sandwich is also very good. For a variation on the Cuban, try the muffuletta. The Gourmettes know muffulettas. The Gourmettes have been friends with muffulettas, and what they call a muffuletta at 43rd Street is no muffuletta. First off, it's not on muffuletta bread, which is, by definition, round. Next, it doesn't have the right kind of meats (capicola, mortadella, and salami), and it doesn't have provolone cheese. It does, however, have an olive spread, which is also at the heart of all muffulettas. So, if you want to try a Cuban sandwich with a muffuletta olive spread, this could be the only place in Florida to try it. It's good. It's just not a muffuletta.

The owner's wife makes the desserts for all three locations (the other two places are at 1505 Northwest 13th Street, 352-373-3354; and 3483 Southwest Williston Road, 352-373-5656), and often they're cakes: chocolate, apple, and pound on one day when we were there. Try a slice, or on your way out, pick up a cookie or muffin by the cash register for the road.

I-75 Exit 382: Just What the Doctor Ordered

Harvest Thyme Cafe & Catering Co.

2 West University Avenue, Gainesville; 352-384-9497; www.harvestthymecafe.com. Open Monday through Friday 8:00 a.m. to 4:00 p.m., Saturday 11:30 a.m. to 3:30 p.m. Closed Sunday. $–$$

From I-75: Take exit 382—SR 121 North/Williston Road. Go east toward Gainesville (2.6 miles). Turn left onto South Main Street/FL-329 (2.4 miles) and left onto West University Avenue/FL-24/FL-26. Harvest Thyme will be on your right, with parking in the rear.

It's been a while since we told you about a health food restaurant, but Harvest Thyme is one of those places that a vegetarian would like and so would a meat eater who wants to feel virtuous. Mike and Jennifer Davidson, who own the restaurant, used to be world-class swimmers. In the 1984 Olympics, Mike swam the 1,500-meter freestyle, and Jennifer swam in the Olympic trials that year. They bring that swimmer's discipline and attention to health into Harvest Thyme, their half funky–half homey deli in downtown Gainesville.

The bread and produce are delivered daily, and the giant blackboard behind the counter entices you with the options: sandwiches, wraps, soups, fresh fruit, shakes, and smoothies. We like the "smoked apple bacon turkey melt" on whole wheat, but the "tuna apple melt croissant" is the favorite at the restaurant. The "nutty raisin chicken salad" sandwich is excellent, but then so is the "Caribbean chicken

wrap" (grilled chicken, a jerk sauce to heat things up, melted jack and cheddar and lots of veggies, all rolled in a sun-dried tomato wrap).

For veggie lovers, they have a garden burger, homemade hummus on a pita sandwich, a "farmers' market pita" with lots of veggies and cheese, and something called a "Veggielicious," which is a sun-dried tomato wrap filled with all sorts of fresh veggies, jack and cheddar cheese, and a honey Dijon dressing. "Mother Nature's Best" is also a restaurant favorite and consists of frozen yogurt and granola with seven different kinds of fresh fruit.

With a sandwich or wrap, try one of the soups du jour. Jane especially liked the chicken gumbo, which is more like a chicken-and-okra stew with some heat thrown in.

Harvest Thyme also uses the locally roasted Sweetwater Organic Coffee, the "100 percent organic- and

shade-grown, gourmet, fair-trade-certified coffee-roasting company." Besides all that, the coffee tastes good, and Harvest Thyme has its own custom blend along with five other Sweetwater roasts.

Jodie of "Jodie's Cookies" fame comes in every week and bakes Harvest Thyme's homemade cookies on the premises—Nancy likes the chocolate chip after such a virtuous lunch. She skips the Zapp's potato chips and goes straight for the cookie. The more consistently virtuous might opt for one of the healthy shakes or smoothies. The "summer breeze" smoothie, with mandarin, papaya, bananas, and pineapple, will leave you satisfied and sanctified.

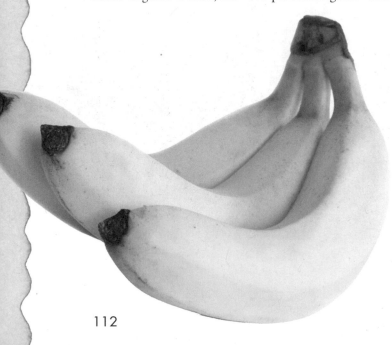

Meals Worth Stopping for in *Florida*

I-75 Exit 382: Mouthwatering Latin Fusion

Emiliano's Café

7 Southeast 1st Avenue, Gainesville; 352-375-7381; www.emilianoscafe.com. Open for lunch Monday through Saturday 11:00 a.m. to 4:00 p.m. and for brunch Sunday 10:00 a.m. to 4:00 p.m. Dinner served Monday through Thursday 5:00 to 10:00 p.m., Friday and Saturday 4:00 to 10:30 p.m., and Sunday 4:00 to 9:00 p.m. $$–$$$

From I-75: Take exit 382—SR 121/Williston Road east toward Gainesville (2.6 miles). Turn left onto South Main Street/FL-329 (2.3 miles) and right onto Southeast 1st Avenue. Emiliano's will be on your right.

The traffic in Gainesville is often onerous except on Sundays or during the summer when the college kids thin out, but Emiliano's is worth whatever traffic you have to fight to get here. On our first visit to this pan-Latin restaurant, we delighted in the casual hip decor: brick walls, cobalt blue trim, contemporary Latin art on the walls, and a neon TAPAS sign over the bar as you enter. You can dine inside or out on the patio in this charming downtown area, where the people-watching possibilities are plentiful and diverse.

We were there for an early Sunday brunch, and our server was friendly and knowledgeable if a bit hung-over—not surprising in a town that's home to the University of Florida. The meal started with an *amuse bouche* of bread pudding, the soft kind without a sauce, but quite tasty. The *tortilla espanol* was also delicious, with lots more chorizo and onions than

Chef Ali dePaz shows off her creations

you usually get in tortillas to season the potatoes and eggs. The tortilla came with small roasted potatoes (more potatoes?) and a fresh fruit cocktail. All good, but we were truly blown away by the brunch special: a riff on eggs Benedict that included the traditional toasted English muffin, Serrano ham, a spinach and Manchego cheese mixture, perfectly poached eggs, and a Dijon-mustard hollandaise sauce. The salty ham balanced out the rich spinach/cheese mixture and sauce, and we mostly quit talking in favor of mindless "mmmmmms." We knew then we had to get the recipe.

Fortunately, Chef Ali dePaz was happy to accommodate (see recipe on next page). Ali and her sister Wanda dePaz-Ibanez and Wanda's son Diego Ibanez now own and run Emiliano's—"One big sister, one little sister, and one big nephew," says Ali.

Emiliano's first opened its doors in 1982 as a bakery. Wanda and her husband, Jorge Ibanez, started the business and named it after Wanda's grandfather, who owned a bakery in Puerto Rico. Ali can still remember the huge brick ovens and the wonderful smell of his bread.

Gradually Emiliano's morphed from a bakery into a restaurant and tapas bar. Ali and Wanda's mother was doing lots of the cooking, primarily Latin classics; many of her recipes are still on the menu. Chef Ali felt she couldn't compete: "Your cooking is never as good as your mom's." So she began using the same ingredients in different ways. This was around the time that Latin fusion cooking was becoming hot, and she was part of that trend.

Ali calls her tapas *nuevo latino* and between 4:00 and 6:30 p.m. (called Sundowner), you can get special prices on tapas as well as beer and wine. Try the hot tapas, such as the empanadas or crab-stuffed portobello or *almejas y chorizos al ajillo* (little neck clams and Spanish sausage in garlic butter), or cold tapas, such as the *alcachofas marinades*, (artichoke hearts in a rich garlicky herb sauce) or *ensalada de pollo al curri* (Jamaican curry chicken salad with green apples and grapes) or *ceviche de vieras* (marinated scallops with lime, cilantro, red onion, peppers, and garlic). On the tapas menu, you can even order *porciones*, a la carte servings of Latin classics, such as *ropa vieja* (shredded flank steak in a red wine/tomato sauce with onions and capers). The Gourmettes wish that all menus were tapas menus, so that we could sample lots of small servings.

Don't forget the regular menu, though, filled with classic Latin dishes and various *nuevo* creations from Ali and the rest of her kitchen.

Things have changed a lot here since 1982. Wanda's mother no longer cooks in the kitchen. Now Jorge is out of the restaurant business and instead is head of the graphics design program at Sante Fe Community College. His brightly colored paintings hang on the brick walls of the restaurant. Ali took a ten-year break to work in the movie industry in LA and the restaurant business in Costa Rica, but since 2005, she's been back heading up the kitchen. It's a family affair, and that adds to both the intimate feel of the place and the commitment to excellence.

Emiliano's Serrano Florentine Benedict

This recipe was created by sous chef David Wallace and has become a favorite at the restaurant!

2 Tablespoons of butter
10 ounces of fresh spinach
1 teaspoon garlic salt
1 cup heavy cream
1 Tablespoon finely minced garlic
2 ounces of Manchego cheese
12 poached eggs
6 English muffins
6 ounces of Serrano ham, thinly sliced
parsley and pimentos (optional)

Creamy Dijon Sauce

1 cup of heavy cream
1 teaspoon of chopped garlic
2 Tablespoons of butter
2 Tablespoons of flour
¼ cup of Dijon mustard

Place all ingredients in sauce pan and cook on medium heat, stirring until it thickens.

The Benedict

Sauté the spinach, minced garlic, and garlic salt in butter for about 2 minutes. Add the cream; cook for another 2 minutes. Remove from heat and add Manchego cheese.

Toast the English muffins.

Set the English muffins on a plate and put a scoop of the spinach-cheese mixture on top, followed by slices of Serrano ham. Carefully place the eggs on top of the ham and finish with the Dijon cream sauce. Garnish with chopped parsley and diced pimentos.

Buen Provecho!!!

—*Courtesy of Ali dePaz, Executive Chef co-owner, and David Wallace, sous chef.*

I-75 Exit 374: Dining the Blue Back Roads

Blue Highway Pizzeria

204 Northeast Highway 441, Micanopy; 352-466-0062. Open Monday through Saturday 11:30 a.m. to 9:00 p.m., Sunday noon to 8:00 p.m. $$

From I-75: Take exit 374—CR 234 east toward Micanopy (1.3 miles) and turn right onto US 441/FL-25 South (.7 mile). Blue Highway will be on your left.

You gotta like any restaurant within shooting distance of the interstate that's named after that great road book *Blue Highways,* by William Least Heat-Moon. The Gourmettes' mission has always been to merge the pleasures of Blue Highway dining with the ease of interstate travel. Something of the spirit of Least Heat-Moon has made its way into this quaint pizzeria run by Frank and Winny Ruffino, socially conscious refugees from the corporate food industry, which Winny unapologetically describes as "one of the greatest evils in this country," responsible for America's obesity.

"Small is good," Winny says. They make sure their philosophy is on the menu: "Eat well . . . . Live well." "We are committed to using only the freshest and best quality ingredients, purchasing locally whenever possible. All sauces, salad dressings, pizza dough, and breads are made in house." It tastes that way too; the freshness shows in their pizzas, salads, and sandwiches.

Frank and Winny got their start in the business when they opened a restaurant called The Pirate's Galley on Siesta Key, Florida, three decades ago. Then Frank decided to try the corporate world, where he quickly rose though the ranks to be an executive chef at University of Florida and a corporate executive chef for Sodexho, the mammoth food services and facilities management company. He was named by

Nation's Restaurant News one of the top fifty research and development chefs in the country.

In 2004 the Ruffinos had a chance to return to Florida, their "first love," and found this tiny place in Micanopy, where one of their best friends lives, an artist whose work is on the restaurant's walls. (Gourmettes' note: We know, the restaurant is a lot newer than other restaurants in this book, but it's truly a Gourmettes' kind of place, so we made an exception.) How do they like leaving the corporate world and being back in Florida? "We love it," says Winny. "The first thing we both did is grow our hair long." They're particularly happy to be away from all the tension, politics, and paranoia of the corporate world. Here in Micanopy, they can focus on turning out great food and pleasing their customers.

And they do. Jane loves the Neapolitan pizzas, although the sauce is too simple and spare for Nancy's taste. Jane likes the crisp crust, the simple fresh tomato sauce, the good quality mozzarella, and the meatball and Italian sausage toppings, although, really, all the toppings seem great to both of us. Giant basil leaves, Gorgonzola cheese, kalamata olives, and sun-dried tomatoes are some of our other favorites.

Nancy especially likes the salads, and the Blue Highway Salad, with garden greens, feta cheese, tomatoes, red onions, kalamata olive, and toasted pecans, is her favorite. The sandwiches are all served Panini style or on fresh-baked country rolls with premium meats and cheese, and they also have calzones and appetizers like cheese bread, bruschetta, hummus, and antipasto.

The food here is great because the people in charge know great food and start with the freshest ingredients. "It's my husband's genius," says Winny. It's nice to have his genius back in Florida along one of the blue highways you can easily reach from I-75.

I-75 Exit 358: Exit Now . . . No, Really!

Jim's Pit Bar-B-Q

7424 West Highway 318, Reddick; 352-591-2479. Open daily 8:00 a.m. to 8:00 p.m. $–$$

From I-75: Take exit 358—FL-326/CR 218 east (.1 mile). Jim's will be on your right.

Okay, so it's not like you wouldn't have found Jim's Bar-B-Q without us. You'd have seen the giant billboards beckoning you off the interstate: EXIT NOW, JIM'S PIT BAR-B-Q, HOT FRESH BOILED PEANUTS. But then when you exited, you would've found a Chevron station with a half convenience store/half barbecue restaurant and you might have just filled up and driven away, assuming that anyplace so unassuming with such big billboards must be a tourist trap. You'd be right a lot of the time, but not this time. Jim's is the real deal, whether you're in the mood for peanuts or barbecue.

Jim Daughtery grew up in Jasper, Florida, and in 1982 opened a fruit and pecan stand on this Reddick property. When the 1984 citrus freeze made oranges scarce, he got a friend to help him get started in the barbecue business. When pecans got so expensive and of questionable quality, Jim started selling peanuts that were locally grown in Williston. "They're healthy for you too," he chimes. Just ask head cashier, the "lovely, young" (as she told us to describe her) Margie North. "I was ten pounds lighter when I came to work here six years ago," Margie proclaims. Her cash register is arm's reach from a sample plate of peanuts fried in peanut oil, sure to pack a wallop on the calorie-ometer.

If fried peanuts *aren't* your cup of nuts, have no fear. You can also get your peanuts roasted, boiled, honey-roasted, butter-toffeed, and about any other way you can imagine. The store is worth wandering around even if peanuts aren't your nut of choice. You can pick up a dried alligator head or maybe a T-shirt with a slogan of questionable taste or perhaps some shell art or Florida treasure maps. But we digress.

The best reason to stop at Jim's is the barbecue. The ribs are our favorite—you just look at the meat and it falls off the bone. Jim's is also one of the few places around that barbecues beef brisket. We like the pulled pork and turkey too. It's hard to go wrong with the barbecue here. And if you're lucky, you'll get a server like Rick, who knew how to take care of us when we ordered the fried corn: "I put a little garlic on there for ya,' then brushed it with butter." Just the way we like it.

The waitstaff here consists mostly of cowboy types who look like they've served up a lot of food back at the ranch but not in any fine-dining establishments. The preferred delivery system is for Rick or somebody like him to call out the items he's carrying and see who in the dining area, which seats maybe twenty-five people, speaks up and claims them. This makes for a lot of comradery among tables too, unless a fight erupts over whose ribs those are. It's not really a fighting kind of place, though. Too laid-back. The uptight folks eat elsewhere.

Jim Daughtery in peanut heaven

Jim's place may not be formal, but they care a lot about food. "We try to make everything we can here," he says. "You can get a little better quality control. We make our own coleslaw [which passed Jane's test], potato salad, pecan pie [which didn't quite make the cut], and beef jerky."

"They make it all in that tiny little kitchen," chimes in Margie.

Jim's Pit Bar-B-Q may have a little kitchen and gaudy signs, but we don't think you'll find better barbecue or a more diverse array of peanuts this close to the interstate anywhere in Florida. And we'd be hawking the place if it were a lot farther away from the exit too.

I-75 Exit 354 or 350: Mas, Mas, Mas!

Latinos Y Mas

2030 South Pine Avenue, Ocala; 352-622-4777. Open Monday through Thursday 11:00 a.m. to 9:00 p.m., Friday and Saturday 11:00 a.m. to 10:00 p.m. Closed Sunday. $$–$$$

From I-75 South: Take exit 354—US 27 South. Turn left onto US 27 South/FL-500 South (2.8miles) and right onto US 27/US 301/US 441/FL-25/FL-500/ Northwest Pine Avenue (2 miles). Latinos Y Mas will be on your right.

From I-75 North: Take exit 350—SR 200 toward Ocala and turn right onto FL-200 North/Southwest College Road (2.1 miles). Turn right onto Southwest 17th Street/FL-464 (1.2 miles) and right onto US 27/US 301/US 441/FL-25/FL-500/ Southwest Pine Avenue (.3 mile). Latinos Y Mas will be on your left.

The building was originally the first Burger King in Ocala, but don't let the exterior architecture fool you. The inside serves Latin fusion with a focus on Spanish and Mexican but with influences from all over the Latin world. Owners Webster Luzuriaga, his wife Fatima, and her mother Maria Pozo are fusions themselves. Luzuriaga is a Basque name; Webster was named after a dictionary given to his father; Webster and Fatima are both from Ecuador, as is Fatima's half-Italian mother Maria Pozo, who helps Fatima supervise the kitchen. These wide-ranging backgrounds contribute to Latinos Y Mas's pan-Latin notions.

"We always try to do a diverse menu," says Webster, "that's why we call it 'Y Mas [and more]—Cuba to Spain to South America or Italy and France because they're Latin countries too. Even the Mexican food is from all over Mexico, not just one place. The tres leche is from Nicaragua, the ceviche is from Ecuador, the paella is from Valencia, Spain." The recipes come from all over, and they even get the bread for their pressed Cuban sandwiches from a Cuban bakery in Tampa.

Most everything else is made in house, though. The salsa, for example, "isn't like most Mexican restaurants with their tomato base," says Webster. "It's chunks of fresh vegetables cut fresh daily with lots of cilantro and lime juice." The Gourmettes are fairly addicted to the salsa, and fortunately, the restaurant sells mason jars full of it to go, although because it's fresh, it has a shelf life of only twenty-four to forty-eight hours.

Besides the salsa, it's the inventive food, the attentive service, and the great values that keep us coming back to this family-owned restaurant that's been a mainstay in Ocala since 1991. Two brothers-in-law and a cousin also work in the restaurant, so lots of people have a vested interest in our dining experience.

Each weekday they have five-to-seven set specials in the well-under $10 range. The Spanish specials are served with salad (house dressing is creamy garlic), rice, beans, and plantains (Yum!), and the Mexican specials are served with yellow rice, refried beans, lettuce, pico de gallo, sour cream, and guacamole. You can't possibly leave here hungry. Try the *pescado* tropical if you're there on Monday. They'll start you off with warm chips and the fresh salsa, light on the tomatoes and heavy on the cilantro. Don't eat too many of them, though. Remember to pace yourself, because your grilled grouper with purple onions and yellow, red, and green peppers in a sweet pineapple sauce is on its way, and it's a killer dish. You get your choice of red or black bean soup—both good—and yellow or white rice. The plantains are crispy and soft, sweet, a bit salty, and delicious. Our Spanish-style steak special wasn't quite as tender as we'd hoped, but the sauce it was in—sautéed pepper, onion, tomato, and cilantro—was so good that we enjoyed it anyway.

For dinner, try the ceviche "*de la casa*" appetizer, which tastes more like a non-food-processed gazpacho that joined forces with a shrimp cocktail. It's delightful. The server tried to take it away before it was finished and Nancy shouted a panicked "No!" The *tostones con chorizo* (fried green plantains topped with slices of grilled Spanish sausage) are a more austere, but also delectable, choice.

Dinner entrees are the most inventive and far-

Danilo, Fatima, and Webster Luzuriaga

reaching, and the choices include mar y tierra (sautéed chicken, shrimp, and mushrooms in a brandy/lobster bisque sauce) and salmon "Caribe" (pan-seared in a citrus marinade and honey marinade). Then again, for the Mexican fans, you can have the old standbys: quesadillas, nachos, fajitas, or chimichangas. On Fridays and Saturdays, try the paella for a real treat. Latinos y Mas's Valencian version is served with Gulf shrimp, clams, mussels, grouper, calamari, chicken, and lean pork as well as the usual other vegetables and spices.

To wash down all the spices, you might choose one of the smoothies or wine-based cocktails advertised on the blackboard in familiar and unfamiliar flavors like mango, guana, bana, lulo, margarita, and moca. Don't be dismayed by the building's distant Burger King past. For almost two decades, the fare inside has been plenty exotic.

I-75 Exit 350: Rich Food in Hiding

Amrit Palace

2635 Southwest College Road, Ocala; 352-873-8500. Open Tuesday through Thursday 11:00 a.m. to 9:30 p.m., Friday 11:00 a.m. to 10:30 p.m., Saturday noon to 10:30 p.m., and Sunday noon to 9:30 p.m. Closed Monday. $$–$$$

From I-75: Take exit 350—SR 200 North/Southwest College Road toward Ocala (1.5 miles). Amrit Palace will be on your left.

Satnam Singh watches cousin Joginder Singh make naan

*Y*es, the Gourmettes bring you another hole-in-the wall in an ugly strip mall, reinforcing what your mama told you about judging books. This time, the bland exterior hides a small tearoom-pink restaurant. Lots of beads, glittery wall hangings, brass elephant heads, and Indian photos quickly distinguish it from a Southern ladies' luncheon spot, as do the rich aromas wafting in from the kitchen.

Here, Satnam Singh Saini and his wife, father, uncle, cousin, and sometimes his daughter, serve up North Indian food, the "food of royalty" according to the uncle. North Indian food apparently focuses more on bread and dairy products while South Indian food focuses more on rice and coconut products.

At the Amrit Palace, everything is made from scratch, says Mr. Singh, "except Coke. The rest is our own." It certainly tastes homemade and royal to us American peasants. The reasonably priced lunch spe-

the old favorite), a delicious vegetable *samoza*, *bhujia* (vegetable fritters, which we liked least), *chooza pakora* (chicken pieces marinated in yogurt, ginger, and garlic), papadam (a wonderful thin bean wafer), sizzling tandoori chicken (great with the curry sauce), *pillaw* rice (sautéed with almonds, cashews, green peas, and raisins), *puri* (a lighter fluffier deep-fried bread that looked like it should have had cinnamon and sugar sprinkled on it—it was tasty nevertheless), cooling *rayta* (homemade yogurt with cucumber), sweet onion chutney, and, for dessert, *gulab jamun* (sweet balls of juicy deep-fried pastry with honey syrup and rose water—lighter, less sweet than it looks).

We also had the rich and spicy shrimp *shaag*, cooked with spinach in curry sauce. Other house favorites include the chicken *tikka masala* (cooked in a creamy tomato sauce) and *rogan josh* (lamb cooked with yogurt, tomatoes, onion, ginger, garlic, and curry sauce).

A local who'd overheard us asking Mr. Singh questions, stopped on the way out to whisper, "This is the best restaurant in town. I'm stuck on the *chicken vindloo*" (boneless chicken in very hot curry sauce).

Mr. Singh and his family have been in Ocala since 1996 after operating Indian restaurants in South Florida and Orlando. They have no intention of leaving Ocala. "On the weekends people come from everywhere," says Mr. Singh, "Tampa, Jacksonville . . . They always want me to open a restaurant where they live, but if I open another branch, I'm going to lose my quality. I like the quiet here and less overhead." Hence the ugly strip mall. Don't be fooled by exteriors.

cials start off with fluffy naan, just out of the tandoor oven.

We're thrilled when later on Mr. Singh invites us back to the kitchen to watch how the bread is made. His cousin slaps a flat round of dough against the side of the cylindrical oven and pretty soon it starts bubbling and browning. A few seconds later it's ready to eat.

Bread is just the prequel to the filling and delicious meal to follow. Choose from any of ten lunch entries, including *aloo palak* (potatoes with spinach), chicken tandoori, lamb curry, and *dal* (lentils and tomatoes). Jane got her *aloo palak* medium hot, which was plenty hot for her.

At night we tried the tandoori dinner, a feast that included a vegetable soup (a rich Indian version of

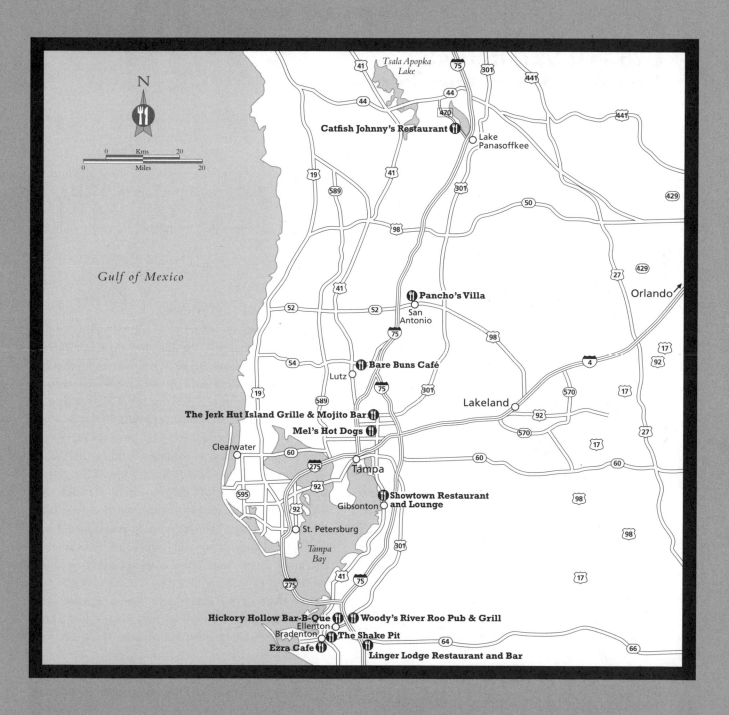

N

Kms 0 · · · 20
Miles 0 · · · 20

Gulf of Mexico

Tsala Apopka Lake

Catfish Johnny's Restaurant
Lake Panasoffkee

Orlando →

Pancho's Villa
San Antonio

Bare Buns Café
Lutz

Lakeland

The Jerk Hut Island Grille & Mojito Bar

Mel's Hot Dogs

Clearwater

Tampa

Showtown Restaurant and Lounge
Gibsonton

St. Petersburg

Tampa Bay

Hickory Hollow Bar-B-Que **Woody's River Roo Pub & Grill**
Ellenton
Bradenton **The Shake Pit**
Ezra Cafe **Linger Lodge Restaurant and Bar**

I-75 Exit 321: Catfish, Country Music, and Gators

Catfish Johnny's Restaurant

2396 CR 470, Lake Panasoffkee; 352-793-2083; www.catfishjohnny.com. Open Monday through Thursday 10:30 a.m. to 8:30 p.m., Friday and Saturday 10:30 a.m. to 9:00 p.m. Closed Sunday. $$–$$$

From I-75: Take exit 321—CR 470 west toward Lake Panasoffkee/Sumterville (3.3 miles). Johnny's will be on your left.

Catfish Johnny Galvin and his wife Pat have been serving fresh farm-raised catfish as well as a host of other fresh seafood, hand-cut steaks, and great burgers since 1990 to folks from all over the world who have ended up in tiny Lake Panasoffkee, Lake Pan to the locals. During football season, carloads of Gator fans drop by on their way to and from the games in Gainesville. During the winter (first Tuesday in November till the last Tuesday in April) old-time country music fans start forming a line at 6:00 a.m. to get a good seat for Catfish Johnny and the Hushpuppy Band when they open the doors at 10:30 a.m. for the all-day open-mic concert. "I tell 'em I wouldn't stand in line at six in the morning for the Pope if I was Catholic," Johnny says with a laugh. And he's not. (DON'T BE CAUGHT DEAD WITHOUT JESUS says the sign behind the cash register.)

Sometimes locals sing, and sometimes Johnny's friends from his music days in Nashville stop by. He's got a whole room full of photos of country music stars who've dropped in, folks like Merle Haggard, Johnny and June Carter Cash, the Bellamy Bros., and Ferlin Husky. People fill up the large banquet room that has a built-in stage, then start setting up lawn chairs outside by speakers in the parking lot, which is next to Ole Amos's double-fenced-in compound.

Who's Ole Amos, you ask? Ole Amos is the 14-foot alligator that hatched in Johnny's hand in 1960 when his parents had an alligator farm. One of the largest alligators in the world, Ole Amos lives out back with RADAR, the blind alligator who'd been shot in both eyes by poachers. The game commission found him in a swamp and Johnny and some other folks rescued him and brought him to live at what used to be a personal zoo.

In the old days, Johnny had a bear, a panther, huge loggerhead and soft-shell turtles, crocodiles, rattlesnakes, even a giant Burmese python. "I used to take

Meals Worth Stopping for in *Florida*

kids out here and tell 'em about critters," says Johnny. That was before the animal rights activists moved to town and started picketing the place. "Finally, one night they cut the lock and chains and let all the animals go at once." Fortunately no one was hurt by the wild animals, and the bear and panther just stayed in the compound despite the freedom. They died of natural causes at twenty-one and twenty-two years old, respectively.

What used to be a private menagerie is down to just Ole Amos and RADAR. The gators are no longer on display for the public, but for many years Johnny and Ole Amos had a road show. On the weekends, Johnny would haul Amos around in a specially made trailer, and they'd make commercial appearances at car dealerships and the like, but during the week, they'd travel to hundreds of schools where Johnny would talk about biology and "critters" and the history of reptiles, then he'd segue into the real purpose of his visit, the antidrugs campaign. "Ole Amos sez no to dope" was the slogan. The link between gators and drugs, according to Johnny, is that everyone thinks gators are so dangerous and kill so many people, but they're not nearly as dangerous as drugs, which kill kids every day. "If you want to be as tough as Ole Amos," Johnny would say, "you should say no to dope." Johnny did the school shows for free.

But enough about country music, alligators, and drugs. Food is the year-round draw to this rustic restaurant where you can eat inside with taxidermy fish and game on the walls or outdoor on the deck under the trees. Three generations of Johnny and Pat's family have hand peeled and butterflied Gulf shrimp;

hand battered catfish, perch, scallops, shrimp, oysters, and gator; and hand cut the steaks. They finally had to take the hamburger off the dinner menu because it was so popular, but you can still get it for lunch . . . if you can divert yourself from the mostly fried seafood, and especially the catfish. Nancy isn't even much of a catfish fan, and she loved it here. Also, don't miss the hush puppies, among the best we've had in Florida.

This isn't the most health-conscious menu in the book, but the food's awfully good, and you'll have a tough time beating the stories that have come out of this place and are repeated frequently by the locals. To what does Johnny attribute all his success?

"My good looks," he deadpans, then laughs. "No, to teamwork. Mostly to my wife, the hardest working person on earth." Raising five kids, being married to a rhythm-guitar-playing husband with a penchant for wild animals, and running a busy restaurant, she'd have to be.

Ole Amos and Catfish Johnny Galvin

I-75 Exit 285: *Nacho Libre* Time

Pancho's Villa

32804 Pennsylvania Avenue, San Antonio; 352-588-3037. Open Sunday through Thursday 11:00 a.m. to 9:00 p.m., Friday and Saturday 11:00 a.m. to 10:00 p.m. $$–$$$

From I-75: Take exit 285—FL-52 east toward Dade City (3.2 miles) and turn left onto Curley Street/CR 577 (.3 mile). Turn right onto Pennsylvania Avenue (less than .1 mile) and Pancho's Villa will be on your right.

*I*n our first trek to Pancho's Villa, we were so stuffed we were ready to pop. We had been trying to fill the restaurant gap along the south part of this chapter, so we ate, we ate, we ate. Restaurants often don't measure up. It was with this stuffed body and miserable mind-set that we stopped into Pancho's to split a quick bite at the end of the day.

The place is Gourmette perfect. Outside, the Old West facade has tromp l'oeil second-story windows with silhouettes of mariachi players and dancers. Inside, the charming beadboard cottage has been converted into a bright Mexican restaurant with serape curtains and valances; murals of desert cacti, cowboys (Gringos and Mexicans), and chili plants; sombreros; and a nearly life-size cutout of John Wayne drawing his gun on you as you head for the restrooms. Cheesy? Heck yeah, but the place is also authentically old enough looking that the cheese is welcome, by Nancy, anyway.

Having lived in Mexico for a year, Jane has the bias of a native against the culinary-bastard-stepchild

Tex-Mex, and Pancho's Villa leans a bit toward Texas, although it's by no means classical Tex-Mex. Nancy has no such compunctions and views orange cheese—preferably cheddar—as a natural accompaniment to Mexican food.

The two salsas—hotish and mild, both with extra

cilantro—were fresh and tasted great with the thin, warm chips. We liked everything about the burrito and the Mexican Rice and frijoles except neither of us was crazy about the ranchero sauce. The place was good enough for another visit for sure.

Our second time at Pancho's, it was crowded as always, with folks sitting outside on benches waiting, but one of the Basquez hosts with a Pancho Villa mustache found a two-top for us. Seven-year-old Jovan Basquez (with no Pancho Villa mustache) had just taken our drink order when Jane looked at the table next to us and gasped: "Oh, my God, Nancy, that's Hector Guerrero!"

"The Mexican Bandito?" Nancy looked over at the dark-haired fifty-something-year-old with the mustache, still good-looking, still fit. "It's him! He looks so much like his brother. Do you remember when he hatched out of that oversize egg and came out as Gobbledygooker, the half turkey–half human wrestler?"

"Sure, and how about that jalapeño powder he used to throw into people's eyes to temporarily blind them?" said Jane.

"Yeah, and the time he accidentally got some in the eyes of his partner, Dr. Diablo, and split up the team forever."

"No wonder he's here," said Jane. "He's a foodie wrestler!"

(The above dialogue is a dramatization of an actual event. The actual event looked more like the following.)

Jovan, the seven-year-old, had just brought the Gourmettes our drink orders when we noticed a man two tables away walk over to a dark-haired man with a mustache at the next table and say, "I'm sorry to bother you. I don't usually do this, but you look so much like Hector Guerrero."

"I am Hector," the dark-haired man said.

"My son is a huge fan of yours. Would you mind saying hello to him?" And by golly, Hector was the nicest guy. He left his date to go over and talk to the man's son and have his picture taken with him. When he came back, the man said, "Thank you so much. You made his day."

"No, you made mine," said Hector.

Why is all this important to a Gourmettes' entry? It's a *Nacho Libre* moment! Those Mexican-American wrestlers know their Mexican cuisine. If Hector Guerrero doesn't mind the orange cheese, neither should Jane. In any case, Jane found a verde sauce and a mole sauce she liked plenty well, and Nancy was particularly partial to the chicken fajitas.

Give this tiny restaurant in the tiny college town of San Antonio a try. It's the kind of place where anything can happen. If you close your eyes, you can almost imagine you're in a Mexican hole-in-the wall with Pancho Villa and his *dorados*, planning their next attack on the *federales* . . . or with Hector Guerrero and Jimmy Valiant plotting their next match against The New Breed.

As we were leaving, the wrestling fan was talking to us about how happy his son was to have seen Hector. "Yeah, he wants to see the Bellamy Brothers next."

"Do they hang out here?" Nancy asked.

"I don't know."

Anything's possible.

I-75 Exit 275: Dare to Go Bare!

Bare Buns Café

20500 Cot Road, Lutz; 877-879-5253; www.lakecomoresort.com. Open Monday through Thursday 8:00 a.m. to 8:00 p.m., Friday and Saturday 8:00 a.m. to 9:00 p.m., and Sunday 8:00 a.m. to 7:00 p.m. $–$$

From I-75: Take exit 275—SR 56 west toward Land O' Lakes/Tarpon Springs (.5 mile). Merge at light onto FL-56 West (.7 mile) and then stay straight to go onto FL-54 West (4.3 miles). Turn left onto US 41 South/Land O' Lakes Boulevard (.2 mile) and take 1st right onto Leonard Road (.5 mile). Watch for sign on fence and go straight onto Cot Road, a private road (.3 mile) to the office on your left.

At Catfish Johnny's, there's a sign behind the cash register that says IF YOUR UNDERWEAR'S SHOWING, KEEP ON GOING. A little farther south, this is where you can go. As a matter of fact, you can show anything you want at the Lake Como Family Nudist Resort.

First off, we should say that the Gourmettes are not "nudists" in any traditional sense of the word . . . or any nontraditional sense, for that matter. But we heard rumor that the grouper sandwiches were good at the Bare Buns Café, and, not being ones to shy away from new dining experiences, we decided to give it a try.

You don't have to be naked to eat at the Bare Buns, but you might wish you were after the initial shock wears off. First thing, stop at the entrance gate and pick up a two-hour restaurant pass that allows you on the grounds, then venture a little farther past the mobile homes and RVs until you see the cafe (next to

the pool) on your left. You'll pick up right away on what a nudist colony is all about as soon as you see people. Lake Como has about three hundred folks who live there year-round and many more during the winter season.

It's not real clear where the entrance to the restaurant is. After our meal, we discovered that the nearest entrance to the parking area is an unmarked door across from the ladies' restroom. Initially, we ended up walking around the side of the building, past a fit middle-aged man holding a towel. We attempted to look confident as we tried to figure out where to focus our eyes. The effect, we're sure, didn't make us look savvy. Conspicuously dressed in clothes, we searched around back for an entrance. There, we found a door to the sweltering screened-in porch, where a group of naked folks were playing cards and another naked man was quietly reading. We walked past them into the cafe and were relieved to be met by a dressed server who said brightly, "Sit anywhere."

Aside from the servers, one table had diners who were conventionally dressed. Besides that, one man wore an open shirt with no pants and one woman wore shorts with no shirt, but the vast majority of folks just wore flip-flops. The cafe looks out onto the pool area, and Nancy's not-usually-nude friend Bob (who has twice run the annual "Dare to Go Bare 5K," which winds up at the cafe) says that "even though they say clothing is optional, that's just not true at the pool." Indeed, everyone we saw at Lake Como was tan, and lots of them were working on their all-over tans by the pool while we ate lunch.

Nudists, as one would guess, come in all shapes and sizes and ages, although the folks we saw seemed to be over thirty, with many over sixty. The great thing about lunch here for non-nudists is that it forces you to confront culturally constructed ideas about "what's proper where" when it comes to the body. We've seen how conventional ideas have shifted over the years as people show more and more of their bodies in public without repercussion. Perhaps the nudists are just ahead of their time. They've been coming here since the 1940s. It's a side of Florida that most tourists don't see.

But back to the grouper. When we ordered the fish sub, we asked what kind of fish it was.

"Either grouper or cod," our server told us, "whichever's in season."

"And which is it today?" asked Nancy.

"Either grouper or cod, whatever the fisherman brings in."

Knowing when to cut our losses, we ordered the fish sub, pretty sure it wouldn't be grouper. Jane ordered the special, a large chicken salad sandwich on white bread, served with tater tots. It was all okay, as were the big basket of french fries (although you always had a great view of just where those fries would end up if you ate too many of them). The menu is extensive, including burgers, sandwiches, salads, thin- or thick-crust pizza, homemade lasagna, liver and onions, Salisbury steak, eggplant parmesan, and roast turkey and the usual suspects in appetizers: wings, mozzarella sticks, etc. They even offer home-made soups and pies. The prices are cheap and the food is decent, but as Jane says, "There are places you go for the food and places you go for the ambience." This is one of the ambience stops.

If you want to find out more about the activities at Lake Como (which are mostly available only to AANR—American Association for Nude Recreation—members), check out their local newsletter, "Como Flash." The resort plans all sorts of recreational activities to keep things lively. Next year Nancy may work up the nerve to "Dare to Go Bare" in the annual 5K—typically held the first Saturday in May in case you're interested. Well, maybe if it were a "Double Dog Dare to Go Bare" . . . .

I-75 Exit 265: Island Time

The Jerk Hut Island Grille & Mojito Bar

2101 East Fowler Avenue, Tampa; 813-977-5777; www.jerkhut.com. Open Monday through Thursday 11:00 a.m. to 10:00 p.m., Friday and Saturday 11:00 a.m. to 11:00 p.m., and Sunday 11:00 a.m. to 9:00 p.m. $$–$$$

From I-75: Take exit 265—Fowler Avenue/FL-582 west toward University of South Florida/Temple Terrace/Busch Gardens (5.9 miles). Make a U-turn just past 22nd Street, and The Jerk Hut Island Grille & Mojito Bar will be on your right across from the University Square Mall. (The old Jerk Hut is 6.3 miles down Fowler Avenue on your right.)

Okay, so you passed on the Bare Buns Café, but you're still up for an adventure as long as everyone wears clothes. Island time at the Jerk Hut is only 5.9 or 6.3 miles down Fowler Avenue, depending on which version you go to. When we first tried this Jamaican treasure, it was bursting out of a former fast-food building and was definitely the most multicultural place so far on our Florida trek. And why not? Jamaican cuisine has been influenced by the Arawak Indians, Spanish, British, Africans, East Indians, and Chinese as the demographics of the country shifted over the centuries.

That Jerk Hut, 6.3 miles down Fowler Avenue on your right, is still in business with all the island treats we love so much, but now they're merging into a soul food menu that includes fried chicken, pork chops, collared greens, pepper steak, stew beef, and homemade corn bread. We haven't tried the soul food yet, but owner Andrew Ashmeade is a heckuva cook, so we have high hopes. Plus, he's planning on adding chicken-and-waffles soon, which have been popular in California and Atlanta. At this Jerk Hut, they no longer have table service, but you can order your food

at the counter and dine in the restaurant, or you can hit the most eclectic drive-thru menu you're likely to find in Florida.

Most of the regulars from that Jerk Hut, though, have moved up the street half a mile to the Jerk Hut Island Grille & Mojito Bar, which is far more spacious and upscale than the old place. A giant fake shark hangs above the bar, but it's been "Jamaican-ified" with a crocheted red, yellow, green, and black cap over dreadlocks. Pretty much everything has been given an island feel: distressed plank flooring, antique painted stools and chairs in island colors, a Jamaican beach mural on one wall, Bob Marley and reggae concert posters on other walls. Oh, yeah, and you'll recognize the external part of the building from its thatched awnings over the windows. Sure, it's kitschy, but cool.

The signature at the Island Grille, as at the old Jerk Hut, is the island jerk marinade, which includes, among Andrew's other secret spices, Jamaican scotch bonnet pepper, thyme, scallions, and pimento. The jerk platter gives you a chance to try the jerk chicken and the jerk pork. Why miss either? You can decide how hot you want it, and if it arrives too mild for you (unlikely but possible), you can always doctor it up with more jerk sauce, the unmarked bottle of brown stuff on your table, or with Andrew's Original Redd Sauce—sweet, hot, and flavorful—that accompanies the platter.

If you're feeling a bit more adventurous, try the curry goat roti. We found plenty of curries on the menu (chicken, shrimp, and veggies) wrapped in roti, an East Indian flat bread, but the goat was the most

exciting. We're no goat connoisseurs, but this version was tender and spicy, more like beef than chicken, and we'd order it again.

We also liked the chicken patty, smooth curried chicken inside a flaky pastry shell, basically a meat pie. The "rootsman special," comes with our favorite side dish, caramelized crispy/soft plantains. We've rarely met a sweet plantain we didn't like, in case you wonder

Andrew Ashmeade at his new mojito bar

why we aren't more discerning—they're a gift from the culinary gods. There's also tasty steamed cabbage with carrots, red and green peppers, and what Jamaicans call rice and peas (which is really rice and red beans—delicious despite the misnomer). We liked everything on the rootsman except the boiled dumpling, which we're sure was an albino hockey puck in a former life. We needed a steak knife to cut it.

The new restaurant also has an expanded menu, including steaks, ribs, crab cakes, conch salad, fish tacos, and a soup on Saturdays called "Mannish Water," which is supposed to be an aphrodisiac and is made from the parts of the goat normally thrown away, like intestines and head, as well as green bananas with

skins and root vegetables. We can't vouch for its taste or it sexual power, but it sounds like an adventure.

With all this Jamaican spiciness, dumpling not included, you need something sweet to wash it down, so don't forget to try one of the many exotic beverage choices. Jane got to drink a white grapefruit version of her favorite Ting soda (even better than pink, she claims), and Nancy couldn't resist the "Solo Banana," a "soda aux extraits vegetaux." Nancy wondered why it didn't have "extraits fruits," but there was no one to ask as it's bottled in Trinidad. Turns out it's a bright orange soda that tastes just like a banana Popsicle. Besides all the cool international sodas, you can also try "Andrew's fruit juices" or any of several "Strongman Nature Drinks for health, strength, and vigor." Hmmmm. Drinks with names like Irish Moss, Peanut Irish Moss, Roots Drinks (sic), and Ginseng Up. No telling what they might do for your drive back to the interstate.

If you don't have to drive, you might consider one of the many flavors of mojitos or martinis on the menu. The new place has a full bar, whereas the old place just had beer. If beer's your thing, there are plenty on tap, including a Jerk Island Redd Ale that Jane likes even better than Jamaica's famous Red Stripe.

Meals Worth Stopping for in *Florida*

I-75 Exit 265: Hot Dog!

Mel's Hot Dogs

4136 East Busch Boulevard, Tampa; 813-985-8000; www.melshotdogs.com. Open Monday through Thursday 11:00 a.m. to 8:00 p.m., Friday and Saturday 11:00 a.m. to 9:00 p.m. Closed Sunday. $

From I-75: Take exit 265—Fowler Avenue/FL-582 west toward University of South Florida/Temple Terrace/Busch Gardens (2.8 miles). Turn left onto 56th Street North/FL-583 South (1.5 miles) and right onto East Busch Boulevard/FL-580 West (1.2 miles). Mel's will be on your right.

You can't miss this place. Not only do you have the Gourmettes' excellent directions, but you also have the world's most phallic Volkswagen convertible hot dog out front to beckon you in. It all started in 1973. Well, actually it started long before that when Mel Lohn was growing up in Chicago, subsisting on hot dogs and rock 'n' roll. He played in a variety of rock bands—none that we would have heard of, he tells us. When he came to Sarasota with one, he loved the warm weather and stayed, eventually migrating north to Tampa, looking for a job playing music. He went out one night to get a dog and was shocked to find that there were no hot dog stands in Tampa.

The rest, as they say, is history, and now, thirty-five years later, the "Wizard of Weiners" is "still waiting for the Stones to call" even though he's "brought the hot dog to perfection" and "created the weiner the world awaited." Mel's wife, Virginia Lohn, works with him and has contributed mightily to his quests.

Humble and reserved, Mel created a T-shirt wall in order to sell more shirts, which say "Mel's Hot Dogs" on the front and "Sit. Stay. Good dog" on the back. Customers wanted their pictures on his wall, so he told them to buy a T-shirt, take their picture with it in an exotic spot, and he'd hang it. So now there are

"Sure," the cashier said, and she yelled over to the next worker, "Dog on the grill." He did nothing.

"Dog on the grill!" she repeated.

He paused. "What does that mean?"

"It means put a hot dog on the grill!" she said. Clearly they don't get a lot of requests for this sort of thing, but here's the main point: They *will* grill the dogs if you ask them to. They'll also grill the buns. We tried asking for that our second time there.

Mel, of course, is aghast at the whole question. "Grilled? It's a travesty! Why would anyone take a beautiful, moist dog and dry it out, make it crunchy on the outside? I can't understand why," he said sadly. Then he perked up a bit. "But if you request it and you've got cash, I'm listening."

Ah, that's why we love Mel's. The dogs are awesome, especially grilled with a grilled bun. The Polish sausage dog (grilled even by Mel) and served with spicy brown mustard and smothered with grilled onions is sublime. Our second time to Mel's we had eaten at four places in a row already. We so didn't want any more food at all. Not at all. But we trudged in and dutifully ordered a slaw dog and a Polish sausage. They took a little extra time because of all the grilling we requested. But when they came, even though we were still stuffed, something magical happened. We each ate a bite, then another, then another. Somehow, Mel's had resurrected our appetites, like the proverbial phoenix. Get your dogs grilled or steamed, but don't miss the chance to eat the wiener that the world awaited.

multiple display cases of folks in Mel's garb in Antarctica, in Afghanistan, in front of the Eiffel Tower, the Statue of Liberty, the Kremlin, London Bridge, on and on. There are even photos of people underwater in Micronesia hawking Mel's. The loyalty of Mel's customers knows no bounds.

Here's the rub, though. Because Mel is from Chicago, he likes his dogs and buns steamed. The Gourmettes? Well, we definitely like our dogs and buns grilled. Our first time there, Nancy admitted it was probably sacrilege but asked for just the dog grilled when she ordered an otherwise classic Chicago hot dog—mustard, onions, neon relish, pickle, celery salt, and sport peppers.

I-75 Exit 250: Carney Haven

Showtown Restaurant and Lounge

10902 US 41 South, Gibsonton; 813-677-5443. Kitchen open daily 6:00 a.m. to 10:00 p.m. Bar is open later. $

From I-75: Take exit 250—Gibsonton Drive west (1.9 miles) and turn left onto Tamiami Trail/US 41 (.4 mile). Showtown Bar and Grill will be on your left.

Gibsonton used to have other choices: Eight-foot-four-inch-tall Al Tomaine and his two-foot-six-inch-tall wife Jeanie (the "half-girl") used to run Giant's Camp down the road on US 41 by the river. A pair of Siamese twins used to run a fruit stand. Percilla the Monkey Girl lived here, as did Grady Stiles, "the Lobster Boy," until he was murdered in the early '90s. Back in the day, you might have seen some of the Munchkins from *The Wizard of Oz* in the local post office. Things are quieter now, though. The town still has its odd zoning laws, so you might see an elephant or tiger in someone's yard, and carnival gear is everywhere during the winter. Nowadays, Ward Hall, one of the great sideshow impresarios, tells Nancy that the only real Gourmettes' choice is Showtown Restaurant and Lounge, and even there, breakfast is your best option.

Showtown is your last real entree into the carnival/sideshow world. Carnies have settled for decades in Gibsonton, and though the sideshow is a declining entertainment option, the ghosts of the past and the people who knew the ghosts are still here. And often they congregate at Showtown Restaurant and Lounge.

The extensive murals on the outside of the building, reminiscent of the old sideshow banners, let you know you're in the right place. You'll have two choices for doors: head through the one with the *trompe l'oeil* bamboo on the outside. The other door, which is to the bar, has a *trompe l'oeil* dwarf door painted on it that we're betting has fooled more than one drunk over the years and maybe even some sober folks.

As we walk inside, where there are more murals on the wall—the Showtown Hall of Fame, the Ringmaster in the Sky—a server yells out, "What're you drinkin'?" so there's no time to feel out of place here. Clearly this is a locals' spot, but the locals didn't waste any time making us feel comfortable. While we were checking out the menu, a newscaster on the television happened to mention something about a town "outlawing lap dancing."

"Outlaw lap dancing?" exclaimed a beer-bellied local who was paying his bill. "I don't see anything wrong with lap dancing." He looked over at us. "Oh, I'm sorry, I didn't see you sitting there. I've never had one, but I don't see anything wrong with it." One of the servers gestured to the clear piggy bank full of quarters on the counter. "No," the man said, "I didn't curse. Really. I just said I didn't see anything wrong with lap dancing."

"So, you have to pay if you curse?" Nancy asked our server.

"Yep, a quarter," she said, pointing at the piggy bank.

"You're gonna have to watch yourself, Jane."

There's a lot of jawing goes on back and forth among the tables here at Showtown, and the only way to escape it is to eat next door in the bar, where you can smoke. A clear glass separates the bar and the restaurant, so you won't miss anything in either place.

Breakfast itself is pretty straightforward: omelets, pancakes, eggs and bacon, home fries that are better than the hash browns. "Strawberry or grape jelly for your toast?" the server yells to us from the kitchen. Everything is hot and competent; nothing is outstanding. It's one of those places you come for the atmosphere and the sustenance, not for the culinary wizardry.

At the end of the meal, when Jane was paying up, she couldn't find the bill she was looking for and said, "Shoot!"

"Did you curse?" our server asked.

"No, she said 'shoot,'" Nancy said, taking up for her.

"Yeah, I've cleaned up a lot too," admitted the server.

"Got too expensive," chimed in one of the regulars at the next table.

"Yeah, and a lot of my customers were leaving my tips in the jar."

If you're nostalgic for the carnivals and sideshows of your childhood, don't miss the chance to check out Gibsonton and the Showtown Restaurant and Lounge. Just be sure to watch your language.

I-75 Exit 224: Head for the Hollow

Hickory Hollow Bar-B-Que

4705 US 301 North, Ellenton; 941-722-3932. Open Tuesday through Saturday 11:00 a.m. to 8:00 p.m. Closed Sunday and Monday. CASH ONLY, ATM on-site. $$

From I-75: Take exit 224—US 301 west toward Gamble Mansion/Ellenton/Palmetto (1.1 miles). Make a U-turn at 45th Avenue East and Hickory Hollow will be on your right.

Hickory Hollow sounds more like it belongs on the back roads of Tennessee than a couple of minutes off busy I-75. The building, nestled in a low spot in the terrain under live oaks with a goat out back, may not be beautiful, but there's some good-looking ribs, pork sandwiches, and homemade vegetables inside.

The decor might be described as craft art busy with a generous nod toward whatever holiday is in season. Owner Donna James changes the decor seven times a year, and she also sells various arts and crafts in her tiny "shop" between the cash register and the restrooms. "If Cracker Barrel can do it, I can do it," Donna says.

This is where any resemblance to Cracker Barrel ends, though. Since 1984 Donna and her husband, Robert, and now their son, Jarrett, have been impressing locals and tourists alike with their North Carolina–style barbeque, prime rib, and seafood, and their plethora of vegetables. When you sit down, you'll be given a menu and a small wooden board

shaped like a pig and Velcroed with the largest selection of sides we've ever seen in Florida. You could eat every meal here for a week and have a different side each meal. There's always a minimum of twenty-five, and it all depends on what's in season. "I go all over looking for the freshest vegetables I can find," says Donna. Nancy fell in love with the rich squash and cheese and the sweet yam cakes, orange puck-style concoctions with brown sugar and cinnamon sprinkled on top. On any given day, you might find spinach soufflé, parsnips, butter peas, fried okra, rutabagas, or any of your other favorite vegetables.

Hickory Hollow's motto is "Every diet, every appetite," and they work hard to accommodate vegetarians, carnivores, seafood lovers, and low-carb or low-fat dieters. It all starts with the barbecue, though. You can get your pork barbecue sandwich traditional style, pulled with a tomato base, or Eastern North Carolina style, pulled with vinegar and seasonings and topped with coleslaw. We love the NC style—tangy and smoky—and Hickory Hollow has made converts out of many. *USA Today* chose Hickory Hollow third in a list of Top 10 Barbecue spots, and one man drove down from Ocala the day the paper came out just for a pulled pork sandwich to go. Worth the trip. Two tomato-based barbecue sauces are on the table, so you can doctor up your meat any way you like: One is mild and sweet, the other hot and spicy, but both are delicious. They've had spareribs on the menu for years, but the *USA Today* article made folks expect baby back ribs, so they added those to the menu and now they outsell the spares.

Dinner platters are served with two vegetables from the wooden-pig selections and big corn fritters that are perfectly crunchy outside and soft inside. The portions are generous and you won't possibly leave here hungry.

Barbecue joints with great vegetables don't usually have good beer and wine selections, but this isn't a dry county in Tennessee, and Jarrett has made it his mission to offer great beers from around the world and also a limited wine list. And if all that's not enough, the local *Weekly Planet* named Hickory Hollow the best reason to shop at the nearby outlet mall, just on the other side of the interstate. Who needs to shop when there's so much great food to eat?

I-75 Exit 224: Waterfront Pub, Grub, and Live Music

Woody's River Roo Pub & Grill

5717 18th Street East, Ellenton; 941-722-2391; www.woodysriverroo.com.
Open Sunday through Thursday 11:00 a.m. to 10:00 p.m., Friday and Saturday
11:00 a.m. to midnight. Bar is open later. $$

From I-75: Take exit 224—US 301 east (.8 mile) and turn right at the light at
60th Avenue East (next to Walgreens) (less than .1 mile). Take the next right onto
18th Street East (.2 mile), and Woody's will be on
your left.

Okay, so say that someone in your car does want to shop at the outlet mall, and you need a place to relax by the water with a cold beer and a delicious sandwich, maybe a little live acoustic guitar in the background. How hard would that be to find? Not too. Just behind Applebee's right off the exit lies an oasis on the Manatee River. You'd totally miss it without us unless you were looking down over the Manatee River Bridge, heading north on I-95. Then you'd see a lively outdoor dining area and dock, a nondescript building, and an L-shaped spit of land that shoots out from the dock, forming a little marina cove for those folks who want to arrive by boat. Heck, Woody's has even had people arrive by horse.

Take whatever transport you have handy and head on over, especially if the weather is good. Woody's has music six nights a week, "hard driving blues and rock" Wednesday through Sunday nights, Tuesday-night karaoke, and laid-back acoustic guitar during the day on the weekends.

Woody Woodring, his wife Christina, and their son, Robert, bought what used to be the Happy Dolphin and turned it into Woody's River Roo in 2002. The name is a logical extension of their other business, an Australian pub in Bradenton called the Lost Kangaroo (427 12th Street West; 941-747-8114), which has twenty-seven beers on tap. Most of the customers at the River Roo, as it's often known, are locals, especially in the summer. We were there on September 1, still brutally hot in Florida, but with the breeze off the water, the fans blowing in the dining area, and the umbrella shading the sun, it ended up a lovely day to be outside.

Woody's is so close to the interstate that it's super easy to get there from exit 224. The problem will be leaving. It's a lot more fun to watch the interstate traffic from under an umbrella while eating a grouper "Roo-ben" and washing it down with, say, a Blue Moon Belgian White with an orange in it or maybe a "boat drink" like a Rum Runner. Their grouper Roo-ben includes a piece of juicy blackened fish served on marble bread with Swiss cheese, coleslaw, and Thousand Island dressing. The fries that come with it are a good battered version but don't compare to the homemade chips—regular or Cajun. Our favorite, sweet potato chips, are often offered as a monthly special. Woody's is also known for its grouper fingers, battered with a Samuel Adams beer batter and deep-fried. We also enjoyed their juicy cheddar burger. If you're in the mood for something a little lighter, the plump peel-and-eat shrimp are a tasty alternative to all this grease, and Woody's also has entree salads. There's a little something for everyone here, especially if you're up for a laid-back spot in the daytime and a party place at night. A big round lighted sign on the end of the L-shaped peninsula says, IT'S ALWAYS A FULL MOON AT WOODY'S RIVER ROO. Don't worry, though. If you get hooked on Woody's, they rent a number of apartments here by the week in the building next door.

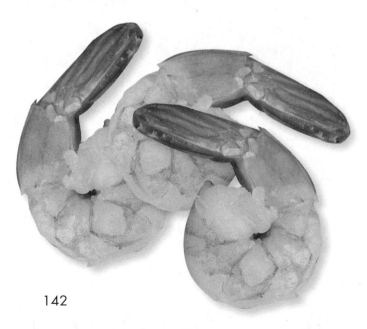

Meals Worth Stopping for in *Florida*

I-75 Exit 220B: Casual Elegance

Ezra Cafe

5629 Manatee Avenue West, Bradenton; 941-792-0990; www.ezrafinefoods.com. Open Monday through Friday 11:30 a.m. to 2:00 p.m. Dinner served Monday through Saturday 5:30 to 9:30 p.m. Closed Sunday. $$–$$$

From I-75: Take exit 220B—FL-64 west toward Bradenton (9.3 miles). Ezra will be on your left in a shopping center.

By day, she's a mild-mannered doctor of biochemistry and molecular biology who works as a research assistant professor in molecular genetics at the Children's Research Institute in St. Petersburg. At night, Dr. Donna D. Easton jumps into the last remaining phone booth in Bradenton, dons an apron, and turns into a restaurant owner and pastry chef extraordinaire. Oh, yeah, and she made the stained-glass EZRA window over the door of the restaurant. We haven't the slightest idea how she manages all her talents, but we're glad she does. We hope she's helping the children of the world with her science, but we know she's helping the eaters of Bradenton with her culinary skills.

Ezra was named "best overall restaurant" in a recent *Bradenton Herald* readers' poll. It's easy to see why. The place is located in yet another nondescript strip mall, but once inside, relaxed elegance predominates. At night, there are white linen tablecloths and napkins, but the servers wear jeans and black button-

down Ezra shirts. During lunch, there's brown paper over the tablecloths and the servers wear jeans and green Ezra T-shirts. The restaurant manages to stay cozy with an open kitchen and original artwork and fairy lights along the walls, but the food is more spectacular than relaxed.

Like Donna, the executive chef, Dave Shiplett, was born and raised in Bradenton. They were once married to each other and both love Ezra. Dave is the son of a commercial fisherman and studied the culinary arts under Asian chefs in San Francisco. The Asian influence meets his Florida sensibilities with delectable results. For lunch, we started with the stone crab corn chowder, lots of crab and hominylike corn with just a little bacon to add a smoky background to the rich cream base. We liked it so much, we were tempted to order another bowl, but fortunately we saved our appetites. Next up was a crab cake, lightly browned with plenty of crab, served on a crisp lightly breaded green tomato surrounded by baby spinach, red onions, and roasted red peppers tossed with creole mustard dressing. The total package was a treat for the eyes as well as the palate. The more "plain Jane" appearance of the chicken picatta sandwich was deceiving. There was nothing plain about the flavor. The toasted French roll was dampened with the lemon butter sauce of the tender chicken cutlet. Delicious.

For lunch or dinner, Ezra's bento box will allow you to check out four wonderful dishes: a yellowfin tuna tempura roll; a crispy crackling and sautéed calamari salad with chopped romaine and a wasabi vinaigrette; gulf oysters pan-fried with lemon, herb aioli and slaw, served with a mango salsa; and Blake's Thai shrimp salad with Asian vinaigrette, cilantro, green tea noodles, mixed lettuce, and peanut dressing. It tastes great with a Cat's Phee on a Gooseberry Branch Sauvignon Blanc from New Zealand. If you need more carbs and fats, try the decadent gourmet version of mac 'n cheese, big enough to split.

Once you've exhausted a meal's worth of Dave's skills—and we've only touched the surface—turn yourself over to Donna's desserts. Nightly, she gives away her famous chocolate chip cookie balls, but if you've got room, try her mousse-filled flourless chocolate cake iced with chocolate grenache, her guava cheesecake, or her key lime pie. At 9.3 miles from the interstate, a fair bit of it in traffic, Ezra is a hike, but we think it's well worth it. You will too!

I-75 Exit 220B: High School Nostalgia

The Shake Pit

3801 Manatee Avenue West, Bradenton; 941-748-4016. Open Monday, Tuesday and Thursday 11:00 a.m. to 9:00 p.m., Friday and Saturday 11:00 a.m. to 10:00 p.m., and Sunday noon to 9:00 p.m. Closed Wednesday. CASH ONLY. $

From I-75: Take exit 220B—FL-64 west toward Bradenton (8.2 miles), and The Shake Pit will be on your left.

The Shake Pit feels like a trip back in time to the after-school burger-and-shake joint in the small town you were from or wish you were from. The current owner, Debbie Crowe—a talkative, pretty blonde—was born in 1959, the same year as the restaurant, so she just knew the place was for her and her husband, Robert, when they went looking for a quiet little pop stand to buy in 2001. They didn't know what they were in for at The Shake Pit. "I wouldn't call it a quiet pop stand," says Debbie. So many generations of Bradentonians have been coming here that the community feels like it has a vested interest in how the place is run. "People say, 'Oh, you own it,' and I like to say we're the keepers of the Pit. People are very protective of the place. The community will let you know how things are going."

You can tell from the posters, pennants, and sanctioned graffiti that The Shake Pit is an ardent supporter of Manatee High School, only three blocks away, and the feeling is reciprocated. Before school lets out on a weekday, the place is crowded with

Debbie Crowe (far right) and her Shake Pit crew

adults (one couple next to us had been coming to the Pit for forty years). The high school kids show up as soon as the final bell rings. "If we see 'em before then, we've got problems," says Debbie. It's clear that she takes a real interest in her patrons and workers, many of whom are from the high school. Members of the Manatee Hurricanes' football team and girls' weight-lifting team work here. Parents also bring in their little kids who have a dangling tooth. Once the tooth comes out, they get ice cream. The young and old love the place. Generations of Manatee alumni come back to the Pit with all kinds of stories, especially during football season. It's truly a community landmark.

From the grill, try one of the burgers. The patties are made fresh daily from the Chop House, and although they have to warn you that the health department says that "undercooked meat could be hazardous to your health," since this is still America, they'll cook them as rare as you like, and grill the buns to boot. The hot dogs are split up the spine and grilled along with their buns. Try some chili on the dogs if you're so inclined. An L-shaped counter wraps around the grill area, so you can sit there, chat with the folks around you, and watch your food being prepared, or you can order from the take-out window and eat on the fly or outside on picnic tables.

Debbie's always running around helping customers with their orders. Before we'd introduced ourselves to her on our second trip there, Nancy ordered a white chocolate and Heath bar shiver. Debbie brought over a side of hot fudge and said, "You might want this." An excellent addition. She talked Jane into the peppermint sauce on soft-served mixed vanilla and chocolate swirl that reminded us of an ice-cream version of a chocolate mint Girl Scout cookie. The mother and son on one side of us had both ordered banana splits, which were mammoth, and as they neared the end, Debbie dropped off straws. "Here, I know you'll want these. Slurping up what's left is the best part." The chocolate malt shakes are also a delicious choice. They're *properly* made with vanilla ice cream and chocolate syrup, and so thick you really do need a spoon.

Stop by and try some comfort food from the past on any day but Wednesday, Debbie's day "to be Mom" to her daughter Hannah, a senior at Manatee High. Debbie has thought a lot about Wednesdays: "This is the day when the town consumes the least amount of chocolate. Wednesday is the decision day. You know women. You might give up chocolate because you've got something going on the weekend and you wanna lose those last two pounds. You eat on Monday and Tuesday. Wednesday is the decision day. I close to give you that moment." You should take it, because any other day of the week, the temptations may be too great.

I-75 Exit 217: Where Weird Rules

Linger Lodge Restaurant and Bar

7205 Linger Lodge Road, Bradenton; 941-755-2757; www.lingerlodgeresort.com. Open Sunday through Thursday 11:00 a.m. to 8:00 p.m. (except Memorial Day through Labor Day, when they close on Monday and Tuesday), Friday and Saturday 11:00 a.m. to 9:00 p.m. $$

From I-75: Take exit 217—SR 70 east (.7 mile) and turn right at the traffic light at Braden Run (.5 mile). Turn right onto Forrester Drive (.7 mile) and right at Oak Hammock Drive, which will turn into Linger Lodge Road (.8 mile). You'll run right into the parking lot of Linger Lodge.

Al Roker named this place one of the five weirdest restaurants in the United States. That's recommendation enough for us. It's not the easiest place to find, but we've tried to simplify the directions as much as possible, and it's only 2.7 miles from the exit, and much closer than that to the interstate if you'd like to pull off onto the emergency lane and bushwhack your way to Linger Lodge. We recommend the more conventional exit, but this place will take you back to Florida's bushwhacking days. First, though, you have to drive through a bit of suburban sprawl.

When you finally make it to the Linger Lodge parking lot, don't be dismayed by the fact that it's smack-dab in the middle of an RV park. This is all part of its charm. The various animal skulls nailed to the light posts out in the parking lot are just a taste of what's to come, and if they're too creepy for you, this might not be your kind of place. Consider them fair warning. Also, don't park in the space that says "Senators only." That spot's reserved for Florida State Senator Mike Bennett, who bought the place a few years ago on an emotional whim after having vacationed here as a boy. Seems fitting somehow; the place is as wild and weird as Florida politics.

Linger Lodge was established in 1945 on the Braden River, supposedly the same year that a giant alligator was killed, the one you can see mounted to the wall over the fireplace. Since then, they've been collecting. What, you ask? Well, the first thing you'll notice is all the critters. They're everywhere, all manner of skulls and taxidermic masterpieces: bobcats,

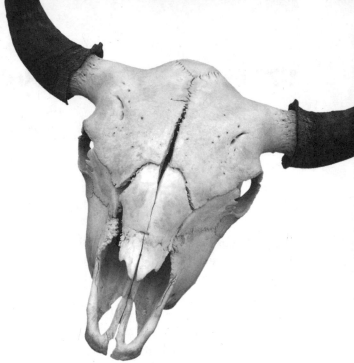

deer, birds, snakes—lots of snakes—fish, boar heads, squirrels, tarantulas; you get the idea. They also have all sorts of tools and traps hanging from the ceiling along with the odd snare drum. License plates hang in the rafters, and beer cans line up just below the ceiling. There's stuff everywhere.

Our first time there, next to our table hung a small framed bit of advice: what you should do if bitten by a pit viper, such as a rattlesnake, copperhead, or water moccasin, all of which can be found in Florida. We love the first suggestion: "Get away from the snake in case it strikes again." We suspect we would have figured that one out on our own, but it's good to have confirmation.

Linger has quite a few dining rooms and a long

Meals Worth Stopping for in *Florida*

bar that snakes through two rooms, including the River Room, which has tables and a big-screen TV. In that room the bar faces a large lighted display of many creatures big and small as well as a mounted copy of *The Dallas Morning News* front page from the day after John F. Kennedy was shot. We'll leave the many possible interpretations of this display to you. Our recommendation is that you head out to the screened-in porch dining area, where if you avoid looking to your left (where the RVs are parked) you'll have a nearly pristine swamp view of Florida's backwoods. It's a wonderful place to linger for a spell and imagine what used to be.

In the meantime, order some food. The menu reflects the locale. There's fried alligator, of course, tender and tasty. We also enjoyed the nouvelle approach to that old standby, alligator chowder. The cream base is loaded with gator and potatoes and, of all things, tarragon. Delicious. Our frog legs came attached to each other, which was just a little disconcerting, although we don't know why it should be amid the decor at Linger Lodge. "It looks too much like the lower half of a human," complained Jane.

"Or even the lower half of a frog," Nancy added. Nevertheless, the legs pulled apart easily enough and the juicy little jumping muscles fell off the bone. We also tried a Philly cheese steak, which won't impress anyone from Philadelphia, but wasn't half bad. For dessert, we would suggest bypassing the French cruller bread pudding with rum sauce, which sounds too sweet and is.

Linger Lodge is the kind of place that fulfills some kids' dreams and gives other kids nightmares. We guarantee, though, that whatever your age, Linger Lodge will be unforgettable.

Interstate 75
Sarasota to Everglades City

7

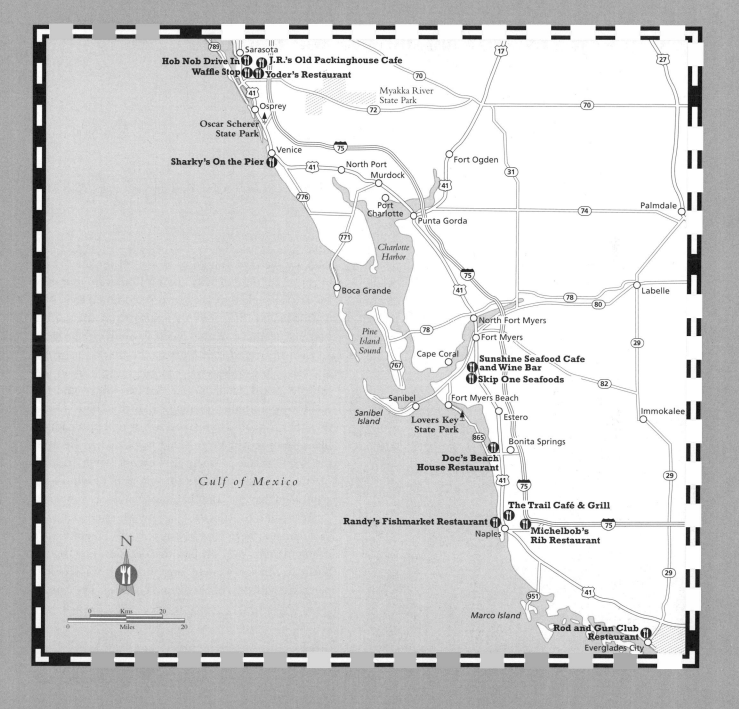

Sarasota

Hob Nob Drive In
Waffle Stop

J.R.'s Old Packinghouse Cafe
Yoder's Restaurant

Myakka River
State Park

Osprey

Oscar Scherer
State Park

Venice

Sharky's On the Pier

North Port
Murdock

Fort Ogden

Port
Charlotte

Punta Gorda

Palmdale

*Charlotte
Harbor*

Boca Grande

Labelle

North Fort Myers

*Pine
Island
Sound*

Fort Myers

Cape Coral

**Sunshine Seafood Cafe
and Wine Bar**
Skip One Seafoods

Immokalee

Sanibel

Fort Myers Beach

*Sanibel
Island*

Estero

Lovers Key
State Park

Bonita Springs

**Doc's Beach
House Restaurant**

Gulf of Mexico

The Trail Café & Grill

Randy's Fishmarket Restaurant

Naples

**Michelbob's
Rib Restaurant**

N

0   Kms   20
0   Miles   20

Marco Island

**Rod and Gun Club
Restaurant**

Everglades City

I-75 Exit 213: Hob Nobbing in the Open Air

Hob Nob Drive In

1701 North Washington Boulevard, Sarasota; 941-955-5001. Open Sunday through Thursday 6:00 a.m. to 8:30 p.m., Friday and Saturday 6:00 a.m. to 9:00 p.m. $

From I-75: Take exit 213—University Parkway west toward Sarasota (4.9 miles) and turn left onto US 301/ Washington Boulevard (2.5 miles). Hob Nob will be on your left.

The regulars get to the Hob Nob Drive In about 5:30 a.m., half an hour before they officially open, just to get an early start on coffee and the news of the day. Regulars have been coming to the Hob Nob for a long time. In 2007 the place celebrated its

50th anniversary. It used to be one of the few places to eat on this end of Washington Boulevard, but now the area is packed with all sorts of commerce.

If you can filter out the noise from the traffic, you can sit here in the open air under the black-and-white striped roof, next to the black-and-white checkered tile walls, and pretend you're back in the fifties. Choose picnic tables that are joined end-to-end for a community picnic feel, or sit at high, round two-tops for a little more privacy, or pull up a padded black stool to the three-sided wooden bar. Because the whole place is open air—except when the big plastic walls go up thanks to cold, rain, or wind—it's a smokers' haven. Take that information as you will.

According to Annette Gargett, who's been a general manager here for a dozen years, the menu hasn't changed much over the past five decades. The bacon-cheddar omelet we had one morning was cooked perfectly with lots of bacon and cheddar. The home-

and cheese in it. The banana pancake special looked pretty tasty as well.

At lunch- and dinnertime, our favorite is the potato-crusted grouper sandwich, but the most popular sellers are the Hob Nob burger and deep-fried hot dogs.

One of the few changes they've made is that they now serve Edie's Ice Cream in their shakes (no malts, to Nancy's disappointment). They're selling a lot more shakes these days. To the Gourmettes' disappointment, they make their chocolate shakes with chocolate ice cream, so be sure to ask for a "black and white" if you want the usual chocolate syrup/vanilla ice-cream matchup.

That's it for the disappointments at Hob Nob. We mostly love the place. It isn't fancy, of course, and if you're not comfortable with Styrofoam plates and cups or plastic cutlery, keep on driving. The Hob Nob attracts all kinds of people, though, which you can tell from the parking lot: motorcycles, Mercedes convertibles, air-brushed corvettes, beat-up clunkers, and the occasional bicycle.

fries on the side were extra thin slices with the skins on—delicate, crunchy, and yummy. They also serve a mean breakfast sandwich on an English muffin: eggs plus a wide choice of cheeses (Swiss, cheddar, provolone, jack, or American), and the usual meats (bacon, ham, and sausage). We also had a great "Nob Scramble" one morning, with onions, spinach, bacon,

Meals Worth Stopping for in *Florida*

I-75 Exit 210 or 207: Rhythm and Blues at OPC

J.R.'s Old Packinghouse Cafe

987 South Packinghouse Drive, Sarasota; 941-371-9358; www.oldpackinghousecafe.com. Open Monday through Thursday 11:00 a.m. to 10:00 p.m., Friday and Saturday 11:00 a.m. to 11:00 p.m. Closed Sunday. $$

From I-75 South: Take exit 210—Fruitville Road/FL-780 west toward Sarasota (.6 mile). Turn left onto Cattleman Road (.7 mile) and left onto South Packinghouse Road (.2 mile). The Old Packinghouse will be on the left side of the street.

From I-75 North: Take exit 207—FL-758/Bee Ridge Road west toward Sarasota (.3 mile). Turn right onto Cattleman Road (1.7 miles), right onto Bahia Vista Street (less than .1 mile), and left onto South Packinghouse Road (.2 mile). The Old Packinghouse will be on your right.

At J.R. Garraus' Old Packinghouse Cafe, the Rosaire family, local animal trainers and circus celebrities, still sometimes ride horses up to the place and tie them up in the parking lot next to limos, Jaguars, Corvettes, hillbilly trucks, Nancy's Honda Civic, you name it, depending on the day. Everyone is welcome at J.R's. It definitely has that old-timey feel that seems attractive across subcultures. If we could choose a spot from among our many finds to pick up and transplant to our own neighborhood, OPC would be among our top choices. Located within spitting distance of I-75, this building used to be next to acres of celery fields, and it served as the administrative offices for a large celery-packing organization.

These days, though, it's a restaurant/bar, sort of a family-friendly honky-tonk. They have no TVs, but they've got live music six nights a week. "Comfort music" is the way J.R. describes it, and it includes bluegrass, rhythm and blues, alternative folk, and soft rock. One night when we were there, a bluegrass band called Swamp Grass played, and it turns out that they all met at J.R.'s in the first place.

Plenty of regulars hang out here, including Frank Nunes, also known as "Cape Man," both for what he wears and where he's from, Cape Cod, Massachusetts. He's a retired firefighter and back in the day at the firefighter Christmas parties, each of the guys had to do a skit. That's where Frank got his start doing his pale-faced James Brown impersonation, complete with gaudy sunglasses and a red cape with gold trim.

J.R. Garraus with Cape Man Frank Nunes and J.R.'s wife, Nancy, in background

After moving to Sarasota, he decided to revive his act here. If you're lucky, you might catch it. "J.R. only lets me do it once a month," admits Frank, so he's been doing it once a month for the last nine years or so.

People come to J.R.'s for the character of the place as well as the characters in the place. J.R. likes to think of the excess stuff everywhere as antiques, but some might mistake it for junk. Lots of it is brought in by customers. "Somebody tells her husband that this has to go, and the husband brings it here," explains J.R. "Some of it's good stuff." Take, for example, the Willie Nelson clock or the red chair on the ceiling (not matching any other chairs in the place and only a very few of those match one another) or the assorted smart-aleck signs, banners, beer bottles, lanterns, old photos, license plates, you name it. There's always something interesting to look at here, whether it's people or paraphernalia.

The service at J.R.'s is great, not necessarily fast if they're busy, but plenty friendly and helpful. And the food's both tasty and reasonably priced. Often you can get out for under $10 with a meal and a drink. "Course if you start drinking a lot of beer, it goes up from there," warns J.R. Besides the three beers on tap, they have almost fifty different bottled beers to choose from. The wine menu is significantly smaller.

For a starter, we loved their Galacian bean soup, a rich, hearty mixture of white beans, pork, and turnip greens. We also recommend the hot-pressed Cuban sandwich, which is as good as any we've had in Tampa. Tender succulent pork, lean ham with a hint of salt, and oozing Swiss make it a winner. The OPC half-pound Church burgers are also a big hit, and if you've got a raging appetite, try the Big Bertha burger, two half-pound patties with bacon, mushrooms, three kinds of cheese, and 999 Island dressing served on toasted Cuban bread. The wings are also great. Jane fell in love with them, and she's not even a wing kind of gal. The original teriyaki wings, spicy and sweet, are baked to a moist, tender perfection, and the sauce reaches a heavenly caramelization that makes for a messy feast.

It might not look at first glance like a kid-friendly place, but plenty of kids show up, and J.R.'s caters to them with a kids' menu, high chairs, coloring books, and a trip to the toy box. "We want a family atmosphere," explains J.R., "with kids running around and everyone having fun." You'd be hard-pressed not to have fun at J.R.'s no matter what your age.

I-75 Exit 210: Elvis Ate Here

Waffle Stop

660 Washington Boulevard South, Sarasota; 941-952-0555. Open Monday, Tuesday, Thursday, and Friday 6:00 a.m. to 2:30 p.m., Wednesday and Saturday 6:00 a.m. to 2:00 p.m., Sunday 7:00 a.m. to 2:00 p.m. $

From I-75: Take exit 210—Fruitville Road/FL-780 west toward Sarasota (5.5 miles). Turn left onto Washington Boulevard South/US 301 (.5 mile), and the Waffle Stop will be on your right.

"Elvis was here February 21st, 1956, and ate three eggs, three pieces of bacon, two orders of toast, pan-fried potatoes, and three glasses of milk." It's no wonder that the King put on weight in his later years if his visit to the Waffle Stop was any indication of his caloric intake. The sign with Elvis's breakfast specifics hangs behind counters on the wall amid all sorts of other Elvis memorabilia. Near the front door, folks often have their picture taken next to a life-size plastic replica of the King sitting on a stool playing the guitar. When we're there in December, Elvis is wearing a Santa hat and Christmas scarf.

The Waffle Stop has been a staple of downtown Sarasota since 1951 and still has a Restaurant Restaurant sign above the building that no longer lights up. We're sure that this unassuming diner on busy Washington Boulevard has lots more stories to tell than the one about Elvis. Regulars get their names up on the back wall's birthday board, and you

can choose to gossip with the locals at the two long counters facing each other with coffee-wielding servers in between or sit at booths or tables in the adjoining space. The menu is on the paper place mats, which have ads for local businesses running up the sides.

Breakfast is king here at the Waffle Stop, and if you're lucky, you might get one of the "double yolkers." "We had a lot this week," owner Dolly Hollinger tells us on one December visit. She attributes all the good luck to the fact that they use only jumbo eggs instead of the large or extra large eggs used by most restaurants. Dolly has owned the restaurant for the past ten years, but she worked as a manager here for six years before that.

For breakfast, it's hard to go wrong with the "Elvis is in the Building" feast, three eggs with ham, bacon, or sausage, potatoes, and toast, but we also like the "All Shook Up Omelette," with onions, green peppers, mushrooms, cheese, ham, bacon, and sausage. From the breakfast specials' list, we've enjoyed the potato cakes—mashed potatoes, hash browns, and onions served with apple sauce—and the blueberry pancake special. The waffles are good, too, if you like them thin and crisp with a light interior, and there's real butter to spread over it all.

Breakfast is served all day and it's always our favorite, but the big sellers on the lunch menu are the "Hunka Hunka Burgers," the patty melts, and the salads, including the "Hard Headed Woman," inexplicably a grilled chicken salad. There's also an "Ain't Nothin' but a Hound Dog," served with chili, cheese, or kraut.

Sometimes it feels like Elvis is still in the building.

Dolly Hollinger with Elvis tribute wall in the background

I-75 Exit 210: Where the Amish Snowbirds Are

Yoder's Restaurant

3434 Bahia Vista Street, Sarasota; 941-955-7771; www.yodersrestaurant.com. Open Monday through Saturday 6:00 a.m. to 8:00 p.m. Closed Sunday. $–$$

From I-75: Take exit 210—Fruitville Road/FL-780 west toward Sarasota (3.4 miles). Turn left onto South Beneva Road/CR 773 (1 mile) and right onto Bahia Vista Street (.2 mile). Yoder's will be on your left.

We made our first trip to Yoder's in February, and winter is definitely the time to come. The food is great all year-round at Yoder's, but in the winter, things are different. The line for dinner was way out the door at 4:30 on a Saturday afternoon. Nancy

had on shorts, and at first wondered if she should go someplace and change when she saw all the Amish families, the women in their plain dresses with small white bonnets, the men in dark pants and blue or lavender shirts with broad-brim straw hats and beards without mustaches. Once we got in line, though, we noticed the modern folks also in line dressed in orange Crocs and Bermuda shorts and rock 'n' roll T-shirts. At Yoder's it's hard to tell who's out of place, the Amish or the "English." Maybe no one is really out of place here.

The Amish began settling in this part of the world in the 1920s and 1930s because of the excellent farmland east of town. Eventually, they and their Mennonite cousins ended up creating this small, charming neighborhood called Pinecrest, and the rest of Sarasota built up around them. During much of the year, Pinecrest doesn't seem especially unusual. The Mennonites look pretty much like the rest of us. It's during the winter—when the Amish snowbirds head south from Pennsylvania, Ohio, and Indiana—that

the contrast between the modern life and the simple life becomes most apparent. These traditionally dressed Amish mostly ride around on adult tricycles instead of in horse and buggies, and on any given winter day at Yoder's, you may see fifteen or twenty trikes parked outside next to the cars. Here, many Amish rent little bungalows and can have electricity, even though they're not allowed it at home. Some even rent RVs and a driver to tour around. In this Sarasota world of bling, Yoder's is a refreshing contrast.

"You can just feel the wholesomeness of this place," said Nancy's friend Jim on his first time to Yoder's. The place may be too country cute for some people, with the Amish quilts on the wall, rolling farmland wallpaper borders, and the servers all dressed in traditional Amish garb, but Yoder's really is a return to a simpler time when food and fellowship were paramount; it's not just trying to look nostalgic for marketing purposes.

Amanda and Levi Yoder started the restaurant in 1975 and now their children, in-laws, and grandchildren run the place. Yoder's doesn't merely offer a counterculture experience; they also offer great home cooking. For breakfast the standout meal is the stuffed French toast: thick homemade bread, oozing with cream cheese and raspberry jam. The Amish scramble with home fries, onions, eggs, and bacon, all smothered with Swiss cheese, is also good. It comes with your choice of bread. They make their own yummy fruit bread—pumpkin and apple the morning we were there—or you can choose the light, flaky biscuits, which go great with butter and jam as a side item or with rich sausage gravy as a meal. Or,

for the hearty, choose one of Mrs. Yoder's homemade sweet rolls.

For lunch or dinner, chicken is a great choice: fried, baked, or barbecued. The barbecue is rubbed on the outside with spices and juicy and moist on the inside. The meat loaf is also popular, and the pulled pork is enough to feed a small Amish family. You get lots of choices of sides. We liked the green beans, the hot baked apples with cinnamon (practically a dessert in itself), the chicken stuffing and gravy, and the Amish noodles, which are a lot like chicken soup without the chicken. The portions are always big, but we caution you ahead of time to save some for a take-home container, because you won't want to miss dessert. Yoder's makes about 25,000 pies a year, all beautiful. We can personally vouch for the fresh strawberry pie and the most unusual peanut butter pie we've ever had: a traditional crust with a layer of vanilla pudding topped by peanut butter and confectioners' sugar mixed to make a crumble.

On your way out, don't forget to pick up some fruit bread or cookies for the road, or best of all, whoopee pies, the Gourmettes' favorite: rich butter cream sandwiched between two devil's food cookies. Picture a gourmet prototype for Little Debby Devil Cremes. Then on your way out the door, take a deep breath before you return to the world of the "English."

I-75 Exit 200 or 193: Tiki Hut Eating and Pier Fishing

Sharky's on the Pier

1600 Harbor Drive South, Venice; 941-488-1456; www.sharkysonthepier.com. Open daily 11:30 a.m. to 10:00 p.m. On Friday and Saturday the deck is open until midnight. Lunch $$, Dinner $$$$

From I-75 South: Take exit 200/FL-681 south toward Venice/Osprey (3.8 miles). Make a slight left (south) at Tamiami Trail/US 41 (4.1 miles). Turn right onto San Marco Drive (.4 mile) and left onto Harbor Drive South (1.1 miles). Sharky's will be on the right.

From I-75 North: Take exit 193/Jacaranda Boulevard west toward Englewood/Venice (.9 mile). Turn right at East Venice Avenue (3.7 miles), left at Tamiami Trail/US 41 (.4 mile), and left onto Harbor Drive South (1.1 miles). Sharky's will be on the right.

In 1986 this was just a small beach concession at the end of the city's fishing pier. The teenagers used to hang out here at night because it was deserted and out of the way. Then two old friends from Detroit, Michigan, Greg Novak and Mike Pachota, won the bid on the place and opened Sharky's in 1987, and it hasn't been the same since. This is about the only place in the book where you can head out on a fishing pier to try to catch supper, and, if you strike out, console yourself with a walk down the pier to get a better fish lunch or dinner than you would have made at home anyway. Then again, you can work things the opposite way: have a big dinner at Sharky's, then walk off some of those calories with a beautiful stroll on the pier out into the Gulf of Mexico.

Meals Worth Stopping for in *Florida*

The sunsets here are often spectacular, and if you eat outside on the wooden deck under a large thatched roof, you'll be at beach level, practically on the sand. You can also choose to sit close to one of the frozen drink machines at the round outdoor bar, just at the end of the pier. Inside, in one of the dining rooms, you'll be cozy and comfortable, no matter the weather, and you'll still have a good view of the ocean, pier, shorebirds—No feeding! Imagine the mess.—and the occasional volleyball game. The place is kitschy with surfboards on the walls as well as kites, and ocean-themed murals. At Christmas they even have a tree decorated solely with gray and blue shark ornaments. The servers wear Hawaiian shirts, and if you'd like a T-shirt to commemorate your time here, they've got lots to choose from.

At lunch we enjoyed the hearty blackened wahoo sandwich with all the trimmings, and a po'boy packed with fried shrimp. Our server, the self-proclaimed "King of Condiments," was happy to help us find appropriate dipping sauces for our fries, both regular and sweet potato. The barbecue sauce and dill ranch were especially tasty with the regular fries. We ended up with melted butter for our sweet potato fries—that'll pack the pounds on, but there's always that walk on the pier or beach to work them off.

At dinner we started off with fresh peel-and-eat shrimp and some large onion rings, both good. We enjoyed the flounder stuffed with blue crab and spinach and topped with a lobster-mushroom sauce;

"Seafood Aruba," a mixture of Canadian sea scallops, lobster, Gulf shrimp, and mushrooms in a rich Parmesan creme sauce; and Walk the Plank: grouper, salmon, and mahi-mahi grilled on a cedar plank and topped with the same lobster-mushroom sauce. All of the entrees were rich and tasty.

For dessert, try the key lime pie. The filling is well balanced between tart and sweet on a traditional graham cracker crust, with strawberry drizzle on the bottom of the plate and a blue gummy shark on top. We warned you the place was kitschy. If you want to eat on the beach in Venice, though, and you don't want to pack a picnic, Sharky's is your only option and an excellent one at that.

I-75 Exit 131: Better Than Its Name

Sunshine Seafood Cafe and Wine Bar

8700-1 Gladiolus Drive, Ft. Myers; 239-489-2233. Open daily 11:00 a.m. to 10:00 p.m. $$–$$$

From I-75: Take exit 131—Daniel's Parkway east (2.6 miles). Turn left onto Ben C. Pratt Parkway, which becomes Gladiolus Drive (4.9 miles). Sunshine Cafe will be in a strip mall on your right at the corner of Winkler Road.

A local magazine voted Sunshine Seafood Cafe the "best kept secret and best seafood" in Ft. Myers. We're here to help spread the secret far and wide. Sunshine is located in—you guessed it!—another less-than-attractive strip mall, and it's on the back side of an L if you're on Gladiolus Drive. It's easy to miss it, which probably has helped keep it secret. They've dressed up the outside a bit with a red and gold awning to try to lure you in, and there is patio seating with a beautiful parking-lot view, but we suggest heading inside where the atmosphere transforms into relaxed elegance with lots of friendly servers and rattan furniture to keep the place from seeming formal.

On Friday and Saturday nights, they have a delightful classical guitarist playing in the small bar area. It's the perfect background music throughout the restaurant, soft enough that you can carry on a conversation if you want to ignore it; complex and beautiful enough that you've always got something to pay attention to if you run out of things to talk about with your dinner companion.

The ambience here is comfortable, but the restaurant is in the book primarily because of its food. Our first time at Sunshine, we had, as is our way, eaten at too many other restaurants already, so we weren't especially interested in a late lunch. When a place impresses us in this sated state, we know it's dynamite. The bread (the only thing they don't make in house) is served with an herb olive oil and makes a good start. Then we went with the dry sea scallops, wood grilled and served with roasted red peppers, hearts of palm, warm herb-crusted goat cheese, crostinis, and a fresh herb olive oil. You don't often see dry scallops on a menu, and they don't necessarily sound all that enticing the first time you hear the description. Here's what you need to know: Most sea scallops in the United States are soaked in water containing sodium tripolyphosphate, which adds weight and helps preserve them. The FDA mandates that "dry" scallops have less than 82 percent moisture content, so producers may still soak them for a little bit if the moisture level is less than that, but basically it means that these are scallops the way Mother Nature intended. Dry scallops, when cooked correctly—and Sunshine cooks them perfectly—are sweeter and more succulent than normal sea scallops, and almost always a good choice. Combined with the wood-oven flavor, the goat cheese, the peppers and hearts of palm, we could hardly speak we were so happy eating on a full stomach.

We also loved the "Blind Pass Shrimp," wood-grilled jumbos in a delicious orange blossom honey barbecue sauce, served with a mixed greens/Mandarin orange salad with a citrus vinaigrette. Once again, we were reminded that people can have either of these spectacular lunches or a number of others for about the same as you'd pay for a typical lunch at T.G.I. Fridays. If you're on a budget, lunch is a great time to get amazing food at great prices. This is especially important in southwest Florida, where the prices seem exempt from gravity.

For dinner, the salads are all fresh and inventive, even the house salad, which comes with an apple vinaigrette and is served with white cheddar cheese and candied pecans. For entrees, we had the Sunshine paella, loaded with those dry sea scallops, jumbo Gulf shrimp, mussels, chicken, sausage, garlic, artichoke hearts, capers, olives, onions, bell peppers, and plenty of rice. It's outstanding, and you'll have extra to take home for lunch the next day. The yellowfin tuna au poivre is also delicious, sprinkled with coarse black pepper and then wood grilled and topped with a red-wine pepper sauce. It's served with scallion mashed potatoes and fresh vegetables. We don't really think you can go wrong with your menu choices here, and there are plenty of steaks to choose from if seafood isn't your thing. They're also happy to accommodate special requests.

For dessert, we tried chocolate fantasia, a cinnamon brownie with one scoop of vanilla ice cream and one scoop of chocolate, topped with a chocolate sauce and whipped cream. Quite the pleasurable indulgence.

We haven't even talked about the wine list, which is decent, but not as good as the food. General Manager Bill Aitken says that some snowbirds come down and head straight for Sunshine. With such a friendly, relaxing place, and awesome food, it's no wonder, even if it is hidden in the back of a strip mall.

I-75 Exit 131: Don't Skip One

Skip One Seafoods

15820 South Tamiami Trail, Ft. Myers; 239-482-0433. Open Monday through Saturday 11:00 a.m. to 9:00 p.m., Sunday noon to 9:00 p.m. $$

From I-75: Take exit 131—Daniel's Parkway east (2.6 miles). Turn left onto Ben C. Pratt Parkway (2.8 miles) and left onto South Tamiami Trail/US 41 South (1.2 miles). Skip One Seafoods will be on your right.

*L*ook for the little dive on Tamiami Trail with a Boston Red Sox flag, an American flag, and a Pittsburgh Steelers flag outside by the two picnic tables. Skip One Seafoods seats only fifty-five, and sometimes the line wraps around the building, so outside may be a good bet. Bring a blanket for the grass if it's during Lent, when lines get the longest. Co-owner Tom Voskuhl tells us that when they see people coming in with "those ashes on their forehead," they know they're going to get busy. The snowbirds and the Catholics avoiding meat on Friday are all in town during Lent, and the rush starts tapering off after Easter.

Skip One has been around since the late 1960s in one form or another. Tom has worked here since the early 1980s, when Skip One was just a seafood market, and then-owner Buddy used it to prep food for his restaurant on Sanibel Island. In the mid-1980s Buddy expanded Skip One into a restaurant as well as a market. Tom worked as a cook and manager and then finally teamed up with Dennis Henderson to

buy the place in 1995. Dennis operates one of the largest shrimp fleets on the west coast, so his boats provide most of the shrimp at Skip One. The majority of the other seafood, they buy from the boats at local docks.

We highly recommend the buffalo-style shrimp, crunchy and spicy on the outside, firm and sweet on the inside. The fried oysters, as a dinner or a sandwich, are also delicious, battered as Nancy likes them, but even Jane thinks they're good. Our very favorite meal, though, may be the gigantic crunchy grouper sandwich, rolled in cornflakes, fried, and served on buttered, grilled sourdough bread made at a local European-style bakery.

Besides the bread and the salad dressings, everything else is made on the premises. They smoke their own salmon for salmon salad in the smokehouse out back. The tuna salad is made from "real tuna, not that stuff out of a can," explains Tom. They make their own cocktail, tarter, and mustard sauces, and everything is cooked to order. They don't start breading or anything until the order comes in. So relax and enjoy the nautical knickknacks and sports paraphernalia in the tiny dining room while you wait. These folks know what they're doing.

The regulars sometimes show up five or six times a week. "I don't get it," says Tom. "I wouldn't want to eat at the same restaurant every day, no matter how good. Some of them even order the same doggone thing every day! I don't get it." It's tough to find good seafood at reasonable prices in a friendly environment. One time a regular asked Tom why he didn't open a steak restaurant. "I don't have no cattle ranch," he answered. The moral of the story is "stick with what you know." Skip One does.

I-75 Exit 116: Sunset Special

Doc's Beach House Restaurant

27908 Hickory Boulevard, Bonita Springs; 239-992-6444; www.docsbeachhouse.com. Open daily 7:00 a.m. to 11:30 p.m. $$

From I-75: Take exit 116—CR 865/Bonita Beach Road (which eventually becomes Hickory Boulevard) west toward Bonita Springs/Beaches (5.9 miles). Doc's will be on your left.

Next to a public park and right on the beach, Doc's Beach House Restaurant offers lots of options for a fabulous break from the highway. You can walk up to the windows, grab some food and a cold drink, and head out to one of the picnic tables on the sand. If you're traveling with kids, they can play while you take a break. There's also an outdoor patio in back with lots of plants that looks inviting. If it's too hot or too cold (unlikely but possible) or you don't like sand or ocean breezes, you can always eat inside, where the temperatures are controlled, and look out the windows. The views are especially good from the upstairs bar area. Or, if you're particularly adventurous, you can eat before or after a parasail ride (single, double, or triple), a kayak trip, a Jet Ski excursion, or a sailing jaunt. Bonita Jet Ski and Parasail camps out on the beach in front of Doc's and has all manner of ocean/beach toys and experiences for rent.

When it comes time to eat, though, try the moist,

Meals Worth Stopping for in *Florida*

of Bonita Beach's gorgeous sunsets, when the deep grays and blues, pinks, and oranges leave the green palms by the beach in silhouette. You can also watch your favorite games on one of a number of TVs in the upstairs sports bar or have a more quiet meal downstairs, where there's also a bar. Early morning is a beautiful time at Doc's too, but we think they serve a better lunch and dinner than breakfast.

Boe has owned Doc's since 1987. Lou came down to help him get it started and then just never left. Many of the servers have also been here for as many as twenty years. They pick their own shorts and T-shirt as a uniform and head to the beach for work every day. It's not a bad gig; no wonder they stick around so long. You may too.

crispy grouper fingers. They're served with tartar sauce, but ask for the cocktail sauce, which has enough horseradish even for Jane. The boiled shrimp are large, perfectly cooked, and well worth the trouble to peel. Nancy's favorite, though, is the Chicago thin-crust pizza they serve. *More* Chicago thin-crust pizza in Florida! Turns out that owner Boe Cibula and general manager Lou Banguest, best friends from Chicago, brought the pizza ovens down from the city, and the sauce is made daily. We're not sure why, but it takes forty minutes to prepare and cook. Who cares? Doc's is a great place to wait for anything. Our pizza came loaded with mushrooms, sausage, and lots of cheese, and the 14" size was plenty of food. We ended up giving the rest of ours to our friendly server for *her* dinner. The half-pound burgers are also supposed to be good, and you can choose from a wide range of traditional appetizers, salads, and seafood selections.

Of course, if you can swing it, be here for one

I-75 Exit 116: Hit the Trail for Breakfast

The Trail Café & Grill

12820 Tamiami Trail North #6, Naples; 239-598-2480; www.trailcafegrill.com. Open daily 7:00 am to 2:00 p.m. $$

From I-75: Take exit 116—CR 865/Bonita Beach Road west toward Bonita Springs/Beaches (1.7 miles). Turn left onto Old US 41/CR 887 (2.7 miles) and left onto Tamiami Trail North/US 41 South (1.2 miles). Make a U-turn at Shores Avenue, and The Trail will be in a strip mall on your right (.5 mile).

The Trail—like many good, bad, and indifferent restaurants in Florida—is located in yet another strip mall. We figured the place would have an outdoorsy theme, but it's named after the Tamiami Trail on which it's located, and the decor is closer to Southern tearoom with pretty curtains and lots of plants, a little on the precious side. But then there's the Egyptian hieroglyphics mural on the way to the restrooms, which adds an air of mystery.

Owners Ron Dean and Vechil Echols retired to Naples from Oklahoma and used to have an antiques store here that they ran during the the winters while spending summers in France buying for the store. In 2001 they found an ad in the paper for this restaurant, saw the place that day, and three hours later signed the papers to buy it. They redecorated, making all their own shelves, upholstery, and curtains, and opened a

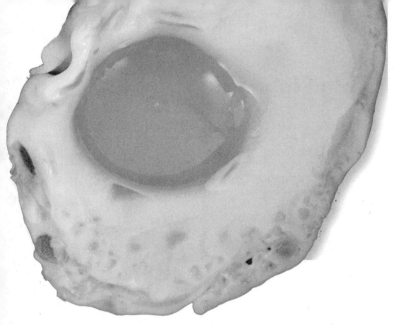

wonderful variations on themes. For example, in the breakfast skillets category, we recommend the Mexican version with scrambled eggs, chorizo, tomatoes, green peppers, onions, potatoes, pepper jack cheese, and salsa. The Greek version, with eggs, spinach, potatoes, tomatoes, olives, scallions, and imported feta cheese, is also a good choice. The eggs Benedict are good, but if you like seafood, try the crab Benedict, delicious and topped with a tomato slice, a crab cake, a perfectly poached egg, and a thermidor sauce. The omelets are tasty as well, and if you're looking for something more adventurous, try the razzleberries (blackberries and raspberries mixed together) pancakes or the cherries jubilee French toast with dark cherries and pecans sautéed in a buttery brandy sauce or the bananas Foster French toast. Or if you're a kid or kid at heart, ask for the mustached Mickey Mouse pancakes that they make on special occasions.

For lunch choose from a variety of salads, soups, pastas, sandwiches, and burgers or try Mom's meat loaf with garlic mashed potatoes and Italian green beans or check out the grouper dusted with pistachio flour, grilled or pan-fried and served with a mango pineapple salsa, rice, and sautéed vegetables. The Trail is not your normal diner fare, no matter how average it looks from the sign outside. Give it a try. You won't be disappointed.

month later. "We wanted you to feel like you were in our home instead of a restaurant," explains Ron. It didn't take long for The Trail to become a destination diner. One Saturday morning, we ate across the restaurant from Dick Gephardt. You never know who might show up.

Both Ron and Vechil were amateur gourmet cooks, so they developed the menu themselves. For breakfast and lunch you can get excellent versions of the traditional standards or you can enjoy more inventive, creative fare. For breakfast we tried our local friend and guide Jim's favorite, the multigrain French toast served with real maple syrup in a jar shaped like a maple leaf to make sure we'd notice. We can see why Jim stops by often for it. The bread gets delivered every morning at 7:00 a.m. from a bakery on the east coast of Florida because they couldn't find any bread closer that suited their standards. They do a number of

I-75 Exit 116: Get Fresh with This Fishmarket

Randy's Fishmarket Restaurant

10395 Tamiami Trail North, Naples; 239-593-5555; www.randysfishmarketrestaurant.com. Open daily 11:00 a.m. to 9:30 p.m. $$–$$$

From I-75: Take exit 116—CR 865/Bonita Beach Road west toward Bonita Springs/Beaches (1.7 miles). Turn left onto Old US 41/CR 887 (2.7 miles) and left onto Tamiami Trail North/US 41 South (2.1 miles). Randy's will be on your right.

According to Executive Chef Richard Miller, Randy's Fishmarket is the only restaurant in town with its own cookbook. "We sell ten a day without trying," he says. It's no wonder. If you wanted, you could buy some beautiful fish (ten to fourteen different kinds every day) and various other seafood at Randy's Fishmarket, but why bother when they cook it up so well here at the restaurant?

The semi-rustic, kitschy restaurant bathed in bright tropical colors even has faux flamingos nesting on the exposed trusses. "I gotta check 'em every morning for eggs," Richie tells kids, who get their meals served on Randy's Frisbeelike discs. The restaurant manages to have a laid-back island feel while focusing seriously on their food. The fish market and main dining room are in the same large room, but don't let that deter you. No fishy smells around this market because they turn over their inventory of fish every twenty-four to thirty-six hours. The always

Richard Miller holds up . . . himself

want 'em back." You can order anything you like from the seafood case, and if you want something special, they're happy to make it for you if it's in the kitchen.

Even without the special orders, the basic menu is plenty tasty all by itself. Rumor has it that snowbirds fly down to Naples for the winter and stop by Randy's for a grouper sandwich before they even go to their condos. For lunch you can also get plenty of other sandwiches—crab cake, oyster, salmon, chicken, or the "Cheeseburger (In Paradise)"—and salads as well. The calamari salad is on our list the next time we go to Randy's.

Dinners start off with good multigrain bread and butter. We weren't crazy for the gumbo the night we tried it, but everything else we've had has been outstanding. You can still get salads and sandwiches at dinner, but we fell hard for the "black and blue"

hopping bar is in an adjoining room. Speaking of hopping, during the winter season, you could easily run into an hour to hour-and-a-half wait if you arrive at prime dinner hour. Show up plenty early (like September) if you're working on your patience.

A likeable, boisterous guy from New Jersey, Richie both heads up the kitchen and makes sure everyone is happy out front. He's not too proud to run salad or pour water at tables, whatever's needed. "We strive for perfection every day," he brags, "and if we don't make it, you won't miss it cause we're so close. If somebody's not happy when they leave here, we don't

grouper, not surprisingly blackened and topped with blue cheese dressing. It was only a wee bit better than the gigantic blackened "Oh my God" shrimp. We ordered them blackened, but you can also get them fried or sautéed in lemon, butter, white wine, and garlic. They were delicious but pricey. If you're inclined toward more subtle flavors, the potato-encrusted salmon is a good way to go. The crispy potato coating gives salmon a new look and taste.

For dessert, have one of Randy's famous key lime pies. Jane adores them and Nancy likes them. The key lime pies have become so popular that owner Randy Essig has opened his own key lime factory, and during the season they sell more than 1,000 pies a week. Nancy's favorite dessert here was the flourless chocolate espresso torte, rich and sweet, topped with chocolate sauce and whipped cream.

We're definitely leaving happy. We'll be back.

I-75 Exit 105: Best Ribs in America? You Be the Judge

Michelbob's Rib Restaurant

371 Airport Pulling Road North, Naples; 239-643-7427; www.michelbobs.com. Open Monday through Friday 11:00 a.m. to 9:00 p.m., Saturday 4:00 to 9:00 p.m., and Sunday 4:00 to 8:00 p.m. $$–$$$

From I-75: Take exit 105—Golden Gate Parkway west (1.9 miles) and turn left onto Airport Pulling Road North/CR 31 North (1.2 miles). Michelbob's will be on your left, across from the airport.

On the building, it doesn't even say Michelbob's (pronounced Micklebob's, a play on Michelob beer); it says in giant letters BEST RIBS IN AMERICA. This pronouncement may be a bit overstated, but not by much. They start out with pigs raised in Denmark in very hygienic pens. For some reason, the ribs end up smaller and leaner and more tender and expensive. We don't know much about Danish pigs, but we do know that the ribs are moist and fall-off-the-bone tender.

People started getting hooked on the ribs as soon as the doors opened in 1979, and Michelbob's has won more than fifty national awards for their barbecue since then. Owners Marsha Gibbs and Bob Mattson used to travel around in the summer and enter their barbecue in various competitions, but winning gets old. They won Best Ribs in America three times and Canada's Best Ribs two times. Yawn. File nails. Celebrities from sports, entertainment, politics, and fishing have stopped by Michelbob's to pay tribute. The barbecue chicken plays a distant second fiddle to the ribs, but it's sweet and smoky, delicious in its own right. We recommend the ribs/chicken combo dinner. They also have sliced smoked pork or beef. Can't decide? Go for "The Feast": ribs, chicken, pork, and beef served with potatoes, corn on the cob, baked

Robin Bruns serves up "The Feast"

beans, coleslaw, and garlic bread. In addition, Michelbob's onion rings are hand cut and hand dipped, which impresses Jane more than Nancy, who cares only about the finished product. These are thick and tasty enough, but nowhere near as good as the barbecue. Of the two sauces they serve, we like the sweet much better. It's perfect for dipping our french fries too. The tangy had too much vinegar and not enough spice for our palates. If you're still hungry after one of Michelbob's generous meals, try the key lime or peanut butter pie for dessert.

The service at Michelbob's is excellent, knowledgeable, and helpful. Both times our servers were ready to answer our prying questions about food as well as change the station on one of the many TVs to a game we wanted to watch. The decor is masculine with pecky cypress separating booths and the largest collection of Coca-Cola paraphernalia south of Atlanta. They also pay tribute to the Master's Golf Tournament and to the Kesagami Wilderness Lodge, Michelbob's very own Canadian fishing lodge in Ontario, where you can fly in to catch fish and eat ribs.

Speaking of flying, for our readers who pilot around Florida instead of driving on the interstates, you can fly into Naples Municipal Airport just across the street and walk over for ribs. And if you get hooked, you can have the ribs shipped to you wherever you live. Arguably the best ribs in America are only a phone call away.

Colonial Outpost

Okay, we know it's way too far off the interstate, and we know that the chef may or may not be around during the hot half of the year, and we know that the service can be a little dicey, but the **Rod & Gun Club Restaurant** is in because we think it's truly one of the coolest places in Florida. An old world frontier lodge and restaurant built on the Barren River, the Rod & Gun Club has been entertaining the rich, famous, and adventurous at least since 1922 when Collier Barren bought the place. The lodge's hardwood floors and pecky-cypress walls sparkle with new gloss, and you kind of expect to see Ernest Hemingway and Teddy Roosevelt engaged in a fierce battle at the billiards table surrounded by all the wildlife trophies. Neither actually made it here to our knowledge, but Coolidge, Hoover, FDR, Truman, and Eisenhower have all been here. We even saw a personalized photo of John Major. In another hand, someone wrote on the photo, "Prime Minister of England." Burl Ives and Mick Jagger have both been here too, although not together.

You do have to be someone adventurous, but you don't have to be rich or famous to eat here. Choose to dine in the dark, elegant indoor dining room or head out to the light, airy porch overlooking the Barren River with airboats motoring by on a regular basis. The menu is limited, and seafood is the star. The fried shrimp is a particularly good choice. Winter is an even better choice, because that's when things come alive at this old outpost teetering stylishly on the edge of the world.

➡ 200 Riverside Drive, Everglades City; 239-695-2101; www.evergladesrodandgun.com. In season (October through April) open daily 11:30 a.m. to 3:00 p.m. and 5:00 to 8:00 p.m. Out of season (May through September) phone ahead because hours are "iffy." $$–$$$

➡ From I-75: Take exit 80—SR 29 (which becomes CR 29) south (21.1 miles). Turn right onto Broadway Street (stay on Broadway around the traffic circle) (.4 mile). Once Broadway Street turns slightly left and becomes Riverside Drive, the Rod & Gun Club Restaurant will be on your right.

Interstate 10
Pensacola to Jacksonville

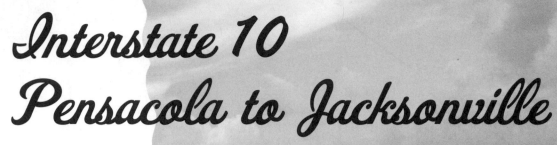

8

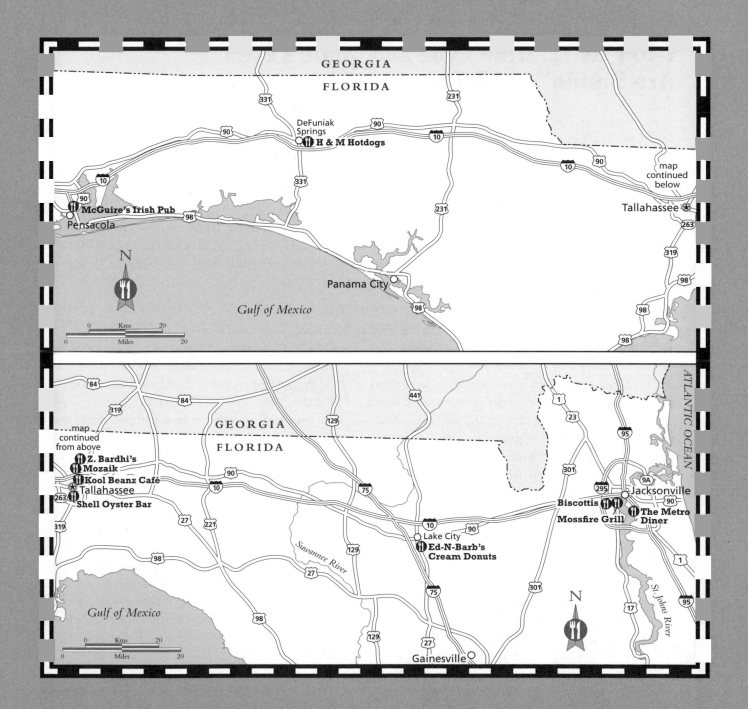

GEORGIA

FLORIDA

DeFuniak
Springs

H & M Hotdogs

map
continued
below

Tallahassee

McGuire's Irish Pub

Pensacola

N

Panama City

Gulf of Mexico

Kms   20

Miles   20

GEORGIA

FLORIDA

map
continued
from above

Z. Bardhi's
Mozaik
Kool Beanz Café
Tallahassee
Shell Oyster Bar

ATLANTIC OCEAN

Jacksonville

Biscottis
Mossfire Grill

The Metro
Diner

Lake City

Ed-N-Barb's
Cream Donuts

Suwannee River

St. Johns River

Gulf of Mexico

N

Gainesville

Kms   20

Miles   20

I-10 Exit 12: Irish Eyes and Moose Eyes Are Smilin' on McGuire's

McGuire's Irish Pub

600 East Gregory Street, Pensacola; 850-433-6789; www.mcguiresirishpub.com. Open daily 11:00 a.m. to "the wee hours." $$–$$$

From I-10: Take exit 12—I-110 south toward Pensacola (6.2 miles). Take exit 1B on the left toward Beaches/US 98/Gulf Breeze (.5 mile). Stay straight onto East Chase Street (.2 mile), and turn left onto North 10th Avenue (.1 mile). Turn left onto East Gregory Street/US 98 West (less than .1 mile), and McGuire's is on your right.

Money, money everywhere. That's the first thing you'll notice when you head into McGuire's Irish Pub. Donors personalize the bills, and then they hang them from the ceiling, paste them to the walls, even wrap the pipes with them. It all started when the place opened in 1977 and Molly Martin taped her first tip to the wall behind the bar. In 1982 she and her husband, McGuire, moved the money and the bar to the old Pensacola firehouse built in 1927, and they've been there ever since. Each year they count the money for tax purposes, and now it's upwards of $730,000. What a retirement fund! It's no wonder they offer half-price food and drinks to the fire department. And they've opened another McGuire's Irish Pub in Destin (33 Highway 98; 850-650-0000) that's filled up with almost as many dollar bills. Smart couple.

Money's not the only weird thing about McGuire's. The moose are also pretty weird. McGuire picked up nine of them (heads only) at an auction and hung them up all over the restaurant. The apocryphal story is that St. Patrick had brought them across the Atlantic. Pretty soon, it got to be a tradition that on your first time here or on your birthday or anniversary, the live entertainer for the night would peg you to come up and "kiss the moose" to great fanfare and maybe a rousing rendition of "The Unicorn Song," which seems to be the anthem of the place.

But money and moose and song aren't the only weird things about McGuire's. The bathrooms are pretty weird too. Our first time there, the Gourmettes had come off a long interstate drive, and the first thing we did, even before being seated, was head to the ladies' room. We walked in the door marked WOMEN'S ROOM and inside we saw swinging wooden doors with a cut-out shamrock in each and another sign hanging on the wall that said STOP

THIS IS THE MEN'S BATHROOM. Nancy read it aloud to Jane, and thinking it was a joke, pushed through one of the swinging doors, only to come face-to-face with a man. "It *is* the men's bathroom!" Nancy exclaimed as she jumped back.

"Yes, it is," said the man. We hustled out of there as fast as we could and looked back at the sign on the door. That's when we read the small print. Above the WOMEN'S ROOM part, it said, TO THE and beside it, it said THIS WAY LADIES with both a hand and an arrow pointing left to a room that had a sign on the door that said TO THE MEN'S ROOM THIS WAY MEN. Apparently almost as many people have been fooled by this gag as have donated dollars. Lots of suckers at McGuires.

The place is enormous and seats four hundred in various rooms, including Nancy's favorite, the Notre Dame room, which of course has its own moose and money in addition to the Fighting Irish memorabilia.

You know the weirdest thing of all about McGuire's? Amid all this silliness, McGuire's serves serious steaks and seafood and has an awesome wine list and its own microbrewery. This isn't to say that there's not plenty of silliness on the menu; there is. How about the Senate Bean Soup, which is a white bean concoction that sells for 18 cents, same as it used to in the Senate cafeteria before they raised their prices to $2.97. If it's all you're going to eat, McGuire will charge you $2.97, but otherwise, you can have it as a side for 18 cents, although we wouldn't recommend it. We also wouldn't recommend the gourmet peanut butter burger or the hot fudge sundae burger, also real choices on the menu.

Don't be lulled by the silly options. Stick with the more serious choices, like Paddy's spinach, artichoke, and cream cheese dip, an excellent version of this bar snack favorite, rich and packed with artichokes. We also loved the seared tuna and the garlic mashed potatoes, although we're not sure we like them together.

Burgers are a good inexpensive option, aside from the above-mentioned versions, and there are twenty-three others to choose from. We liked the spicy black 'n blue burger, huge and truly blackened. Steaks are king here, though, and they serve only USDA Prime. Our filet was wonderful and didn't need the merlot mushroom sauce or the blue cheese crumbles, both available on request.

For dessert, the bread pudding was a perfect texture, not too dry, not too mushy, and it was served with—what else?—a delicious Irish whiskey sauce.

McGuire's is as far west as the Gourmettes can take you. Beyond here lie dragons. Best eat up, drink up, and kiss a moose while you've got the chance.

I-10 Exit 85: Dog Day Afternoons

H & M Hotdogs

43 North 9th Street, DeFuniak Springs; 850-892-9100. Open Monday through Friday 9:00 a.m. to 5:30 p.m., Saturday 10:00 a.m to 4:00 p.m. $

From I-10: Take exit 85—US 331/Freeport Road north toward DeFuniak Springs (2 miles). Turn right onto US 90/Old Spanish Trail/FL-10/Nelson Avenue (.2 mile) and left onto North 9th Street/FL-83. H & M Hotdogs will be on your right.

We know, we know. There's a big gap between Pensacola, where our last restaurant was, and DeFuniak Springs, where we'll introduce you to some outstanding hot dogs and Italian beef. And there's another big gap before you make it to Tallahassee and more Gourmettes' choices. It's not because we haven't tried. We've eaten more bad food within 10 miles of I-10 in the Panhandle than you can imagine. It's not that there's no good food in the Panhandle. It's just that the vast majority of it is more than 10 miles off the interstate, often a lot more than 10 miles off the interstate. We'll keep you from starving, though, by telling you about a truly world-class hot dog joint: H & M Hotdogs.

To give you an idea of how tough it is to find great food in this part of the world, consider the fact that folks start eating hot dogs, hamburgers, pulled pork, and Italian beef sandwiches at 9:00 in the morning here. H & M serves no traditional breakfast food, but

we were there at 9:00 on a Thursday morning, and we can vouch for how good everything tastes, early or late. We had to fight for two of the seven stools in the place. How does owner Dan Pinson explain this? "People love good food. They're tired of the same damn food in the South. In Chicago, there is no bad food. There're too many people doing it right. They'll go out of business if they don't." Hyperbole, to be sure, but we think Dan has a point in this neck of the south. People eat his Chicago dogs at 9:00 in the morning even with the neon green relish and sport peppers because they taste good. One reason is that he's improved the Chicago dog! He's still got the usual condiments on it: tomato, kosher spear, neon relish (imported from Chicago), onion, mustard, sport peppers, and celery salt. But finally a Chicagoan has done what Chicago hot dog stands should have done decades ago: He's started grilling the dogs instead of steaming them. Certainly, many in his former city will consider this heresy, but we defy you to place two hot dogs with the same dressings side-by-side, one steamed and one grilled, and, with a straight face, tell us that the steamed one is better. It just ain't so.

Dan moved down from Chicago and stayed in the Panhandle, not because of the food but because "you get used to a more civil, nicer way of life here." He realized the slim pickin's when it came to restaurants, though, and bought H & M from Dan Bodiford, a man he credits with saving the place from going under. You see, the H & M has been here since 1947. Harley and Margaret Braxton owned it from 1947 to 1964, and Harold and Hilda Carpenter owned it from 1964 to 2002, although two sisters, Merle Carter and Maggie Davis, actually ran it on a day-to-day basis from 1972 to 2001. After the new millennium, things started going south, and for a while it looked like the hot dog stand would go out of business. Bodiford bought it, though, and updated it a bit (you won't think it's ever been updated when you see it), adding a take-out window. It's Pinson, however, who updated the food, adding, among other things, the Chicago dog, Italian beef, and pulled pork. Pinson and his wife, Phyllis, run the place now along with their young daughter, Emily, who helps with serving and restocking, and their younger son Andy, who stands on an upside-down pickle container and washes dishes.

The white tin-roofed shack trimmed in red has two wooden angels on top of the roof: one says peace; the other says earth. As you walk inside, the ceiling slopes down from the front door, so that if you're in the rear, the ceiling is only a little more than six feet high. If you're claustrophobic, you may want to stick with the take-out window and sit in the outdoor area that's larger than the restaurant itself. In one narrow room, the grill and all the cooking are done on the left side of the counter. The drink case with all sorts of glass bottle choices, including old-fashioned creme sodas and root beers, takes up a big chunk of the right wall, and there's an aisle between the drink case and the seven stools that's only wide enough for folks to squeeze past one another sideways, being careful not to knock the chips off the rack. What's Dan going to do when people start pulling off the interstate in droves because this is the best food between Tallahassee and Pensacola near the highway? We don't know, but we have faith in his ingenuity. He'll think of something.

Emily, Phyllis, Dan, and Andy Pinson keep the customers happy

I-10 Exit 203: Pearls from Apalachicola

Shell Oyster Bar

114 Oakland Avenue, Tallahassee; 850-224-9919. Open Monday through Saturday 11:00 a.m. to 6:00 p.m., except on FSU home football game days, when they open at 8:00 a.m. Closed Sunday. CASH ONLY. $$

From I-10: Take exit 203—Thomasville Road/FL-61 south toward Tallahassee (4 miles). Make a slight left onto US 27/FL-61/FL-63/North Monroe Street (1.3 miles) and turn right onto Oakland Avenue. Shell Oyster Bar will be on your right, behind Maner's Garage.

You wouldn't just run into the Shell Oyster Bar. It's not too far from the state capital or the FSU campus, but you've got to go behind the Subway on Monroe Street and walk around the back of Maner's Drain and Change Service Center and through a chain-link fence to a gray cement-block building. It's

got a couple of small SHELL OYSTER BAR signs on it, so you'll know you're in the right place.

Walk up the ramp inside, and you can take a seat at a few scattered tables in a pine-paneled room or, better yet, sidle up to the bar, where the shucking is likely already in progress. Their specialty is raw oysters fresh from down the road in Apalachicola, and they'll set you up with some before you can get a napkin in your lap. The shuckers and servers are friendly and happy to see new faces, but lots of folks have been coming here for decades, even back to the 1960s when it was just five stools, a counter, and buckets of oysters. Back then it was in an old Shell gas station, hence the name, and it was located around the corner on the property now occupied by the Subway. That's how it ended up so hidden. Cheaper dirt.

Vann Brackin and his family have been coming up from Eustis, Florida, to see FSU games for decades. They and some other diehards start every FSU home football game day with a round or three of oysters at

Top 5 Food Souvenirs from Florida to Take to the Folks Back Home

Why save all this good eating for yourself? Here are some ideas of great Florida food to take home to family and friends:

1. Citrus, of course. See citrus variety sidebar, page 242.

2. Honey. Florida has lots of apiaries, and hence plenty of local honey for sale. Thanks to Van Morrison, everyone knows the mild Tupelo honey grown in the Panhandle. Orange blossom is probably the most popular and, with its distinctive sweet, mild flavor, a sure crowd pleaser. Give some others a try, though. Saw palmetto has a darker, more complex flavor, as do the winter wildflower and the gallberry honeys. Mangrove and the old standby, clover, are other possibilities.

3. Jams and jellies. You'll see plenty of orange marmalades, but also be on the lookout for muscadine or scuppernong grape varieties, and, if you're in the northern part of the state, be sure to pick up some mayhaw jelly. This old southern delicacy is made from the red berry of some varieties of the hawthorne tree that are found growing in wetlands and swamps.

4. Key lime anything. You can find key lime saltwater taffy, cookies, hard candies, sauces, and, naturally, the pies. Almost every food in Florida gets made in a key lime flavor at one time or another.

5. Boiled peanuts. Some call them slimy, some call them great. The Gourmettes think they are slimy and great. They come with all sorts of additional spices added. We're partial to the Cajun.

8:00 a.m., when Shell opens on game days. Normally, folks don't start eating oysters around these parts till 11:00 a.m., but fans get pumped up for Seminole games and sometimes need early fortification. It's the kind of place that could get into your soul if you spent much time here. It's not so much the surroundings as it is the staff and the food and the history.

If you're not into raw oysters, you can have them "nuked." We prefer steamed, but these "nuked" aren't nearly as bad as they sound; they come swimming in butter with Parmesan cheese on top. We also recommend the fried oysters, which are fat and lightly battered just like Nancy likes them. Try the cheese grits for a side item or the house-made onion rings. The hush puppies too are good if you like them sweet as Nancy does. Jane's particularly sold on the shrimp burger: lightly floured fresh shrimp, fried to a crisp, and piled on a hamburger bun with lettuce, tomato, and tartar sauce. We like them to hold the tartar sauce because we're so fond of Shell's special cocktail sauce.

They don't sell any beer or wine, but you can bring your own in a brown bag or cut a deal for a free beer if you order enough oysters. If you like oysters, that won't be a hardship.

I-10 Exit 203: More Than Kool Beanz!

Kool Beanz Café

921 Thomasville Road, Tallahassee; 850-224-2466; www.koolbeanz-cafe.com. Open Monday through Friday for lunch 11:00 a.m. to 2:30 p.m. and Monday through Saturday for dinner 5:30 to 10:00 p.m. Closed Sunday. $$–$$$

From I-10: Take exit 203—Thomasville Road/FL-61 south toward Tallahassee (3.8 miles). Kool Beanz is on the left.

At Kool Beanz Café, the decor matches the food: eclectic and hard to pin down, but always interesting. In 1996 Englishman Keith Baxter set out to create a restaurant with a fun, casual atmosphere but serious food, the kind of place where he liked to eat. Keith has traveled all over the world and was in the restaurant business for almost thirty years before he opened Kool Beanz, whose menu draws on ethnic food from the southern United States, Mexico, Europe, the Middle East, Africa, and Asia. The squat building is totally plain on the outside, but inside, the bright blue, orange, and green walls are covered with all sorts of art, mostly created by employees and friends. The servers' station is camouflaged with a broken tile mosaic, and the customers are as likely to wear jeans and T-shirts as anything dressier. The wine list is taped to wine bottles and the beer list is taped to beer bottles. We think Keith has pulled off his mission.

We were there first on a hot summer day and ordered the perfect antidote to the weather: a cool honeydew and mint soup—smooth, sweet, and chilling—which was topped with pepper-spiked sour cream for a little kick. The salads, which are huge, can be ordered by the half size. We loved the blueberry spinach

Keith Baxter relaxes in his Kool Café

The menu changes every day except for five or six favorites that have become fixtures by popular demand. The art, too, changes often. On our second visit, Keith had just taken down photographs of the post-hurricane Ninth Ward in New Orleans, a reminder of what little has been done there, and he was off to find more "misfit" art in his home. "The room is so esoteric," he says, "that you can stick anything on the wall and it works."

Socially conscious, brightly decorated, and filled with fresh, eclectic concoctions: what's not to like about Kool Beanz?

salad with sprouts and candied pecans, dressed with orange-sherry vinaigrette. The "meaty" bean cakes with a chipotle pepper sour cream and a salsa fresca are spicy and smoky, and would please even carnivores. Vegetarian options abound at Kool Beanz, but meat eaters still get more than their share.

Our next time there, on one of the coldest days in Florida, we opted for a hearty linguini with crawfish, mushrooms, and tasso ham in a roasted garlic-cream sauce. Rich, spicy, and delicious, it contrasted well with the blustery cold outside. We also ordered the Louisiana andouille-and-shrimp skewer, served over tasty red beans and rice. We loved the andouille and shrimp, but the best thing on the plate was the fried kale that came with it, fresh and tender, yet crispy. We hope to find more fried kale in our futures.

For dessert, try the key lime pie if they have it, traditional with the graham cracker crust and just the right balance between tart and sweet.

Meals Worth Stopping for in *Florida*

I-10 Exit 203: Broaden Your Culinary Horizons

Mozaik

1410 Market Street #D1, Tallahassee; 850-893-7668; www.dinemozaik.com. Open Monday through Saturday for lunch in dining room 11:00 a.m. to 2:30 p.m. Dinner served Monday through Thursday 5:30 to 9:30 p.m., Friday and Saturday 5:30 to 10:00 p.m. Take-out area open Monday through Saturday 11:00 a.m. to 8:00 p.m. Closed Sunday. $$–$$$

From I-10: Take exit 203—Thomasville Road/FL-61 north toward Thomasville (.4 mile) and turn left onto Market Street (.1 mile). Mozaik will be on your right in a strip mall.

Mozaik is aptly named both for the decor, which features shiny glass and mirror mosaics on walls, bars tops, and posts, and for the way the chef mixes bits of taste into artistic creations. Less than half a mile from the interstate, this dual deli and casual fine-dining room is a slam dunk. If you're in a hurry, stop by the deli and take out or eat in a variety of taste sensations. When we were last there, the deli choices included standard sandwiches and wraps, plus shepherd's pie, Waldorf chicken salad, roasted peppers in baked ziti, buttermilk-fried drummettes, a variety of side dishes, and lots of sweets from the in-house pastry chefs: hummingbird cupcakes, Amaretto cheesecake, mango-coconut rum crème brûlée, wild berry Napoleons, and mint chocolate torte, just to name a few.

If you have a little more time, it's worth spending it in the main dining room, where lunch is reasonable and eclectic, and dinner is romantic and eclectic but still a great value. General Manager Brian Hudgens explained their mission: "We want people to be comfortable and casual while they're here in a funky atmosphere, and we want to broaden people's culinary horizons." Broaden they do. Their cornmeal-fried oysters, for example, were plump and juicy, and even Nancy thought the oyster taste held up perfectly inside the cornmeal. The broadening, though, is that they serve the oysters on a pool of heirloom anson mill grits, sautéed peppers, and among the best rémoulade sauces we've ever tried. The sesame and coriander seared ahi tuna, a fairly standard rare tuna, is served with a delightful salad of mixed greens, marinated haricot verts, tomatoes, and sesame wakame (the green Japanese seaweed), all in a ginger scallion vinaigrette, with crispy wontons thrown in for good measure. Even a standard salad like a Caesar rises to new heights at Mozaik with its shaved Parmesan, homemade peppercorn Parmesan croutons, fresh lemon juice, and anchovies served on the side for those poor folks who have missed the anchovy bandwagon. If you want a funkier salad, though, try the baby spinach and romaine with fried green tomatoes. The chopped red onions, apple-cured bacon, and sweet Vidalia dressing complete this salad that pleased even Nancy, who is rarely impressed by fried green tomatoes.

At dinner the bright colors of the place soften, and the quirky lighting, including lighted vines creeping up the walls and a copper Medusa tube lamp with Christmas tree lights on the end, gives the place an off-beat romance that marks the evening as special even before you have your first bite. You may also choose to sit outside in a quiet courtyard, weather permitting.

We started off with the Steele "Writer's Block" Pinot Noir for obvious reasons. Beer and wine are currently available, but Mozaik should have a liquor license by the time the book is printed. Call ahead if it's important to you. We then proceeded to nearly spoil our appetite by gorging on the fresh sliced baguette and addictive honey basil balsamic vinaigrette dipping sauce. The bread is free at dinner, but well worth the nominal surcharge at lunch. Mozaic has its own herb garden, so of course the basil is fresh picked, but we're not sure what else makes this sauce fodder for a 12-step program.

We would have been satisfied with just the bread and sauce, but in your best interest, we continued eating, and we're so glad we did. The next dish inspired prelanguage moans and ahhhhhhs: ravioli stuffed with port-braised apple and wild boar sausage, served with crisp pickled purple cabbage—a contrast in both color and texture—and rosemary-whipped Brie. We vowed to start herb whipping our Brie the next chance we got, but we don't think we could possibly duplicate the ravioli.

Next up was the crispy goat cheese (rolled into balls, breaded, and baked) and duck confit salad, a delectable concoction of mixed greens, candied pecans, dried cranberries, and cherry tomatoes in a vanilla-lime vinaigrette, topped with the duck confit. For an entree, Jane chose the monkfish bouillabaisse, which wasn't much like a bouillabaisse, but was delicious nevertheless. The firm, sweet fish, lighted breaded and browned, was served atop a non-stew-like medley of red bliss potatoes, leek hearts, pearl onions, roasted garlic, baby spinach, house-made ricotta, and lemon zest gremolata. The tastes were elegant and subtle, exactly the opposite of Nancy's "seven dusted Atlantic salmon," whose flavors exploded in the mouth like a tiny but loud symphony. The salmon topped a snow pea/shitake/carrot stir-fry, Chinese black rice, peanut/celery/cilantro relish, and a soy glaze. The tastes were bold and dynamic. Jane liked her monkfish better and Nancy liked her salmon better, but each of us liked them both. It's just hard to go wrong at Mozaik. Mix and match from the menu and create your own culinary mosaic.

I-10 Exit 203: Z Best Italian Around

Z. Bardhi's

3596 Kinhega Drive, Tallahassee; 850-894-9919. Open Monday through Saturday 5:00 to 9:00 p.m. Closed Sunday. $$–$$$

From I-10: Take exit 203—Thomasville Road/FL-61 north toward Thomasville (5.1 miles) and turn left onto Kinhega Drive (.1 mile). Z. Bardhi's will be on your right.

On a crowded Friday night before an FSU-Clemson football game the next day, Zeke Bardhi wandered from table to table with a water pitcher, making sure everyone's meal was perfect. Our table of six had only praises for the owner. Casual in jeans and a polo shirt, he apologized for not having on a Seminoles' shirt and said, "Go Noles" in an Italian accent as he left to check on another table. This place is one of FSU football coach Bobby Bowdon's favorite haunts, so Zeke is familiar with the lingo even though he was born in Kosovo, grew up in Rome, and spent fifteen years in the northeast United States before moving to Tallahassee in 1984. A decade later he and his wife, Carla, opened Z. Bardhi's in a small cottage on a wooded lot next to what is now another of Florida's ubiquitous subdivisions. It wasn't long before Z. Bardhi's became known as one of the finest restaurants in Tallahassee.

The interior mimics a log cabin, masculine and dark with exposed beams, greens, golds, and burgundies, and wine bottles in all sorts of nooks and cran-nies. Lace curtains and antique plates above the walls give the place a feminine touch. The effect is warm and welcoming, but you can also choose to dine on the terrace in front of the building and enjoy a bonfire if it's a chilly north Florida night.

The relaxing setting is only to ensure that you're in the proper frame of mind for the cuisine to come. We keep trying different things every time we go to Z. Bardhi's, and we just keep finding more and more that we like. All the meals start off with warm Italian bread with sun-dried tomato-herb olive oil. The Wedding Soup is one of Jane's favorites, and Nancy fell in love with the roasted red pepper salad, mixed greens covered by a big roasted red pepper, capers, and garlic, with swirls of balsamic vinaigrette.

If pasticcio is one of the specials, don't miss it. Grouper, shrimp, and tomato in a lobster cream sauce, all hidden in a giant sheet of pasta and topped with goat cheese. Incredible! The fruitti di mare is also a great seafood choice, and so is the Shrimp Zeke. The veal piccata—sliced and pounded by hand—is tender and tangy, and all the ravioli concoctions we've had were good. So were the eggplant Florentine and the pizza, if you're looking for less expensive options. The pizza is hand-tossed, medium thick with plenty of sweet tangy marinara and mozzarella, and topped with yummy eggplant and pepperoni in our case, but they have plenty of options.

We think the dining experience at Z. Bardhi's is so good because the Bardhi family works so hard and Zeke thinks in legacy terms. His three children all work in the restaurant: Son Enver is a chef, daughter Shanna is a general manager, and daughter Khara is a hostess. "I'm trying to give it to the kids one day. I hope they want it." We hope they want it too, so Z. Bardhi's will be here for decades to come.

As much as we like everything at Z. Bardhi's, we think they save the best for last. We're mostly hooked

Zeke and Carla Bardhi and the world's best pumpkin cheesecake

on the cheesecakes. First, we fell for the ricotta cheesecake with blueberries and a raspberry topping. It's not as sweet, creamy, or rich as a New York-style cheesecake, but it's fresh, clean, light, and delicious. But then, one night at the end of a long road trip with too much mediocre food, we stopped by Z. Bardhi's for a sure thing. Our meal was spectacular, but for dessert that night, Zeke had his pumpkin cheesecake on the menu. After our first bites, we swooned and started plotting immediately for the recipe. Fortunately Zeke was gracious enough to give it to us . . . and you. Truly food for the gods. Enjoy.

Z. Bardhi's
Pumpkin Cheesecake

Crust

½ cup of food-processed ginger snaps
6 ounces of melted butter

Mix together and spread on the bottom of a buttered-and-floured springform pan.

Filling

16 ounces mascarpone
24 ounces cream cheese
1 can (15 ounces) pumpkin pie mix
5 eggs
½ cup sugar
touch of vanilla

Let the cream cheese, mascarpone, and eggs get to room temperature. Combine cream cheese, mascarpone, sugar, and vanilla with a wisk. Add eggs one at a time and mix slowly until there are no lumps. Add pumpkin slowly and gently.

Bake in a springform pan at 375 degrees for about 45 to 50 minutes or when a toothpick comes out clean.

—Courtesy of Zeke Bardhi.

I-10 Exit 303 or 301: Donuts and Bust

Ed-N-Barb's Cream Donuts

567 Southwest Main Boulevard, Lake City; 386-752-1901. Open daily 5:30 a.m. to noon. $

From I-10 West: Take exit 303—US 441 south toward Lake City (4 miles) and turn right onto Southeast Camp Street (.1 mile). Turn left onto Southwest Main Boulevard/US 41 North. Ed-N-Barb's will be on your left before long.

From I-10 East: Take exit 301—US 41 south toward Lake City (about 5.1 miles). Ed-N-Barb's will be on your left.

(See the write-up in Chapter 5, page 102.)

Meals Worth Stopping for in *Florida*

I-10 Exit 360: Big City Bistro Charm

Biscottis

3556 St. Johns Avenue, Jacksonville; 904-387-2060; www.biscottis.net. Open Monday through Thursday 10:30 a.m. to 10:00 p.m., Friday 10:30 a.m. to midnight, Saturday 8:00 a.m. to midnight, and Sunday 8:00 a.m. to 9:00 p.m. $$–$$$

From I-10: Take exit 360—FL-129/McDuff Avenue onto Rayford Street (less than .1 mile). Turn right onto McDuff Avenue South (1.5 miles) and right onto St. Johns Avenue (.5 mile). Biscottis will be on your left.

This little neighborhood bistro and wine bar is tucked between an antiques shop and a Peterbrooke Chocolate store in the charming Avondale business district. Stroll the area if you have time, then step into the dim gold, beige, and brown interior of Biscottis. Metal lizards wander down the brick exterior wall, and original paintings from Roberts Gallery don the interior walls. Fans and track lighting hang from exposed wooden beams and complete the half-rustic, half-chic decor. Check out the incredible desserts in the glass case as you walk in the door. We recommend you order wisely or get some of your lunch or dinner in a doggie bag so you can save room for a slab-size piece of cake. Biscottis does not do slivers.

The place got its more modest start in 1993. Barbara Purcell had been working for a corporate chain in Nashville and Karin Tucker had moved to Jacksonville from San Francisco. They met at their apartment complex in the pre-Starbuck's days and decided that Jacksonville needed a decent place to get a cup of coffee, so, they opened up Biscottis as a neighborhood coffee shop with breakfast sandwiches. The menu and the square footage kept growing, and now even the *New York Times* has recommended Biscottis. The women, fifteen years apart in age, love the hard work and success and have managed to still remain

friends. "We'll be the only seventy-five and ninety year olds running a restaurant," Barbara says.

Biscottis offers far more than coffee and sandwiches these days, with a very reasonable set menu for lunch and dinner and daily specials that are a bit more expensive. The sweet potato red pepper soup is velvety and sweet with just enough pepper to spice it up. We loved the fresh, crisp field greens tossed with balsamic vinaigrette and topped with a lightly mayonnaised apple dill chicken salad with grapes and walnuts. It's particularly refreshing on a hot day and light enough that you can claim your dessert prize at the end. Biscottis has no less than nine salads to choose from, including your old favorites like Caesar and tomato mozzarella and some new concoctions like roasted salmon on baby spinach and field greens with shiitake mushrooms and red onions, topped with a warm lentil bacon vinaigrette. Or try the goat cheese salad, warm pumpkin-seed-crusted medallions of goat cheese with field greens, fresh berries, red onions, and raspberry vinaigrette.

For the heartier eaters, try one of the 8-inch char-grilled pizzas as an appetizer or meal in itself. The wild mushroom and Spanish chorizo with wilted spinach, roasted garlic, and Asiago cheese is particu-

larly good, and they also have even more exotic combinations like balsamic marinated duck confit pizzas with caramelized onions and Dijon topped with Parmesan, field greens, and diced tomatoes. Or try the rock shrimp pizza with goat cheese, baby spinach, and sun-dried tomatoes.

In terms of sandwiches, the servers' favorite and perhaps the Gourmettes' favorite as well is the Biscottis meat loaf on focaccia bread, topped with mozzarella and apricot marinara sauce. This ain't your momma's meat loaf; it's newfangled and delicious. Other possibilities include the Ancho honey–glazed salmon BLT, served on focaccia bread with bacon, field greens, and smoked tomato rémoulade, and the grilled portobello panini with blue cheese, spinach, and pancetta bacon, drizzled with thyme vinaigrette on focaccia bread and served hot.

Wash all these delicacies down with a glass of wine or beer. The two big blackboards hanging over the jars of various biscotti behind the bar announce the forty-two wine-by-the-glass options and eighteen bottled-beer selections. You're likely to find quite a mix of people in the bar and the dining room, young and old, well-to-do and bohemian.

Don't forget the desserts, though. Bypass the exquisitely beautiful mixed-nut chocolate torte—a pleasure to behold, but difficult to eat—and instead head for one of the cakes. Our favorite is the chocolate éclair cake, a gigantic yellow layer cake with éclair filling and dark chocolate icing, topped with a whole mini éclair. Biscottis has come a long way from its coffee shop days.

I-10 Exit 362: Southwestern Fire

Mossfire Grill

1537 Margaret Street, Jacksonville; 904-355-4434; www.mossfire.com. Open Monday through Thursday and Saturday 11:00 a.m. to 10:00 p.m., Friday 11:00 a.m. to 11:00 p.m., and Sunday 11:00 a.m. to 9:00 p.m. $$–$$$

From I-10: Take exit 362—Stockton Street. Turn left onto Stockton Street (.5 mile), left onto Park Street (.4 mile), and right onto Margaret Street (less than .1 mile). Mossfire will be on your left.

Two words: fish tacos. We'll come back to them, though. Mossfire Grill is a small southwestern gem in the Little Five Points section of Jacksonville. Nancy lived in the area when it was still a little on the seedy/crime-ridden side, but now it's revitalized, hip, and charming. Mossfire Grill is a big part of the charm.

It all started in 1998. After working in the corporate restaurant industry in Denver, Drew Cavins and his wife, Scooter, moved to Jacksonville and opened a little restaurant called the Tumbleweed Grill. Somebody else apparently had the rights to the name, so they held a renaming contest and one of the regulars came up with Mossfire Grill in honor of the great Jacksonville fire of 1901. So, maybe that's when it really started. A fiber factory that processed moss, which they used to stuff mattresses, ended up being the principle fuel for the early stages of the fire that consumed much of the city. A century later, the city is better than ever, especially its fish tacos.

Close your eyes and imagine blackened rare sushi-grade tuna on top of fresh pico de gallo, shredded cabbage, and sour cream, served in a soft flour or crunchy corn tortilla, with homemade salsa and spicy black beans and rice on the side. It'll make you forget every other fish taco you've ever had, and it costs little more than an entree at Denny's. Head cook Jonathan Dwelle tells us that when the 2005 Superbowl was in Jacksonville, Mossfire's pulled pork tacos were repeatedly mentioned on ESPN radio by some commentators who'd eaten here. The pork tacos are probably excellent, but we think ESPN missed the great story of Superbowl XXXXI: the *fish* tacos. We would stop the entry with the fish tacos if Mossfire didn't serve so much else that's delicious.

For starters, Jane's favorite is the chile-fried plantains, dusted with chile powder and served with fresh guacamole and an addictive hot mango dipping sauce. Nancy can't get enough of the tortilla-crusted goat cheese, which is actually a puck of goat cheese encrusted with pesto, topped with sun-dried tomatoes and pinion nuts, and served warm on grilled flour tortillas and field greens tossed with Mossfire's special red chile vinaigrette.

For an entree, try the grilled mahi-mahi topped with pepper pesto if it's on the specials menu. Virtually all their fish is fresh, and with the creative south-western sauce possibilities, it's hard to go wrong. The Mayport chicken and shrimp, pan seared and finished with poblano pesto alfredo, is also excellent. So is the spice-rubbed pork loin, grilled and topped with ancho cherry glaze. The mashed potato side is rich and buttery, and the steamed vegetables are among the best we've ever had. We haven't tried the empanadas, but they're also supposed to be terrific, and we're going back soon to try the slow-roasted pulled pork in a chipotle orange barbecue sauce.

Each table's condiments include Iguana Red Cayenne Pepper Sauce, Iguana Mean Green Jalapeño Pepper Sauce, and Bee Sting Honey n' Habanero Pepper Sauce, enough to heat you up. If you need a little sweet after all the flames, Scooter's crème brûlée will put out the fire. Scooter's the pastry chef, and her concoctions include key lime pie, coconut cake, pumpkin cheesecake during the holidays, and Mossfire's famous chocolate chip and oatmeal cookies every day.

Indulge yourself in Mossfire's glow in their downstairs dining room, decorated in southwestern browns, golds, and blues, or try the upstairs, a former apartment that they transformed into a bar/dining room five years ago. Sources tell us that the bar serves a mean margarita, and they've got a variety of tequilas and a dozen beers on tap to choose from. You won't go thirsty. Happy hour runs all day on Sunday and from 3:00 to 7:00 p.m. all other days. For maximum comfort, drink inside on one of the blue, rust, or gold leather couches or outside on the upstairs balcony if the weather's beautiful. But don't leave without trying the fish tacos.

I-10 to I-95: Yo, Check Out This Diner!

The Metro Diner

3302 Hendricks Avenue, Jacksonville; 904-398-3701; www.metrodinerjax.com. Open daily 7:00 a.m. to 2:30 p.m. $$

From I-10: Merge onto I-95 south toward Jacksonville Beaches/Daytona Beach (2.5 miles). From I-95, take exit 348—US 1/FL-5/Philips Highway. Make a slight right turn onto St. Augustine Road (less than .1 mile), turn right onto River Oaks Road (.3 mile), and turn left onto Hendricks Avenue/FL-13 (.5 mile). The Metro Diner will be on your right.

(See the write-up in Chapter 1, page 7.)

Interstate 4
Tampa to DeLeon Springs

9

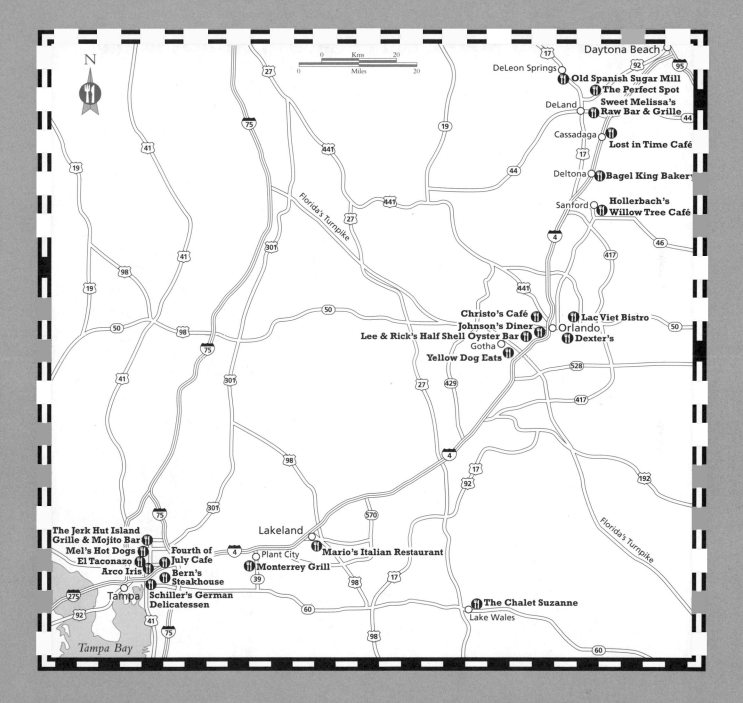

N

Kms
0   20
0   20
Miles

27

Daytona Beach

DeLeon Springs
17
92
95
Old Spanish Sugar Mill
The Perfect Spot
DeLand
Sweet Melissa's
Raw Bar & Grille
44
19
Cassadaga
Lost in Time Café
17
44
Deltona
Bagel King Bakery
441
Sanford
Hollerbach's
Willow Tree Café
4
46
417
75
41
19
41
98
19
301
Florida's Turnpike
27
50
98
441
441
50
Christo's Café
Lac Viet Bistro
50
Johnson's Diner
Lee & Rick's Half Shell Oyster Bar
Orlando
Gotha
Dexter's
Yellow Dog Eats
528
75
301
27
429
417
4
570
17
92
Lakeland
The Jerk Hut Island
Grille & Mojito Bar
4
Mario's Italian Restaurant
192
Mel's Hot Dogs
Plant City
Florida's Turnpike
Fourth of
July Cafe
El Taconazo
Monterrey Grill
Arco Iris
Bern's
Steakhouse
39
98
17
275
Tampa
Schiller's German
Delicatessen
60
The Chalet Suzanne
92
Lake Wales
41
75
98
60
Tampa Bay

I-4 onto I-275 South: Old Friends in Little Havana

Arco Iris

3328 West Columbus Drive, Tampa; 813-879-1357. Open daily 11:00 a.m. to 9:00 p.m. $–$$

From I-4: Exit onto I-275 south toward Tampa International Airport/St. Petersburg (3.6 miles). Take exit 41B—Dale Mabry north (.9 mile) and turn right onto West Columbus Drive (.5 mile). Arco Iris will be on your right in a strip mall.

With a name like Arco Iris (rainbow in Spanish), one might expect a romantic, other worldly hideaway in Tampa's "Little Havana" along Columbus Drive. This would be a far cry from the reality of Arco Iris, which is more like a crowded neighborhood coffee shop in a strip mall that's seen better days. Don't worry, though, there's a pot of gold inside.

When you open the door, you're hit with the smell of the "holy trinity" of Cuban cuisine (garlic, bell peppers, and onions) and the loud conversations and laughter of many friends. Everyone seems to know each other, but smiles welcome us newcomers and we quickly feel at home. Almost all the conversation is in Spanish, but there's no mistaking the good time being had by all. Owners Madeline and Jorge Gonzalaz are friendly, welcoming folks, and their attitude is reflected in their customer base. They came to the United States from Cuba in 1970 and 1980, respectively, and opened Arco Iris in 1983. Madeline tells us that some folks come in every day, and if they're going out of town, they let Arco Iris know so that nobody worries. In the front room, the tables are packed so close together that you can hardly help getting to know the folks around you. You'll likely be scooting up your chair again and again, so that people can get by you. Large murals of bright Cuban scenes decorate the back room, which is a bit more spacious. It didn't take us long to see why so many people congregate here. We'd spend a lot more time at Arco Iris if we lived closer.

The menu is extensive enough that you'd never grow tired of trying new things, unless you're Jane, who is so hooked on the *chicharitas* (super garlicky fried plantains) and the *puerco asado* (roast pork) that she has trouble branching out. The roast pork is swimming in au jus with lightly cooked onions on top and is served with fresh buttered Cuban bread and your choice of two side dishes. We also can recommend the *ropa vieja*, which means old clothes, but don't let that discourage you from ordering it. The dish is actually shredded beef with a tomato sauce and the "holy trinity," and Arco Iris's version is delicious. The *bistec de palomilla*, a thin steak marinated in garlic and citrus juice, sautéed and served with grilled onions on top, is also a great traditional choice, flavorful and filling. Then, of course, there's the requisite Cuban sandwich, with plenty of pork, ham, Swiss cheese, and pickles. You can watch them squish the sandwiches in the hot press behind the counter. The baked chicken and the lamb shanks are also big sellers.

Side dishes include *caldo gallego*, an excellent white beans and collard greens soup; *chicharo*, a rich spicy split pea soup with lots of chorizo and ham; our favor-ite *platano maduro* (fried sweet plantains); three other soups; three kinds of rice; two kinds of beans; *yuca con mojo* (yuca in a garlic sauce), which Jane loves; *papitas frita* (ordinary French fries); and *ensalada* (tossed salad).

If you're not in the mood for Cuban, and we can't imagine why you're not, there are also some Chinese dishes to choose from, basically fried rice, which you can top with any of your Cuban favorites. Jorge, the chef here, had a close Cuban-Chinese friend who taught him these dishes.

So, why is this down-home Cuban restaurant named after a rainbow? Well, when the Gonzalazes were starting out, they put everything they had into the restaurant. The sign was out front from the previous establishment, and they couldn't afford to change it. By the time they could afford a new sign, it was too late. They were too well-known to fool around with the name. Oh, well, what's in a name? It's the food that counts.

I-4 onto I-275 South: Bavaria West

Schiller's German Delicatessen

4327 West El Prado Boulevard, Tampa; 813-839-6666. Open Monday through Saturday 8:00 a.m. to 6:00 p.m. Closed Sunday. $$

From I-4: Exit onto I-275 south toward Tampa International Airport/St. Petersburg (3.8 miles). Take exit 41A—US 92/Dale Mabry south (3 miles) and turn right onto West El Prado Boulevard (.7 mile). Schiller's will be on your right.

If you don't like the smell of sauerkraut, well, Schiller's Deli is a good spot to learn to like it. You'll have plenty of incentive because the food's so good and the groceries are so exotic (by American standards). In fact, our first time there, before we could even get to the counter to order, we were side-tracked by the wondrous selections of coffee, beer, wine, candy, cookies, sausage, herring—all things to make Germans in Tampa think they've died and gone to deli heaven. Jane is still raving about finding tomato paste in a tube at Schiller's. She immediately bought enough to get her through the summer.

Hanging over the cash register at Schiller's, a sign says, OUR MOTTO: HONESTY IS THE BEST POLICY. BE HONEST IN ALL YOU DO.... TELL THE TRUTH AND TREAT PEOPLE FAIRLY AND THEY'LL DO THE SAME FOR YOU. It's a nice motto, of course, but they put it into practice here. You order at the counter between the deli cases, you pick up a drink or whatever else you want from anywhere in the store, they bring your food to your table when it's ready, and it's up to you to head up to the counter to tell them what you ordered and what you picked up, and pay for it all at the end.

Tampa's oldest German delicatessen, Schiller's has been cooking up sausages and sandwiches since 1952.

Meals Worth Stopping for in *Florida*

Café con Leche?

Looking for a traditional Cuban café con leche that's just an infield fly away from the interstate? Look no farther than the **Fourth of July Café**, which got its start in 1905 by two men who moved to Tampa from Key West with the cigar factories. This isn't the original building, but you might think it is, with its high pressed-tin ceiling, closed dark wood shutters, and old black-and-white photos of Tampa's Cuban history. The menu itself is pretty limited, but the Cuban bread is fabulous: Order simple buttered bread, a Cuban sandwich (delicious and heated in the oven, but not pressed), or a Cuban hamburger (like the ones you're familiar with except served on Cuban bread). Deviled crab, sugar cookies, and pound cakes are other options, but it's the café con leche that made Fourth of July famous. They still boil the coffee on the stove, strain it through a sock (not a real one), and boil the milk on the stovetop too. They make it individually according to the customer, and it's all cheap. Fourth of July Café is a great slice of Cuban culture and coffee with hardly a hiccup in your progress along the interstate.

➡ 1611 North Howard Avenue, Tampa; 813-254-2278. Open Monday through Friday 5:00 a.m. to 2:00 p.m. Closed Saturday and Sunday. CASH ONLY. $

From I-4: Exit onto I-275 south toward Tampa International Airport/St. Petersburg (2.1 miles). Take exit 42 toward Armenia Avenue/Howard Avenue, merging onto West Green Street (less than .1 mile). Fourth of July will be on your right. Park on the south side of the building; you can enter through the parking-lot door.

The Trunk family, Elisabeth and Erhard, their son Craig, and his wife, Amy, has owned it for a quarter century. They all manage to get along, a feat which Craig attributes to his wife, who's "a wonderful buffer," and the fact that they've all mellowed. Amy is also the prime baker. She makes fresh apple strudel every day and developed their carrot cake recipe herself. We'll come back to desserts.

If you're here at breakfast time, don't miss the German pancakes—*think* thick crepes made with cottage cheese in the batter. Better yet, don't think about the cottage cheese in the batter, just enjoy it. They roll up the pancakes and top them with confectioners' sugar and red current jelly. These babies will make you reconsider your entire pancake belief system. For lunch, we loved the bratwurst Reuben, sliced bratwurst served on perfectly grilled rye with Swiss, kraut, mustard, and Russian dressing. The Black Forest ham—lean, sweet, and slightly smoky—and cheese came on excellent pumpernickel, and was likewise grilled. No matter what sandwich you choose, and there are lots more options, pick up a side of German potato salad. It's creamy and tart and comes topped with bacon.

After the meal, it's time for the homemade strudel: chunks of apple in a delicate pastry topped with confectioners' sugar. One piece to split was definitely not enough. Next time we hit Schiller's, we're getting the large strudel and a variety of *hefeweizens* to go.

If you need a German fix or just like a great sandwich, Schiller's is the spot. You'll hear plenty of German spoken in the place, but lots of non-German locals have gotten hooked on the place too. "We know lots of people by name," said Craig, "especially my mom, she's really good at that. I know what people eat. They just look at me and I make their sandwich."

I-4 Exit onto I-275 South: Steaks in a Brothel

Bern's Steakhouse

1208 South Howard Avenue, Tampa; 813-251-2421; www.bernssteakhouse.com. Open Sunday through Thursday 5:00 to 10:00 p.m., Friday and Saturday 5:00 to 11:00 p.m. $$$$

From I-4: Exit onto I-275 south toward Tampa International Airport/St. Petersburg (2.1 miles). Take exit 42 toward Armenia Avenue/Howard Avenue, merging onto West Green Street (.2 mile). Turn left onto Armenia Avenue (1.3 miles), left onto West Swann Avenue (.1 mile), and right onto South Howard Avenue (.4 mile). Bern's will be on your left.

*D*uring a good two years of roaming around Florida, eating at hundreds of potential Gourmette spots, many wonderful, many much less so, we always saved Bern's Steakhouse for last. Nancy's family used to go there on extra-special occasions when she was a child, so it held iconic status for her. It was where she learned that she liked her steaks rare with a warm center—one of four designations for *rare* at Bern's—and where she first saw a waiter massaging baked potatoes tableside. Although she hadn't been there in years, that didn't stop her from jabbering about it a lot to Jane, so plenty of pressure was riding on Bern's when we headed there on a busy Saturday night for our last supper. Could it live up to its legend?

Before you even get to your table, you start to figure out the theme for the evening: over the top. It starts with the decor, which Jane describes as tastefully excessive house-of-ill-repute: red walls with

Oh, Captain, our Captain, Kirnes

lots of mahogany, marble, gilt, mirrors, statuary, and paintings. When you walk in the door, you see the stairs to the right, which lead directly to temptation. More about that later.

We are seated fairly quickly. Bern's will serve 900 to 1,200 people on a typical Saturday night, but they give such attention to each table, and it takes so long to eat here, that you'd never know. We begin by trying to make our way through the labyrinthine menu, thinking about what to have as an appetizer and what wine to order with it. Our waiter is one of five captains with gold ties in a group of fifty-two waiters in gray ties, including women, all in black suits. Our captain stops by to see if we're ready. We ask for more time. He graciously gives it. Finally, it dawns on us that perhaps we should just choose the appetizer and let him help us with the wine selections. We're forgoing the 172-page wine-by-the-bottle list and are concentrating on the more than 200 wine-by-the-glass options, which overwhelm us along with the 33 appetizer options divided by type (fish and shellfish, beef, poultry, foie gras, vegetables), which doesn't include the 26 caviar options divided by country (America, Japan, Iran, Russia, Sweden). Yikes!

When our captain comes back, we're ready.

"I'll have the ceviche," says Nancy.

"Let me tell you about the appetizers," says our captain. "The crab cakes are probably the best you've ever had in your life. The grilled shrimp are excellent and so is the spicy seared yellowfin tuna."

"Are you telling me I shouldn't order the ceviche?" asked Nancy, confused.

"I can strongly suggest, but the final decision is yours."

"Uh, I'll have the crab cakes," Nancy surrenders. Our captain approves Jane's choice of six oysters on the half shell, each a different type from the northwest. Then she asks for wine recommendations. He suggests a Chateau de Sancerre, which she orders. When Nancy asks for help with the wine selection, he pauses, thinks for a moment, then says, "I'll bring you something," and hustles away.

He returns with a Gary Farrell sauvignon blanc. The wine and the crab cakes with a Choron sauce (picture a tomatoish bérnaise sauce) are wonderful. Jane's eyes glaze over as she eats five of her oysters, offering Nancy only one, having conveniently forgotten that the Goumettes are *equal* partners in this venture.

Our captain stops by and says with a twinkle in his eyes, "I heard that you ladies were complaining about the wine."

"No, we were complaining about our waiter." Nancy grins.

"Hey, it's only my second day," he deadpans. The truth is that all of the waiters at Bern's go through a twenty-four-month training period before they get their gray ties. They work all the stations in the kitchen, they bus tables, they work for months on the Bern's farm where they grow their own herbs and vegetables, and they work in the dessert casks upstairs—the temptations we mentioned earlier. We ask how long he's really been there, and he admits that he's been at Bern's for almost thirty years. When we ask his name, he says if we like everything it's Kirnes; if we don't, he rattles off some other names we might try.

Suddenly Jane reads the first page of the menu where it says that you should reserve your own private "wine cask" for dessert at the start of the evening. A mild panic rises in her, and she asks Kirnes about reserving one. "I've already booked it," he tells us. "You ladies just had that look in your eyes."

By now we realize that we're dining "omakase" style, putting ourselves not into the hands of our chef but in the hands of our captain. Best decision we've made in a while. He helps us through the steak choices, which seem more like differential equations. You've got to choose the cut of steak, then the size (by weight or thickness), then the temperature. What you will get in terms of crust varies depending on how thick the steak is and what temperature you choose, and there are charts and explanations for all of this in the menu. We naturally end up just discussing it with Kirnes, who says he's going to do something special for Nancy: "Ten-ounce sirloin bone-in charred Pittsburgh rare warm garlic butter." She nods. He gets to Jane and helps her with her chateaubriand choice: "Seven-ounce medium rare garlic butter?"

"Can I have béarnaise?" she asks.

"Yeah, let's do the butter," he says, but later, when the steak comes, not only has Kirnes brought the béarnaise sauce for Jane, but he's added another choice too, a mushroom-port reduction that we both loved. Kirnes is not a sauce guy, but he takes care of the desires at the table. When we have to order wine with dinner, he quizzes us about what we like, says he'll serve us anything but merlot. When we totally leave ourselves in his hands, he brings two glasses of wine, with two extra glasses, and splits them equally into the "preview" wine, a Parducci '74 petit syrah from Mendocino, and a Berringer cabernet sauvignon for our steaks. Heavenly.

Now we start the feast in earnest. Kirnes brings us the French onion soup, topped with four different cheeses. "Just have a few bites and push it away," he tells us. "You'll thank me later." He gives us a similar warning when he brings our house salad, which he doctors up with extra Maytag blue cheese, and some

citrus vinaigrette in addition to the house blue cheese dressing. "You only get to eat half." Thank goodness for the warning. Both the soup and the salad seemed absolutely too good to leave any in the bowl or plate. Had we done what our taste buds said instead of what Kirnes said, we never would've had room for our steaks, much less our dessert upstairs.

The truth is, we could write a whole chapter on Bern's, but we probably ought to move toward a close here. Suffice to say that the steaks were perfect, the wines were a real treat, and the sides were serious. The baked potato comes with tableside service for the add-ons, the fried onion rings are thin and perfect (Bern's goes through 300 to 500 pounds of onions a day), and the beans and carrots are fresh from Bern's garden. After dinner downstairs, diners get a tour of the kitchen and wine cellar. Various small groups are moving through each all night. Waiters in training lead us through, describing what's happening at the various kitchen stations, and then one of the wine gurus explains the amazing cellar possibilities, including a 1851 Bordeaux that you can pick up for ten grand or the 1790 Constantia, a bargain at $4,900.

After the tour, if you or your waiter has made a reservation, you head upstairs to one of the dimly lit, giant "wine casks." They vary in size to match the number of people in the party, and the effect is that you have your own semi-private room. A phone in your cask connects you to your pianist for requests or allows you to choose several different kinds of background music. Kirnes is no longer our waiter upstairs, but we so came to depend on him that we got dessert recommendations before we made the transition. The banana cheese pie is light and dainty, and the macadamia nut ice cream with Valrhona hot fudge might be described as decadence itself. Rich on top of rich on top of rich. Jane can't stop eating it. We each have a coffee—try the cappuccino Bern's Steakhouse, whose grounds have been marinated in Kahlúa for weeks. Four hours into the last supper, it's over and time to pay the bill, about the cost of a small house in some third world countries. Worth every penny, though. The Bern's legend lives on.

I-4 Exit 7: Taste of Mexico in a Bus

El Taconazo

913 East Hillsborough Avenue, Tampa; 813-232-5889. Open Monday through Saturday 7:00 a.m. to 9:00 p.m., Sunday 7:00 a.m. to 6:00 p.m. $–$$

From I-4: Take exit 7—US 301 toward Busch Gardens/US 92 West/Hillsborough Avenue (.9 mile). Keep left at the fork toward East Hillsborough Avenue/US 92 West (.3 mile). Keep right at the next fork and follow signs for and merge onto East Hillsborough Avenue/US 92 West (5.4 miles). El Taconazo will be on your left.

El Taconazo could have been airlifted straight from any number of spots in Mexico and plopped down on Hillsborough Avenue in Tampa. The old school bus that houses the kitchen is now permanently parked out back with a real restaurant attached. In nice weather, choose the outdoor seating option, a little pebble-floored patio with homemade wooden tables and stools, and a roof and walls made of bamboo and bougainvillea to separate you from the busy street and an Advanced Auto Parts parking lot. There's even a sink and soap on the bus's front bumper for you to wash your hands before or after you eat.

We were infatuated by the ambience, but we fell in love with the food. Best of menu was the *cochinita pabil*, which Jane is almost as obsessed with as Johnny Depp's character is in *Once Upon a Time in Mexico*. Nancy had never tried it, but one bite made her a devotee. The

Rene Valenzuela, Pruedencia Espinoza, and Maria Serrano

pork is marinated in citrus and herbs, then slow roasted in banana leaves before being shredded and served in a taco. Owner Rene Valenzuela based his recipe (see sidebar) on the way the Mayans made the dish in the rain forests 5,000 years ago.

Rene learned to cook from "a lot of women," he told us. "Most of the knowledge is in the hands of the housewives," so Rene learned from the women in his family, friends of his mother, and the mothers of his childhood friends in Monterrey, Mexico, where he grew up. At nine years old, he had his first business, selling tacos his grandmother helped him pack. By high school, he had his own taco stand, and by college he had his first real taqueria. He moved to the States after college in 1991 and had a small truck at the Hillsborough Farmers Market before he moved to this location permanently in 2002. He and his wife, Lladira, also own a taqueria (see the entry later in this chapter on page 213) and Mexican grocery store in Plant City.

You definitely shouldn't miss the *cochinita pabil* if it's on the menu when you're there, but this little bus has lots more to choose from. We can vouch too for the *barbacoa* (slow-cooked shredded beef) taco, and the *pollo* (chicken) burrito, which we loaded up with both the red and the tomatillo hot sauces on the table. Other options in your taco, burrito, or quesadilla included *carne asado* (grilled beef), *puerco asado* (pork roast), *lingua* (tongue), and shrimp. The homemade salsa is a great complement to any choice. On Saturdays and Sundays, they also serve tamales and *menudo*, a spicy soup that some folks think cures a hangover. If you party hard on a Friday or Saturday night in Ybor City, you can stop by Taconazo the next day and test out the theory.

The ceviche, based on a recipe from Northern Sonora, Mexico, is a thick mixture of tomatoes, onions, cilantro, lime juice, shrimp, and octopus, and has an extra kick thrown in for good measure. Nothing a rice *agua fresca* can't ease, though. The Mexican agua frescas here also come in pineapple or tamarind flavors. Nancy could eat ceviche all day, but unfortunately, she had to save a little room for the *tres leche* cake. El Taconazo makes their version with a strawberry filling and topped with whipped cream and pecans. It was deliciously rich and heavy with milk. We haven't tried the breakfast here yet, but they open at 7:00 a.m. and have plenty of options for early risers, including *huevos rancheros*, *huevos con chorizo*, *huevos con carne asada*, and *huevos a La Mexicana* (scrambled eggs with tomato and onions). You can also get a *burrito norteño* (scrambled eggs with choice of chorizo or steak, tomatoes, onions, jalapeños, and cheese) or a *sunrise torta* (a Mexican sandwich with scrambled eggs and a choice of chorizo or steak). Considering all the delicious food we've tried so far, we can't imagine that Rene and the Mexican women in the bus kitchen don't do a great job with *desayuno* too.

Rene Valenzuela's Cochinita Pabil

5 lb pork shoulder (Boston butt), diced into 1″ cubes
3.5 oz. Achiote paste (El Yucateco brand is good)
Juice from one orange
Juice from one lime
Juice from ½ grapefruit
10 allspice berries
1 garlic head
1 teaspoon whole cumin seeds
1 teaspoon whole oregano
½ teaspoon black pepper
2 Tablespoons sea salt
¼ cup white vinegar

Mix everything except the pork in a food processor, then marinade the pork cubes overnight in the mixture.

The next day lay two banana leaves in the form of a cross in a Dutch oven. Put the pork in the middle and fold the leaves over the pork.

Slow roast the uncovered Dutch oven in a smoker at 275 degrees or until the meat gets to be 170 degrees.

—*Courtesy of Rene Valenzuela.*

I-4 Exit 9: Hot Dog!

Mel's Hot Dogs

4136 East Busch Boulevard, Tampa; 813-985-8000;
www.melshotdogs.com. Open Monday through Thursday
11:00 a.m. to 8:00 p.m., Friday and Saturday 11:00 a.m.
to 9:00 p.m. Closed Sunday. $

From I-4: Take exit 9—I-75 north toward Ocala (3.7 miles). From I-75, take exit 265—Fowler Avenue/
FL-582 west toward University of South Florida/Temple Terrace/Busch Gardens (3.2 miles). Turn left onto
56th Street North/FL-583 South (1.5 miles) and right onto East Busch Boulevard/FL-580 West (1.2 miles).
Mel's will be on your right.

(See the write-up in Chapter 6, page 135.)

I-4 Exit 9: Island Time

The Jerk Hut Island Grille & Mojito Bar

2101 East Fowler Avenue, Tampa; 813-977-5777; www.jerkhut.com. Open Monday through Thursday
11:00 a.m. to 10:00 p.m., Friday and Saturday 11:00 a.m. to 11:00 p.m., and Sunday 11:00 a.m. to
9:00 p.m. $$–$$$

From I-4: Take exit 9—I-75 north toward Ocala (3.7 miles). From I-75, take exit 265—Fowler Avenue/
FL-582 west toward University of South Florida/Temple Terrace/Busch Gardens (5.9 miles). Make a U-turn
just past 22nd Street (less than .1 mile), and Jerk Hut Island Grille & Mojito Bar will be on your right.

(See the write-up in Chapter 6, page 132.)

I-4 Exit 19: An Authentic Taqueria

Monterrey Grill

1302 West Reynolds Street, Plant City; 813-752-6862. Open daily 8:00 a.m. to midnight. CASH ONLY. $

From I-4: Take exit 19—FL-39 South/Plant City, merging onto Thonotasassa Road (1.2 miles). Make a slight right onto North Lemon Street (less than .1 mile) and continue on Thonotasassa Road (.5 mile). Monterrey Grill will be on your right when Thonotasassa Road merges into West Reynolds Street.

Looking for a real taste of Mexico on your I-4 drive? Look no further than Rene and Lladira Valenzuela's Monterrey Grill. It's even more ethnic than their El Taconazo in Tampa. Here, nobody speaks English, hence the taqueria glossary. The restaurant is an exact replica of the taqueria Rene owned in Monterrey before immigrating to the United States. The lime green walls, red roof, and red picnic tables outside make this former convenience store hard to miss. Inside, its bright yellows, limes, oranges, and blues match the bright smiles of the staff as we try to order in our well-broken Spanish. Through lots of pointing and their patience, we arrive at our orders, tacos on one trip, burritos and quesadillas on another.

Here's the way things work. Your tacos or burritos or quesadillas will arrive on handmade tortillas with whatever meat you ordered and with *arroz* (rice) and *frijoles* (beans) if you got that far on the menu. Then you load them up at the salsa bar, sort of a mini salad bar with fixings for your tacos. There are nine dif-ferent salsas to choose from with very pronounced flavor differences, so this is a great chance to explore. Be warned, though, that none would be described as "mild." There's also shredded cabbage, marinated onions, pico de gallo, limes, cilantro, sliced radishes, and jalepeños. It's all fresh and delicious. We took

Nancy's eleven-year-old niece, Ellie, on one of our trips there, and she said, "This is like an adventure!" And it is. She loved it, especially the flan and Mexican candy for dessert. No alcohol is sold, but check out the variety of Mexican pop: *mandarin* (orange), *pina* (pineapple), mango, and *limon* (lemon). You won't be disappointed if you're looking for authenticity at the Monterrey Grill.

Strawberries are king in Plant City, with most of Florida's strawberry production within thirty miles of the city. A large Mexican population lives here to work with the strawberry crops, so Monterrey Grill tends to get very busy on the weekends. They stay open till midnight because a lot of the strawberry truck drivers get in late and want to pick up dinner. The strawberry season generally runs from November to March, so be sure to pick up some for the road on your way to or from the taqueria.

Taqueria Glossary

When you head into a real Mexican taqueria in Florida, you may want to have a bit of Spanish under your belt. Monterrey Grill is one of those all-in-Spanish places. Here are some translations that will help:

adobo—a sauce made from various peppers, spices, and vinegars, usually used as a marinade.

asada—usually carne asada, meaning spiced, thinly sliced beef that is either grilled or fried.

arroz—rice.

barbacoa—meat that may have been either wrapped, pit cooked, or slowly steamed. It all depends on what part of Mexico the cook is from, but it's almost always good.

borrega—lamb.

carne—meat, can be *res*-beef, or *puerco*-pork.

carnitas—usually pork that has been boiled, then cut into chunks and fried (delicious).

chicharrones—fried pork rind.

cochinita pibil—pork that has been smoked while wrapped in banana leaves, then used as taco filling. Order at every opportunity.

frijole—beans.

lingua—beef tongue.

menudo—tripe soup.

pescado—fish.

pollo—chicken.

pozole—a pork and hominy stew.

tripa—tripe.

Meals Worth Stopping for in *Florida*

I-4 Exit 32: You Don't Have to Be Italian

Mario's Italian Restaurant

1833 East Edgewood Drive, Lakeland; 863-688-9616; www.meetmeatmarios.com. Open for lunch Monday through Friday 11:00 a.m. to 2:00 p.m. Dinner served Monday through Thursday 5:00 to 9:00 p.m., Friday and Saturday 5:00 to 10:00 p.m. Closed Sunday. $$–$$$

From I-4: Take exit 32—US 98/FL-35 south, staying straight as it becomes Florida Avenue (5.6 miles). Turn left onto East Edgewood Drive (1.8 miles), and Mario's will be in a strip mall on your right.

"When you take over a favorite old established place in a town, people are looking for something to complain about," explains Julie Marshall, one of the three owners of Mario's Italian Restaurant. "You're the enemy."

"And Lakeland's had a history of independent owners coming in and ruining good places," pipes in Tony Guinn, one of the other owners and the guy who takes care of the vastly expanded wine list here at Mario's.

The place doesn't look like much from the outside, sandwiched as it is between Larry's Locksmith and Signs and Specialties, Inc. in yet another boring strip mall, but the locals are fiercely attached to it, for good reason. Tony, Julie, and her husband, Michael Srednicki, bought the place in 2006 from Mario, who'd opened it in Winter Haven in 1976 and moved it to Lakeland in 1987. When it comes to a town's favorite restaurant, transitions can be dicey, but this trio worked closely with Mario to make sure they kept all his recipes, and the basic menu stayed exactly the same: traditional Italian fare cooked to perfection. They made their imprint on the place by expanding into the former doctor's office next door and splitting it into two rooms, the front one with more seating and a six-stool wooden quarter-circle bar, the back with long tables for large private parties. Then they went from four wine-by-the-glass choices to close to twenty and doubled the number of choices of wine by the bottle. Finally they gave the chefs carte blanche on the five to six specials offered every night, which aren't necessarily Italian. This is the spot where the chefs can add more creativity to the menu: Mediterranean, French, Indian, Spanish, whatever stirs their sauce that day.

"There's not an Italian among us," admits Tony, and that includes cooks, servers, hostesses, you name it. Nevertheless, you'd swear there's an Italian grand-

mother back in the kitchen simmering tomatoes and secret herbs, and there's a great selection of mostly Italian wines. The place even feels Italian, with dim romantic lighting, violin music, white tablecloths, and Italian paintings and black-and-white photos hung on rough plastered walls. In any case, the interlopers passed the test, and the transition went smoothly. Now they're the darlings of Lakeland's doctors, lawyers, and business moguls, and more people than ever dine at Mario's, which is now also open for lunch.

We stuck with traditional Italian favorites the times we were there, but one of these days we'll give the specials a try. The house salad is fresh and served with a balsamic vinaigrette, and the *insalata caprese* (buffalo mozzarella, sliced tomatoes, and strips of basil on a pool of extra virgin olive oil) is also a great start, fresh and delicious. When we asked Tony where he managed to find good tomatoes in Florida, he said that

he handpicked 150 to 200 every week at the farmers' market. And that doesn't include the thirty to thirty-five gallons of sauce, which uses crushed tomatoes.

The fried eggplant was one of our favorite entrees: thin slices of eggplant, lightly battered and fried, then baked with lots of marinara and melted mozzarella on top. Tender and delicious. The heavy hitters will enjoy the rich gnocchi Sorrentino with toasted pine nuts in a creamy pesto sauce. The lightest dish on the menu is the chicken Florentine. The boneless, skinless breast is butterflied and grilled with a sprinkle of Italian seasoning and a generous basting of olive oil. It's served on angel-hair pasta whose only sauce—and a very tasty one—is the drippings from the chicken. All this is surrounded by barely wilted fresh spinach. You won't be disappointed with the beauty or the taste of this dish. No matter what you get, though, the portions will be large, plenty to feed the hungry hordes or take home for later. If you somehow manage to have room for dessert, the tiramisu is supposed to be awfully good.

Try Mario's for a fine romantic dinner, or show up for an elegant lunch at a very reasonable price. Or, if you happen to be there on the first or third Monday of the month, call ahead to get in on one of Tony's wine tastings at 6:30 p.m. Your very knowledgeable host gives a lively class on wine while you're tasting. "Everything here that has anything to do with the wine program is about enjoyment," says Tony, "not being snobby about wine." We'd say that's true of the restaurant in general: fine dining in a friendly atmosphere with a group of locals who are more than happy with the new ownership.

Meals Worth Stopping for in *Florida*

Classic Florida Gourmet

Before Duncan Hines became known as a box of brownies, he was first known as a road-trip foodie, one of the great American pioneers who paved the way for travel restaurant guides. In homage to Mr. Hines for his contributions to the field and to **The Chalet Suzanne** for its Soup Romaine® and liver-topped broiled grapefruit, we include Chalet Suzanne here just as Mr. Hines included it in many incarnations of his seminal book, *Adventures in Good Eating*, first published in the mid-1930s.

This 100-acre estate—22 miles from the interstate!—includes an odd conglomeration of Swiss fairy-tale buildings, a lake, and a private airstrip, home to aerobatic planes whose pilots often thrill the guests with their maneuvers overhead. The Chalet Suzanne has been serving up gourmet food since 1931 and has hosted some of the world's most glamorous people. It's also among the most expensive restaurants in our book, so make sure you've budgeted accordingly if you stop here for breakfast, lunch, or dinner. The recipes have stayed largely the same for decades, so it's not a cutting-edge version of gourmet food, but what they do, they do well—king crab thermidor is our favorite. You can order a la carte or their traditional prix fixe menus at lunch and dinner, which include their homemade potato rolls, broiled grapefruit (topped with liver at dinner or by special request at lunch), famous Soup Romaine® (which Apollo astronauts ate in space, and The Chalet Suzanne sells by the can in the soup cannery on the property) and dessert. You won't leave hungry or lacking in stories.

The dining room itself is multileveled thanks to a fire that destroyed the original building during World War II. They rebuilt on a shoestring budget that added much character. We like the sloping hardwood floors and low ceilings, and we like watching the army of turtles in the lake the dining room overlooks. It's not hard to imagine why Duncan Hines was so attracted to the food and setting here. The same Hinshaw family has owned it since the beginning, and The Chalet Suzanne is still satisfying people with its quirky elegance and consistently good meals.

➡ 3800 Chalet Suzanne Drive, Lake Wales; 800-433-6011; www.chaletsuzanne.com. Open Sunday and Tuesday through Thursday 8:00 a.m. to 8:00 p.m., Friday and Saturday 8:00 a.m. to 9:00 p.m. Closed Monday. Dinner jackets suggested for men at dinner; reservations suggested. $$$$

➡ From I-4: Take exit 55—US 27 south toward Haines City (20.4 miles). Turn left onto Chalet Suzanne Road (1.6 miles) and right onto Chalet Suzanne Drive.

I-4 Exit 78: Yellow Dogs Are Still Eating

Yellow Dog Eats

1236 Hempel Avenue, Gotha; 407-296-0609; www.yellowdogeats.com. Open Tuesday through Saturday 11:00 a.m. to 9:00 p.m., Sunday and Monday 11:00 a.m. to 5:00 p.m. $$

From I-4: Take exit 78—Conroy Road west (4.7 miles) and turn right onto South Apopka-Vineland Road (1.8 miles). Make a left onto Westover Roberts Road (.9 mile) and a right onto Hempel Avenue (.6 mile). Yellow Dog Eats is on your left.

Nancy, with her missing dog gene, wants you to know that our inclusion of two Yellow Dog restaurants in this book (See also Yellow Dog Café in Chapter 2, page 53) has nothing to do the fact that Jane has a great affinity for her two yellow labs. It just so happens that both our Yellow Dog restaurants are quintessential Gourmettes' spots.

This one, Yellow Dog Eats, resides in an old home built in the late 1800s—super old for Florida. Eventually folks turned the home into a country store, which it still was when the inimitable Chef Fish Morgan and his mother, Lee Morgan, decided to lease the place in 1996. In 1993, Fish had started a tiny Winter Park version of Yellow Dog Eats, so named after Fish's golden retriever Scarlett, but he and Lee decided to move the operation to tiny Gotha and have both a cafe and an antiques store. The success of the inventive food quickly overwhelmed the antiques business and now both floors of the building and a rustic outdoor courtyard are available for the steady stream of restaurant customers.

You can see Fish's creative imprint everywhere. Regulars bring in photos of dogs and tape them all over the place. Every inch of wood, including walls, tables, and chairs, seems to have graffiti on it. Fish

Chef Fish Morgan

got it all started by writing "Pen goes here" on a notch in a bit of window trim. Postcard-size Yellow Dog wisdom signs hang all over: YELLOW DOG SAYS OLD WINE FOR OLD FRIENDS. YELLOW DOG SAYS DRINK WINE BE HAPPY. YELLOW DOG SAYS THE GRAPE IS GOOD. Yellow Dog is clearly a wino, and you may be too before you leave here. Fish has held more than three hundred wine tastings over the years. "I look for esoteric, eclectic wine from smaller purveyors," says Fish. Washington and Oregon are particularly well represented, but he buys wine from all over.

Fish is talking to Yankee baseball god Johnny Damon one day when we arrive, but he turns to greet us like the long lost friends that we aren't. Lots of celebrities show up at Yellow Dog because it's near some of the super-wealthy gated communities, like Isleworth, and, hey, even multimillionaires have trouble finding a great sandwich. Fish's philosophy is, "We treat everybody like they're famous. That's the way it should be. Now that Orlando's become a big city, we still have that old-school charm."

Actually spending time talking to Fish is a little like trying to interview a firefly. Long hair in a ponytail, sunglasses on his head, flip-flops on his feet, he looks every bit the surfing dude he is, but he's also got a Culinary Institute of America degree in his back pocket, and he's justifiably proud of his food and marketing abilities. He sits for a minute and a half, answering a question, then he bounds up to greet someone new at the door. He comes back to sit, and then a baby at the next table starts crying. "I've got Animal Crackers," he exclaims, and runs over to get them. The baby stops crying. He answers another question

or two, then jumps up to greet the Chick Fil-A managers who stop by often for sandwiches and salads. He answers another question, then hawks the Lobster bisque special to another regular who's walked in. His manic personality is all part of the charm of Yellow Dog Eats.

It's finally the food that seals the deal, though. The sandwiches are large, inventive, and uniformly excellent. The "Club Elvis" is always a great choice: their own pulled pork topped with thickly sliced bacon, Gouda, and fried onions on a bun with coleslaw and chips on the side. Feel free to add coleslaw to the sandwich if you're so inclined. The "Black Lab's Lunch" shows off all their fresh veggies burrito style in a spinach wrap: hummus, local tomatoes, cukes, sprouts, caramelized onions, shredded carrots, shredded lettuce, artichoke hearts, roasted yellow bell peppers, sunflower seeds, a light drizzle of feta dressing, and topped with feta. The list is making us hungry. The "Classic Yellow Dog Club" is also delicious: honey mesquite turkey with Gouda cheese, applewood bacon, lettuce, and cucumber with a delicious orange-Cointreau mayonnaise, all on multigrain bread. They also serve a variety of fresh salads that are as interesting as the sandwiches. We haven't had anything at Yellow Dog Eats that wasn't delicious.

On your way out, you can also pick up some boutique wine or homespun goodies for the folks back home. Yellow Dog Eats has its own line of barbecue sauces, Bloody Mary mix, salsas, and mustards. And feel free to bring a photo of your dog or a Sharpee to leave your mark on the place.

I-4 Exit 82: Old School Fresh Oysters

Lee & Rick's Half Shell Oyster Bar

5621 Old Winter Garden Road, Orlando; 407-293-3587. Open Monday through Saturday 11:00 a.m. to 11:00 p.m., Sunday 3:00 to 10:00 p.m. $$–$$$

From I-4: Take exit 82—SR 408 and merge left onto the west exit. Head west on FL-408 (3.7 miles). (Pay those pesky tolls! The oysters are worth it.) From FL-408, take exit 6—Pine Hills Road. Turn left onto North Pine Hills Road (.5 mile) and right onto Old Winter Garden Road (.7 mile). Lee and Rick's will be on your right.

Consider the oyster. Now consider 50,000 of them. Oyster lovers stood in line for hours to eat that many during one three-day Lee and Rick's anniversary celebration held in September, when they sell buckets for $5 a piece. The Gourmettes personally found gastronomical homes for some

two hundred of the crustaceans during the feeding frenzy. This, of course, was nothing compared to Joe Dixon—the reigning Lee and Rick's champ, who ate fifty dozen oysters in one sitting in 1976—but it wasn't bad. We waddled out happy, chased by the manager who was sure we'd stolen his pen. He confronted us between our cars and the old boat facade of the ancient building. We dutifully checked our purses for the pen. "What does it look like?" (We were thinking maybe a Cross pen or a family heirloom.)

"It's got Ace Hardware on it," he said.

"Sorry, we didn't take it." He left, shaking his head, and we burst out laughing.

You never quite know what you're going to find at Lee and Rick's, aside from the great oysters. The place opened in 1950 with nine stools and one item on the menu: oysters. If you wanted a beverage, you had to bring your own. Leah would keep your beer cold for you in the icebox. It was Central Florida's first oyster bar, and people flocked there to eat the spoils of Rick's weekly oyster run to Apalachicola. Nowadays, Lee and Rick's son, Gene Richter, owns the place, and it's managed by his children, Gene Richter Jr. and his sister, Tricia Blunt. Gene Jr. started as a dishwasher at age eleven, was shucking by age fifteen, and has been the general manager for the last seven years. He's proud of being the third generation and hopes that his son Ryle or nephew Cole will eventually take over.

Lee & Rick's has expanded since the early days, and now the concrete shucking bar is eighty feet long and seats fifty, the oysters get delivered from Apalachicola (or Texas or Louisiana if the Apalachicola beds get closed), and the menu is considerably expanded, including beverages. The rough-around-the-edges shuckers wear Lee & Rick's T-shirts that say "Oysters a must so your ding-dong don't rust" or "I eat 'em raw." The juke box has George Thoroughgood singing "One Bourbon, One Scotch, One Beer," a big marlin hangs over the bar, and an American flag looks down on the cash register. It's that kind of place.

Nancy used to come here on her birthday when she was a kid, and she and her brother, John, still hit Lee & Rick's on special occasions. It's a tradition for a lot of folks in Orange County, even celebrities. "Some celebrities come in," said Gene Jr., "but we keep it all real low key, no photos on the wall, and we try to keep our prices down. We don't want to be millionaires living in Isleworth, we just want to keep the family doing okay."

They're doing okay by us. We like the oysters steamed medium or raw when we're living dangerously, which is a fair amount of the time. The clams casino are also fabulous if you care to stray from the main fare. When we asked our waiter A.J. if he'd heard anything about the Red Tide clam problem, he smiled big and said, "I'm sure you ladies'll be safe." And we were. Safe and sated.

Gourmettes' Public Service Announcement: Oysters and "R" Months

It's time, once and for all to dispel the myth that oysters should only be eaten in months with an "r" in them. That was true in the very old days before modern refrigeration. Oysters were brought from the beds to boats to trucks, and it was tough to keep them iced down enough during the summer heat. Nowadays, oysters go immediately from the water to a refrigerator on the boat to a refrigerator on the truck to a refrigerator in your favorite oyster bar. Problem solved.

Even though they're just as safe in the summer months, that's when oysters spawn, so they might be a little softer and more fatty. Fall and winter are still the premium times for eating oysters, but a cold beer and a bucket of oysters is awfully hard to beat in the summer. Deny yourself no longer.

I-4 Exit 83 or 82C: Food for Your Soul

Johnson's Diner

595 West Church Street, Orlando; 407-841-0717; www.johnsonsdiner.com. Open Monday through Thursday 7:00 a.m. to 7:00 p.m., Friday and Saturday 7:00 a.m. to 8:00 p.m., and Sunday noon to 5:00 p.m. $–$$

From I-4 West: Take exit 83 (on the left) and merge onto West South Street (.4 mile). Turn right onto South Division Avenue (.1 mile). Make a left onto West Church Street (.1 mile). Johnson's Diner will be on your right.

From I-4 East: Take exit 82C—Anderson Street East. Merge onto Boone Avenue (.1 mile) and turn left onto West South Street (.3 mile). Make a right onto South Division Avenue (.1 mile) and a left onto West Church Street (.1 mile). Johnson's Diner will be on your right.

Our friend Bonnie has already decided that when she dies, she wants to be reincarnated as a Johnson's Diner smothered pork chop. We agree that the chops are the all-too-rare real thing, cooked to fall-apart tenderness with dark, thick pork gravy. You could never go wrong ordering them, but there are too many other fabulous home-cooked items to limit yourself to only the chops.

We're sure that the Orlando Magic and half of the rest of the NBA—plus lots of other rich-and-famous folks like Wesley Snipes, Danny Glover, and Johnnie Cochrane, who've been known to pop into this tiny cafe—have also tried the meat loaf, the fried chicken, the fried catfish, and the ribs—all tasty. Don't scrimp on the side dishes either; everything's cooked southern style (long with plenty of flavor—no crisp green beans here). All entrees come with your choice of three sides and corn bread or dinner rolls. We particularly recommend the steamed cabbage, the mashed potatoes, and the green beans, but they also offer creamed corn casserole, black-eyed peas, mac 'n cheese, collard greens, and more. The menu changes daily, but you can always get the perennial favorites: the tenderest stew beef you've ever tasted and those delectable smothered pork chops. The oxtails were the only main dish we weren't crazy about. Make sure you don't leave without a taste of the sweet potato pie. Since the crust is store-bought, you can save a few calories by scooping out the creamy innards. Delicious. They also offer peach cobbler, and on Wednesdays only, you can finish up with banana pudding, and on Thursdays only, red velvet cake. You'll get way more food than you need at Johnson's at very affordable prices.

For decades the restaurant was in a beat, tiny, cramped two-room building just blocks from Orlando's Amway Arena, but a couple of years ago, they moved uptown to this spacious West Church Street location, which coincidentally will be very close to the new arena Orlando has planned. The new place has a bigger kitchen and about five times as much seating. Also, the ceiling is much higher and easier to negotiate for the basketball players who stop by. The Polaroid collage of the famous folks whose souls have been fed at Johnson's Diner still graces the walls of the new place, but now so do tributes to Martin Luther King Jr., Ray Charles, and many jazz greats. There's no longer a mural out front of founder Lillie Johnson announcing, "Soul food to please the tastes," but her granddaughter Andrena Daniels and grandson Clarence Taylor, who now run the place, are still busy pleasing people's tastes with their soul food. They'll be happy to please yours too.

I-4 Exit 84 or 83B: Where Everybody Knows Your Name

Dexter's

808 East Washington Street, Orlando; 407-648-2777; www.dexwine.com. Open Monday through Thursday 11:00 a.m. to 10:00 p.m., Friday and Saturday 11:00 a.m. to 11:00 p.m., and Sunday 10:00 a.m. to 10:00 p.m. $$–$$$ (mostly $$)

From I-4 West: Take exit 84—Colonial Drive/FL-50/Ivanhoe Boulevard toward Centroplex (.2 mile). Keep right at the fork and follow signs for Ivanhoe Boulevard (.2 mile). Turn right onto South Ivanhoe Boulevard (.2 mile) and stay straight onto North Orange Avenue (.9 mile). Then turn left onto East Robinson Street (.6 mile), right onto North Summerlin Avenue (.1 mile) and left onto East Washington Street (less than .1 mile). Dexter's will be on your right.

From I-4 East: Take exit 83B—Amelia Street toward Centroplex/SR 50/US 92/US 17. Turn right onto West Amelia Street (.2 mile), right onto North Orange Avenue (.3 mile), left onto East Robinson Street (.6 mile), right onto North Summerlin Avenue (.1 mile), and left onto East Washington Street (less than .1 mile). Dexter's will be on your right.

Nancy has been hanging out at Dexter's Thornton Park location for years because one of her oldest friends, Lissa, and her husband, Paul, live nearby. It feels like *Cheers* to them, and nearly so to Nancy. Jane thinks it's a little on the hip side for the Gourmettes, but the food and the neighborhood won her over. Gay-friendly Thornton Park is perhaps the most charming area in downtown Orlando, with its tree-lined brick streets and quaint renovated bungalows and cottages. It's a part of the downtown scene that many visitors miss.

Dexter's is a fun spot whether you're outside at one of the sidewalk tables watching the world go by or inside the high-ceilinged dining room with its exposed ductwork, large center-stage bar, and noisy crowd. On the walls hang work by local artists. One wall rotates every month. The opposite wall's artwork stays for longer, and the artistic choices for both seem skewed toward brightly colored acrylics on large canvases, which tends to give the place a hip, festive feel for the crowd that's mostly in their 20s, 30s, and 40s.

In 1983, Dexter Richardson started Dexter's as a wine shop on trendy Park Avenue in Winter Park, just outside Orlando. By 1988, Dexter's had moved and started selling food. It moved again to its current Winter Park location (558 West New England Avenue, 407-629-1150), then Dexter opened this Thornton Park location in 1995. We like both of these Dexter's a lot but are less crazy about the latest Dexter located in a neotraditional shopping center in Lake Mary (950 Market Promenade Avenue, Suite 1201, 407-805-3090). The food and service are just as good at the Lake Mary location, but the overall setting feels too corporate for our taste.

Once you've gotten to a Dexter's, start off with one of the many reasonable wines by the glass or choose from an excellent imported beer selection. Next, if you want to live dangerously, try Dexter's homemade chips, Cha Cha and/or sweet potato: crunchy, caloric, and addictive. The real danger is that they might spoil your dinner, and, trust us, you wouldn't want that to happen.

For entrees, Nancy is a huge fan of the chicken tortilla pie. They take crisp flour tortillas, stack them up, and layer them with chopped sautéed chicken breast, tomatoes, jalapeños, and melted provolone. They bake it till the provolone is oozing, then top it with sour cream, chopped scallions, and sun-dried tomatoes. Unless you're allergic to one of those ingredients, you'll love it. Jane fell hard for the hot duck wonton stack, listed as an appetizer but big enough to be an entree. The crisp wonton skins are stacked with lots of duck confit and sweetly caramelized onions and topped with a mango and papaya salsa. Delicious.

Another of our favorites is the eggplant Napoleon, thinly sliced eggplant coated with buttermilk and flour, fried crisp in olive oil, then layered with spinach, ricotta, provolone, and Parmesan cheeses and baked on a bed of sweet delicious marinara until the cheeses start to bubble and brown.

Try also the inventive sandwiches, including the pressed duck with grilled onions and melted Brie cheese or the grilled veggie sandwich. Or check out one of at least nine different salads, depending on the specials, including their Matanzas sour orange salmon salad and Peter's grilled mahi-mahi and sun-dried cranberry salad. Best of all, the prices are incredibly reasonable for all this creative culinary work. Dexter's is a hip setting with great food, but it won't put a hurting on your cash or credit. Show up a few times, and they'll know your name.

I-4 Exit 84 or 83B: We Lac This Viet Bistro

Lac Viet Bistro

2021 East Colonial Drive, Orlando; 407-228-4000. Open daily 10:00 a.m. to 10:00 p.m. $$–$$$

From I-4 West: Take exit 84—Colonial Drive/FL-50 toward Centroplex (.5 mile) and turn left onto West Colonial Drive/FL-50 (1.7 miles). Lac Viet Bistro will be on your left.

From I-4 East: Take exit 83B—Amelia Street toward Centroplex/FL-50. Merge onto Garland Avenue (.2 mile) and turn right onto West Colonial Drive (which becomes East Colonial Drive)/FL-50 (1.6 miles). Lac Viet Bistro will be on your left.

*T*rust us. Just say F1 and you'll be happy. Or E6. Or A9. Or D1. Okay, the truth is that we haven't found a letter-number combination that we didn't like. And the rest of the truth is that we can't pronounce anything on the menu, and we have a hard time finding all the Vietnamese characters so that we can type out the names. We know what we like when it comes to Vietnamese food because we recognize freshness and flavor, but we just have a hard time talking and writing about what each dish is called.

With that confession out of the way, we can tell you that Lac Viet Bistro is a relative newcomer to the ViMi District of Orlando, where lots of Vietnamese restaurants have clustered near Mills Avenue. We like Lac Viet best, though. Located in a freestanding brick cottage with a Spanish tile roof, Lac Viet offers both traditional Vietnamese fare and sushi. Everyone speaks English well, and the service is terrific: friendly, knowledgeable, and helpful.

Inside, the space is lush with flora, fountains, and a display of traditional Vietnamese musical instruments. You can eat inside or outside on the patio surrounded by bamboo and banana trees. The owners, Loan and

Meals Worth Stopping for in *Florida*

Andre Bui, second-generation Vietnamese-Americans, love plants and like for everything to have a green look. They had wanted a restaurant for years and finally opened Lac Viet Bistro in 2004 with Loan and Andre's brother-in-law overseeing the kitchen. Andre, after twenty years as a computer analyst, runs the front of the restaurant. He's a people person with a great sense of humor and diplomacy. Besides, Loan tells us, "If he were in charge of the kitchen, we'd lose our customers." Thankfully, the kitchen is running just fine.

To start, you might try a 33 Export, a Vietnamese lager, or if you're more adventurous, one of the Vietnamese specialty drinks, like lemonade with pickled plum. "Let me make it little bit special for you," our server says. Apparently he adds Sprite to it. We're not sure how it compares to others of its ilk, but it's tangy, sweet, and sour *in the extreme*. Full of flavor, but not for the faint of palate. For an appetizer, you might try *Bánh Xèo* (A9), a crispy golden pancake/crepe with pork, shrimp, scallions, bean sprouts, mixed greens, and mint. All fresh and crunchy, this is a meal in itself. We also like the rice paper rolls with shrimp or grilled tofu, served with the usual peanut dipping sauce.

That famous F1 is actually *Bún Lặc Việt Đặc Biệt*, a bowlful of goodness: vermicelli noodles topped with grilled pork, grilled beef, a sliced fried spring roll, shrimp paste, lettuce, herbs, and fish sauce. One of the rules here is that anything with grilled pork is going to be delicious. We also like D1, *Bánh Cuốn Lạc Việt*, which is actually a combination of D2, D3, D4, and D5 plus a shrimp cake. We're not going through all these names, but suffice to say that this roughly translates to rice crepes with the shrimp cake; marinated pork, mushroom, and onions; marinated shrimp; and green onions and shallots. The marinated pork is a little like Vietnamese bologna, and it tastes a lot better than it looks. Another star is J1, *Cơm Lạc Việt Đặc Biệt*, jasmine rice with shredded-pork grilled pork chop, steamed pork loaf, "sun shine egg" (poached), and grilled shrimp. For those with more of a Thai than a Vietnamese bent, try E6, *Bún Măng Gà (Vịt)*, which is a vermicelli soup with chicken, bamboo, and lemongrass. Its flavor is much like Tom Yum Goong. For those of you with more of a Japanese bent, try the fresh and flavorful (if a bit expensive) sushi.

If any of this seems confusing, you should remember two things. First, everything here is so good that you're unlikely to make a choice you'll regret (except perhaps the lemonade with pickled plum). Second, the staff at Lac Viet is so helpful that if you have any questions, they'll be delighted to guide you.

As for the name of the restaurant, Lac Viet has many deep meanings, explains Loan Bui. Thousands of years ago, Viet Nam was known as Lac Viet. "Lac" means you are happy but it can also mean you are lost. It depends on the context. Here at the bistro, it means, "We are Vietnamese, we love our country, we lost our country, but we are happy to be here in America, to be Americans where we have so many opportunities to resettle, to be happy. We want always to remember our roots, where we came from. Lac is also the name of a bird that, like the U.S.'s bald eagle, when you see it, you know, that's Viet Nam, that's our country." It seems to us that the heartfelt name of the restaurant, with all its meanings, is somehow transferred into the food, even if we can't pronounce it.

I-4 Exit 85: Christo's of the Great Greek Omelets

Christo's Café

1815 Edgewater Drive, Orlando; 407-425-8136; www.christoscafe.com. Open Monday through Saturday 6:30 a.m. to 9:00 p.m., Sunday 7:00 a.m. to 3:00 p.m. $–$$

From I-4: Take exit 85—Princeton Street/FL-438 west (.8 mile) and turn left onto Edgewater Drive/FL-424 (.3 mile). Christo's will be on your left.

*T*his Edgewater landmark still has the feel of a 1950s neighborhood diner. The building has had all sorts of incarnations: Rumor has it that it was the first Edsel car dealership in Florida and a fried chicken place somewhere along the way and a restaurant called Cupie's. On one of our visits we sat next to a regular who'd been coming there since the 1970s, before it was bought by a guy named Christo more than twenty years ago. Although it's been through several owners after Christo, this is one of those diners that's really owned more by the neighborhood than by the person who signs the paychecks. It's an institution that belongs to the people of the College Park area of Orlando, who've been coming here for years. You'll see lots of their photos up in collages on the wall.

On a given morning, you'll find a range of locals inside, from Moms with toddlers on their laps to businessmen in suits to blue-collar workers in paint-stained overalls to a couple of sleepy-headed women in their early twenties, chins in hands at the counter, barely managing to lift the heavy Christo's mugs. Everyone seems to be talking at once and the room is buzzing with early morning energy. The smiling servers keep the mugs filled with good diner coffee with real half and half available. You can sit outside on one of the picnic tables and watch the traffic, but then you'd miss sitting at the counter or grabbing one of the ten indoor tables, and eavesdropping on the group of retired gentlemen discussing the latest football scores before they move on to politics and the one topic that seems to stir the most interest among them: the various surgeries they and their pals have had or are about to undergo.

On our first visit to Christo's, we sat at the counter between wrapped slices of red velvet cake and a cake plate full of yummy blueberry muffins. Turns out that an eighty-something-year-old woman named Dottie has been making the cakes here for years. The menu is fairly standard diner fare. We ordered eggs

Benedict and a Greek omelet, not because either of us are big Greek omelet fans, but because it looked like the most exotic thing on the menu. It arrived bursting with lamb slices, ripe tomatoes, feta, and olives. This omelet was definitely the best Greek one we've ever had and perhaps one of the best omelets of any kind. The eggs Benedict, too, were delicious, with big slabs of ham instead of Canadian bacon, perfectly poached eggs, and rich hollandaise. The home fries were discs of crunchy-on-the-outside, moist-on-the-inside Idahos. Yummy.

On another morning visit, our waitress Terry, whom we found out later is a former owner and in charge of pies at Christo's, arrived to take our order. Like the other server, she wore a bright red T-shirt and matching lipstick. Each had blond hair pulled back in a ponytail. When we asked Terry which of the two French toasts on the menu is best, grilled or fried, she suggested the deep-fried, admitting that she may be partial because it's her invention. That was good enough for us, and we added a side of crispy bacon to the French toast order. When you're having deep-fried white bread, you might as well go all the way. We loved Terry's invention. They coat thick slices of white bread with cinnamon and sugar, then plunge them into boiling fat. It's great as it is for Jane, but Nancy likes to add the syrup that comes with the French toast. The saltiness of the crisp tasty bacon is a perfect complement to the sweet. When we tell Terry how much we like it, she tells us about the dessert spinoff, Christo's a la mode. They take the same French toast, put a scoop of ice cream on top, drizzle it with chocolate sauce, and top with whipped cream and a cherry. Mmmmm.

Breakfast isn't the only meal at Christo's, but we think it's the best, and you can get it until 3:00 p.m. They also do a lively lunch and dinner business with plenty of sandwiches, burgers, and home cooking like pork chops, catfish, and country fried steak. Nancy's favorite nonbreakfast item is the sweet potato fries, which they serve with apple butter, like one of the server's grandmothers used to do. The menu is extensive, and they've tried to simplify it, but they can't figure out what to cut. Every item is the favorite of somebody in the neighborhood. The neighborhood rules at Christo's.

I-4 Exit 104 or 101 BC: "Where Gemuetlichkeit Happens"

Hollerbach's Willow Tree Café

205 East 1st Street, #C-D, Sanford; 407-321-2204; www.willowtreecafe.com. Open Monday 11:00 a.m. to 3:00 p.m., Tuesday through Thursday 11:00 a.m. to 9:00 p.m., and Friday through Sunday 11:00 a.m. to 10ish. $$–$$$

From I-4 West: Take exit 104—US 17-92 toward Sanford (3.6 miles). Turn left onto West 1st Street (which becomes East 1st Street)(.4 mile) and Hollerbach's Willow Tree will be on your right.

From I-4 East: Take exit 101 BC—FL-417/FL-46 toward Mount Dora/Sanford (.5 mile) and then take exit 101C—FL-46 on the left toward Mount Dora (1.4 miles). Turn right onto West 1st Street (which becomes East 1st Street)/FL-46 (4.2 miles), and Hollerbach's will be on your right.

In 2001, the Hollerbachs bought the Willow Tree Café and served about four hundred guests per week with seven employees. Now, more than fifty employees serve more than three thousand guests a week. We think it's mostly due to the *Gemuetlichkeit*, what the Hollerbachs describe as "a sense of well-being and happiness that comes from enjoying the company of friends and family while savoring good food and drink." Oh, and music too. Thursday through Sunday nights, call ahead to reserve your spot at the *Schunkel Abend. Schunkel* means interlocking arms with your neighbor and swaying back and forth to the music—in this case accordions and other folk instruments—and *Abend* means evening. They provide the music sheets, and you show up for the singing and swaying. It'll be a night you won't forget. They also sometimes have a guitarist on Saturday afternoons playing popular covers outside.

You can sit inside in one of two large rooms or outside along a quaint downtown street in historic Sanford. Clearly the *Gemuetlichkeit* starts with the staff because the servers are all helpful and enthusiastic. They'll patiently explain all the sausages and schnitzels and give you tastes of wine to make sure you like it—lots of German Rieslings on the menu, both dry and sweet, as well as well as other German varietals and a few American and Romanian wines. No, we're not sure about the Romanian wines. Beer is really the major house drink, though, especially with all that locking of arms and swaying. Nancy is happy because Hollerbach's has a spectacular selection of hefeweizens, but you can also find plenty of pilsners, dunkel lagers, festbiers, doppelbocks, or helles lagers. It's fun just naming the beers here, but if you're not so adventurous, they'll sell you a Bud or Bud Light.

On to the food, which is wonderful. Theo Hollerbach was born in Cologne and grew up in tiny Kyllburg, Germany, working at his family's butcher shop, hotel, and bakery, so he learned about German food the old-fashioned way. He moved to the United States in 1970 for school but still went back to Germany in the summers to work for his grandparents. He and his wife, Linda, both worked in German restaurants here in the States before they bought the Willow Tree and, along with their daughter Christina, transformed it into the hot spot for fun and great food in Sanford. Most of the recipes here have been handed down from Theo's aunt and grandparents. We like to start out with their potato pancakes and the great sunflower seed bread. Then we move on to more protein and carbs. They sell five different types of sausage—Bratwurst and Nürnberger are our favorites, but we wouldn't discount the Weisswurst, Mettwurst, or Knockwurst. They also have an inventive Schnitzel Bank, with eight different choices, each with a pork, veal, or chicken option, except for the Jaeger Schnitzel (sautéed without breading and smothered with sautéed mushrooms and Rahm sauce), which is only available for pork or chicken. You can get the basic Wiener Schnitzel (lightly breaded and pan-fried), but we think that's a little boring compared to the rest of the choices. The

Gemuetlichkeit *in action*

Zigeuner Schnitzel (rubbed with Opa's Gypsy spices and sautéed with butter, onions, and green peppers) is delicious and mixes well with the Gourmettes' Gypsy spirit. If you're an anchovy person, you might try Schnitzel Holsteiner Art (breaded with a sunny-side-up egg, capers, and anchovies). All the Schnitzels come with your choice of two sides. Besides the great sauerkraut and sweet red cabbage, which they cook with tart Granny Smith apples, we especially like "Heaven & Earth" (yummy mashed potatoes with sautéed onions, bacon, and apples) and Käse Spätzel (homemade egg noodles sautéed with onions, butter, and Emmenthaler cheese), basically the German improvement on mac 'n cheese.

If for some crazy reason, you're not a big fan of German food, there are plenty of American options at lunch and some at dinner and lots of salads and sandwiches that you can pronounce. They do a good job with American food too. In any case, make sure you save room for dessert. Creating tasty and artsy desserts is one of Linda Hollerbach's passions. We loved the blueberries and cream cheesecake: layers of cheesecake, fresh blueberries, and a cream cheese and whipped cream topping. Linda also is a genius cake designer/decorator. Check out their Web site to see some of her creations.

The only reason not to go to Hollerbach's is if you're in a lousy mood and you're intent on staying there. The *Gemuetlichkeit* could pose a serious threat to your misery.

Where Bagels Are King

If you're from New York City and are looking for a bagel that tastes just like the best the Big Apple has to offer, you're in the wrong state. However, **Bagel King Bakery** may very well get you through your cravings till you get home, or at least make it palatable for you to stay here. In any case, these bagels are as good as the Sunshine State has to offer. Nancy's friend Howie, a Jewish New Englander, swears by Bagel King now that he lives in Central Florida. The King has provided a refuge for many exiled bagel fanatics, which you can tell just by listening to the dialects of the customers around you. An institution in the area, Bagel King has two locations, one in Casselberry at SR 436 and Howell Branch Road (take exit 92 off I-4 and travel west on SR 436 for 5.9 miles; Bagel King will be on your right) and the one we're talking about here, only a mile off the interstate.

Take your pick of nineteen different types of bagels with all sorts of spreads, including pineapple, nut and raisin, and guava, besides the traditional ones. Or try Nancy's favorite, a knish, served with spicy brown mustard or stuffed with turkey or corned beef. The kosher bagel dog is hearty "everything" bagel dough around a hot dog and stuffed with your choice of onions, kraut, mustard, or whatever else sounds good to you.

If you've got more of a sweet tooth, try the ragulach, the cinnamon buns, or the danishes. There's always plenty to tempt you.

The bakery itself is nondescript and located on the corner of an even less descript strip mall, but the service is always helpful and friendly. They don't rush you through your order like the bagel shops in NYC. It's a lot warmer down here in the winter too. Hey, life's a trade-off, but don't think you have to live without bagels just because you flew south.

➡ 777 Deltona Boulevard #32, Deltona; 386-574-5729. Open Monday through Friday 6:00 a.m. to 4:00 p.m., Saturday and Sunday 7:00 a.m. to 2:00 p.m. $

➡ From I-4: Take exit 108 — Debary/Deltona. Turn east onto Debary Avenue/CR 4162 East (.2 mile). Make a left onto Deltona Boulevard (.8 mile). Bagel King will be on your right in a strip mall.

I-4 Exit 114: If the Spirit Moves You

Lost in Time Café

355 Cassadaga Road, Cassadaga; 386-228-0508. Open Monday through Thursday 11:00 a.m. to 3:00 p.m., Friday and Saturday 11:00 a.m. to 6:00 p.m., and Sunday 11:00 a.m. to 5:00 p.m. $$

From I-4: Take exit 114—SR 472 west toward DeLand/Orange City (.6 mile). Turn right onto Dr. Martin Luther King Beltway/CR 4101 (.4 mile) and right onto Cassadaga Road (1.8 miles). Lost in Time will be in the Cassadaga Hotel on your right.

Where else, for just a little over $200, can you get a past-life regression and a better-than-decent mushroom burger? For less than half that, you can get a full spirit contact and a chicken quesadilla. For even less, you can bring in Fido for a pet reading to find out what that running in circles is all about and get a patty melt yourself. Nancy keeps trying to get Jane to bring in her mischievous (Jane's word, not Nancy's) yellow lab Jasper for a reading to find out why he's so ill-mannered (Nancy's words, not Jane's), but for some reason Jane won't do it. Don't let that stop you, though.

Cassadaga is one of the most unusual and fascinating places in Florida, and Lost in Time Café, located in the haunted Cassadaga Hotel, is a great way to start to get a sense of the town's spirit . . . er, so to speak. Established in 1894, the Southern Cassadaga Spritualist Camp Meeting Association owns fifty-seven acres of this community on which less than one hundred residents live. The Cassadaga Hotel, built in 1927, isn't part of the camp but is a central hub of the community, and from there it's easy enough to set up a reading, check out the spiritualist gift shop with one of Florida's "largest selections of metaphysical books, CDs, and gifts," or just grab a burger and a beer and take in the surroundings. Cassadaga welcomes skeptics and the curious, as well as those more in tune with the Spiritualists' traditions. On Sundays, if you really want to learn more, the camp holds an adult lyceum from 9:30 to 10:15 a.m. There's also a healing service at 10 a.m. and a church service at 10:30 a.m. Lost in Time Café opens at 11:00 a.m. on Sunday, so you could attend a service and then stop over for a sandwich.

As for the restaurant itself, loosely named after the 1980 Christopher Reeve movie *Somewhere in Time*, it's located off the lobby of the hotel and decorated like a Southern tearoom: hardwood floors, Renoir prints on pink walls, curtains on the windows. You may need a psychic to figure out what the kitchen is thinking because what comes out doesn't always match the menu description. Sometimes it's worse, like the grilled four-cheese chicken quesadilla that didn't seem very grilled and appeared to have only one cheese—overall a bit bland, but acceptable. Sometimes what the kitchen does is better, though: the patty melt, which was supposed to come on rye showed up on Texas toast, which was delicious. Once, when we asked our server about the diet Coke we had ordered, she said, "I'm sorry, I forgot. I'm losing my psychic abilities today," and scampered off to get the drink. The "spirit burgers"

are always a good choice, as is the egg salad sandwich on toasted wheat. The French onion soup was pretty tasty, but the Caesar salad seemed past its life. For dessert, try the decadent Hershey almond pie: mashed up Hershey's almond milk chocolate candy bars mixed with a cross between chocolate mousse and chocolate pudding in a graham cracker crust, topped with chocolate sauce and whipped cream. Indulgent.

When you finish eating, you might consider the "Official Encounter with the Spirits Tour" at the bookstore across the street, or you might just want to drive around town and see if the spirit moves you to stop by one of the many houses with a small shingle outside that says something like CERTIFIED MEDIUM HEALER or SPIRITUAL COUNSELOR. On the weekend, you'll likely need to make an appointment to get a reading with a psychic, but at other times you can often get in on the spur of the moment.

At the hotel, some of the folks do double duty. One of the chefs is a Reiki master, and one of the waitresses photographs spirits in the hotel. Owner Donna Morn assures us that although the hotel is full of spirits, "we don't have anybody mean here; they're all friendly spirits." If you decide you want to get a room in the hotel for the night, you too can try your hand at photographing them. Lost in Time may not have the most inventive of menus, but you won't go hungry, and there's plenty to keep things interesting in this tiny southern spiritualist town.

I-4 Exit 118: Come for the Food, Stay for the Fun

Sweet Melissa's Raw Bar & Grille

1046 East New York Avenue, DeLand; 386-736-4006; www.sweetmelissasrawbar.com. Open Wednesday 11:00 a.m. to 6:00 p.m., Thursday through Saturday 11:00 a.m. to 11:00 p.m., and Sunday noon to 7:00 p.m. Closed Monday and Tuesday. $–$$

From I-4: Take exit 118—FL-44 west toward DeLand (3.5 miles). Sweet Melissa's will be on your left.

Sweet Melissa's isn't the kind of place where one expects an amuse bouche, but before you order, they'll likely drop off a little plastic cup of their crawfish bisque, rich, thick, with lots of crawfish and a hot kick to it. If they forget to give you one, just ask. It'll whet your appetite for all the delicious creations to come. Sweet Melissa's, located in a little building next to a gas station, has had lots of different incarnations, but it's finally found its niche as an oyster bar/barbecue/home-cooking/hamburger joint with Melissa Mathews and Big Mike Dapice at the helm. Just the two of them run it—all the waiting tables and cooking and quirky hometown hospitality—so you can see how they might forget the amuse bouche. One of their many mottos is "Come here early, be assured to eat; come here late, be prepared to wait." If you're fun loving, though, you won't mind the wait. They'll bring a bucket of beer to your table, and Big Mike will keep you laughing and wondering with his bullhorn trivia.

This open-air spot has a covered, screened-in, small dining room (think one long table and a short counter), but most of the action happens in the front part of the building around the large polyurethaned cable-spool tables or along the two outside bars, one an oyster bar and the other next to the 73-inch TV screen. On Thursday nights, you can be assured of a crowd. That's the night Johnny drives the Allen Brothers Seafood truck into town from Apalachicola. The regulars wait patiently for him to get here, usually sometime between 7:00 and 9:00 p.m., and when he arrives, they often chant, "Johnny! Johnny! Johnny!" and help him unload the precious cargo—this weekend's oysters, shrimp, and crawfish. "Johnny thinks he's Cary Grant," says Mike. And why not with a reception like that? The regulars include everyone from international skydivers to state senators to bik-

ers to faculty from nearby Stetson University. What do they all have in common? They "come for the food, stay for the fun," another of the mottos around here.

Sweet Melissa's is named after the Allman Brothers Band song and Melissa Mathews, a pretty blonde who is indeed very sweet. She used to be an advertising executive in sales, but through the quirks of life, now finds herself in charge of a thriving restaurant with outstanding food.

Of course we love the oysters: raw; perfectly steamed (just cooked through, still plump, moist, and tasting of the sea); freshly shucked, floured, and pan-fried; or in a "booger beer." What's a "booger beer," you ask? Picture a large shot glass with a freshly shucked oyster at the bottom, a secret combination of horseradish and hot sauce, and beer poured on top. You count down and throw it back in one gulp, often in a festive small group. When the Gourmettes and Jane's husband, Gary, made our "booger beer" debut, Mike and Melissa were right there to cheer us on. "In about five minutes, you'll feel like you just got eight hours of sleep," said Melissa mysteriously. Funny thing was, she was sort of right. It did give us a second wind.

Although we are obviously enamored of the oyster in all its guises, there's so much more great food on the menu. In the seafood category, try a peel-and-eat trifecta (a third of the shrimp in garlic, a third in Old Bay seasoning, a third in Cajun seasoning) or try the clams or crawfish. Everything is fresh, and sometimes by Sunday night, they've run out. If you're open to possibilities, though, there's always something else

Big Mike Dapice and Sweet Melissa Mathews making "booger beers"

good on the menu. Mike barbecues the pork, brisket, and chicken on the smoker out back. It's tough to find brisket in Florida, especially this good. The burgers are juicy and fresh, never frozen. Try the "Melissa" burger with A-1 sauce, cheese, and an onion ring. If you're in the mood for comfort food, the pot roast is delicious, served swimming in gravy with some veggies, and you can get it with the scattered potatoes (hash browns grilled with onions, peppers, and sausage), greasy, but flavorful and addictive. We also recommend the wings, roasted with a neutral dry rub after marinating in an apple cider–vinegar base— unusual, tender, and flavorful. We've never had anything we didn't like at Sweet Melissa's. The bottom

line is that Mike and Melissa are talented cooks who know what tastes good and know how to coax people into having fun.

"Name the song, name the artist, win a beer!" says Mike on the bullhorn while a song we've all heard many times plays in the background. No one knows the artist. The more obscure the band, the more likely Mike will offer a beer. "It's 'True,' by Spandau Ballet."

"I thought it was Wham," said a woman nearby.

"You'd be wrong," says Mike on the bullhorn.

"Are you sure?"

"If I'm wrong, I'll pick up your whole check." Mike is rarely wrong, about trivia or good food.

I-4 Exit 118: Burgers, Beers, and Skydiving

The Perfect Spot

1600 Flightline Boulevard, DeLand; 386-734-0088. Kitchen open daily 8:00 a.m. to 8:00 p.m. Bar is open until it feels like time to close. $$

From I-4: Take exit 118—SR 44 west (2.1 miles). Turn right onto Kepler Road/CR 4101 (2.6 miles) and left onto US 92/International Speedway Boulevard (.7 mile). Make a right onto Langley Avenue, which becomes Flightline Boulevard (.5 mile), and you'll run into The Perfect Spot parking lot.

*I*nside, "The Perfect Spot" looks pretty standard: long bar against the wall on the left, booths and tables taking up the rest of the space. But then you notice that the walls are decorated with skydiving posters and awards, and the mounted TVs display nonstop skydiving videos. If you walk in the door and look across the restaurant through the plate-glass windows at just the right time, you might see a color-

ful parachutist or two or three swoop down for a landing just beyond the deck out back. This place is "the perfect spot" to stop and people-watch. We send you to lots of places with great views that usually include water, but here, the view is of beautiful people as they fall from the sky (parachutes attached) or prepare to fall from the sky. DeLand is a Mecca of skydiving, and although the locals still show up in force, the skydivers are the real draw here, speaking everything from Finnish to Portuguese. It's one of the few Gourmette choices that has a cosmopolitan feel, although it's totally casual . . . as is the service, so be ready to relax and take your time.

Most people chomp on the burgers (called Swoopers) while watching the skydiving show, but the avocado and Swiss or baked tofu sandwiches are also decent choices. The menu is wide, with lots of healthy and less-healthy alternatives, and it includes a kid's section, but besides the burgers, nothing is killer. If you're not that hungry, you could stop in just for a

beer—there's a broad selection, domestic and imported, bottle and draft—or a glass of wine from a tiny selection.

It's really all about the skydiving, though. The landing area is only a few feet from the long outdoor picnic tables on the deck outside, but you can also sit on a rooftop deck or indoors and watch through the windows. As the daredevils swoop in for a landing, the vicarious thrills are free with any purchase, but you could decide to participate. One of those spots could be yours. Tandem jumps go for less than $200.

Once when we were there, one of the servers was making her first jump, so all the other servers and manager came out to watch. When she landed, the manager said, "I guess we'll have to keep her on the schedule. She lived."

An older man watching nearby piped in, "It's like they say, 'If at first you don't succeed, skydiving ain't for you.'"

One beautiful winter day when we were munching on Bleu Swoopers (bacon, Swiss, and blue cheese), we heard whispers that a ninety-two-year-old woman was jumping in the group that had just taken off. Pretty soon, she wafted down, her instructor attached to her back, and landed just as softly as if she had stepped off a curb. The whole crowd cheered. Less than six miles from I-4, this is "the perfect spot."

"Load five, fifteen minutes. One slot available," the loudspeaker announces.

"Jane, where are you going? Come back!"

Meals Worth Stopping for in *Florida*

Citrus Varieties

Florida grows lots of citrus beyond the kinds you find in grocery stores throughout the world. If you know what to look for, you can taste sensational flavors that never leave the state. Even the more common varieties taste a lot better just off the tree. Check out roadside stands, farmers' markets, vegetable stands, farmers who sell directly from their groves, or, the best tactic of all, make friends in one of the local diners with a Floridian who has a few backyard trees. Here are some varieties you might like:

Oranges

1. Valencias are late ripening and excellent for juicing.

2. Navels are large, good for sectioning or juicing, and they also come in red.

3. Hamlins are a Gourmettes favorite. They ripen early and are grown mainly for juicing. They make for great eating, though, if you don't mind rivers of juice running down your chin.

4. Gardners are less readily available, but excellent for juicing when you can find them.

Grapefruit — The best are available after Christmas, with the very best flavor usually in February.

1. Duncans are seedy, but tops on flavor.

2. Marshes are seedless, most widely grown throughout the world, and also come in a pink variety.

3. Reds include several varieties, such as Ray Ruby, Red Blush, Star Ruby. They're seedless and sweet.

Mandarins and Related Hybrids

1. Satsumas are very early ripening, from September to November. They're sweet and often ripe when green. They don't keep long, though.

2. Ponkans are easy to peel, incredibly sweet tangerines that will not ship, so eat them here. A Gourmettes favorite.

3. Murcotts are very sweet, late season fruits, another Gourmettes favorite

4. Minneolas are another very, very sweet fruit, often called the honeybell and in the tangelo family.

There are, of course, lots of other citrus varieties, from Myers lemons (large, thin-skinned lemons, bursting with a less acidic juice than normal lemons have) to calamondins (a small, orange-colored, sour fruit good for making marmalades or drinks) to kumquats (a small sweet fruit eaten rind and all), but we think this gives you enough to get started on your search.

Meals Worth Stopping for in *Florida*

I-4 Exit 118: Flipping on Your Own Griddle

Old Spanish Sugar Mill

601 Ponce DeLeon Boulevard, DeLeon Springs; 386-985-5644; www.planetdeland.com/sugarmill. Open Monday through Friday 9:00 a.m. to 4:00 p.m., Saturday and Sunday 8:00 a.m. to 4:00 p.m. Entry fee to DeLeon Springs State Park is $5 per car. $–$$

From I-4: Take exit 118—FL-44 west toward DeLand (2.4 miles). Turn right onto Kepler Road/CR 4101 (2.7 miles), left onto US 92/International Speedway Boulevard (2.6 miles), right onto US 17 North/North Woodland Boulevard (5.8 miles), and left onto Ponce DeLeon Boulevard (.8 mile). The Sugar Mill will be inside DeLeon Springs State Park. (Note: we cheated because we like the place so much. It's 14.3 miles off the interstate.)

Every morning of the year, even when it's cold, even when it's raining, even when hurricanes are approaching, unless DeLeon Springs State Park closes down, the Mermaids/Merpeople/Merfolk are out swimming in the springs. "Merpeople come and Merpeople go," says Mary Smithwick, their eighty-nine-year-old unofficial leader. "Some of us have been doing it over twenty years." And every third Wednesday of the month, after swimming, they get dressed and head into the Old Spanish Sugar Mill to flip pancakes and eggs and do their Mer-Cheer: "Pure spring water, Rah! Rah! Rah! Do we love it? Zis boom bah! Merpeople, Merpeople, Stroke! Stroke! Stroke!" They have other cheers and pledges, which they seal "with a flick of our fishy tales."

It's all part of the colorful flavor of the Sugar Mill in DeLeon Springs State Park, one of the most beautiful spots in Florida with its centuries-old live oak trees dripping Spanish moss, its clean blue water at seventy-two degrees year-round, and its plentiful

Mary Smithwick (standing) leads the Merpeople in food and song

wildlife, including the occasional alligator. Peter and Marjorie Schwarze started the Sugar Mill in 1961. Peter, a fifth-generation grist miller, had a bakery in New York City in the 1920s where he flipped pancakes as well as made bread, and that place provided the concept for the eventual Sugar Mill. When the couple moved to Kissimmee, Florida, Peter heard about the sugar mill slated for demolition. He couldn't bear the idea, so they bought it and the springs. Both were privately owned until 1982 when daughter Patty sold the springs to the state. Patty had come down from Maine in 1980 on vacation and ended up sticking around and running the place. The water-fueled mill still functions.

Once in the state park, you can swim (with or without the Merfolk, depending on time of day), hike, or rent kayaks before or after a meal at the Sugar Mill, but don't miss a meal, even if you have to wait in line. Have a seat in the fireplace-heated or fan-cooled restaurant and get to work. Yep, you're going to be doing a chunk of the work here. In the center of every table is a large griddle. The friendly staff will bring you cooking spray, a pitcher of pancake batter, homemade bread, and/or eggs, and you'll cook them right there at the table. Your server will patiently provide instructions on grilling procedures if needed, and any bacon or ham you order will be cooked in the kitchen. "It would be easier to cook everything in the kitchen," explains Patty, "but it's a lot more fun to give instructions to customers, stand back, and let them explore. Some folks take a little while to get the hang of it."

We have yet to decide which pancake batter we like better, the hearty five-grain or the lighter white batter. Both are excellent, and you can get mix-ins to make them even tastier. Our favorites are blueberries and pecans, but you can also choose bananas, chocolate chips, apples, apple sauce, or peanut butter to create idiosyncratic pancakes of your own. The pancakes are served all day, and we highly recommend them, but if you must stray from breakfast, they also serve sandwiches.

What's the best thing about running the Sugar Mill? "Seeing people coming here, then returning," explains Patty, "some bringing third, now working on fourth generations, being a part of their family traditions." Start a pancake-flipping family tradition today and throw in a swim for good measure.

Index

About the Authors

Nancy Barber, a native Floridian and lifelong foodie, began her writing career at the *West Orange Times* in the center of the state. She ate her way through an MA in English and an MFA in creative writing, and currently she teaches English at Stetson University. When not on the road, she typically eats in DeLand, FL, where she resides.

Jane Bolding, a native Arkansan, grew up in a family of talented home cooks and has been a dedicated eater since childhood. She first worked in the restaurant business in Little Rock, followed by a decade of restaurant work and dining in Manhattan. Since the early 1990s, she has lived and eaten primarily in Florida, taking a year to live in Mexico and spice up her culinary education.

Notes

Travel Like a Pro

gpp travel

To order call 800-243-0495 or visit thenewgpp.com